Behavioral Interventions with Brain-Injured Children

CRITICAL ISSUES IN NEUROPSYCHOLOGY

Series Editors
Antonio E. Puente
University of North Carolina, Wilmington

Cecil R. Reynolds
Texas A & M University

Current Volumes in this Series

AGING AND NEUROPSYCHOLOGICAL ASSESSMENT
Asenath La Rue

BEHAVIORAL INTERVENTIONS WITH BRAIN-INJURED CHILDREN
A. MacNeil Horton, Jr.

BRAIN MECHANISMS IN PROBLEM SOLVING AND INTELLIGENCE: A Lesion Survey of the Rat Brain
Robert Thompson, Francis M. Crinella, and Jen Yu

BRAIN ORGANIZATION OF LANGUAGE AND COGNITIVE PROCESSES
Edited by Alfredo Ardila and Feggy Ostrosky-Solis

HANDBOOK OF HEAD TRAUMA: Acute Care to Recovery
Edited by Charles J. Long and Leslie K. Ross

HANDBOOK OF NEUROPSYCHOLOGICAL ASSESSMENT: A Biopsychosocial Perspective
Edited by Antonio E. Puente and Robert J. McCaffrey

NEUROPSYCHOLOGICAL EVALUATION OF THE SPANISH SPEAKER
Alfredo Ardila, Monica Rosselli, and Antonio E. Puente

NEUROPSYCHOLOGY, NEUROPSYCHIATRY, AND BEHAVIORAL NEUROLOGY
Rhawn Joseph

THE NEUROPSYCHOLOGY OF ATTENTION
Ronald A. Cohen

THE NEUROPSYCHOLOGY OF EPILEPSY
Edited by Thomas L. Bennett

A PRACTICAL GUIDE TO HEAD INJURY REHABILITATION: A Focus on Postacute Residential Treatment
Michael D. Wesolowski and Arnie H. Zencius

A Continuation Order Plan is available for the series. A continuation order will bring delivery of each new volume immediately upon publication. Volumes are billed only upon actual shipment. For further information, please contact the publisher.

Behavioral Interventions with Brain-Injured Children

A. MacNeill Horton, Jr.

Psych Associates
Towson, Maryland

With Contributions by
William G. Miller

Western Maryland College
Westminster, Maryland

Plenum Press • New York and London

Library of Congress Cataloging-in-Publication Data

Horton, Arthur MacNeill, 1947-
Behavioral interventions with brain-injured children / A. MacNeill Horton, Jr. ; with contributions by William G. Miller.
p. cm. -- (Critical issues in neuropsychology)
Includes bibliographical references and index.
ISBN 0-306-44438-0
1. Brain-damaged children--Rehabilitation. 2. Behavior disorders in children--Treatment. 3. Behavior therapy for children. 4. Behavior disorders in children--Physiological aspects. I. Miller, William G., Ph. D. II. Title. III. Series.
[DNLM: 1. Brain Injuries--in infancy & childhood. 2. Brain Injuries--therapy. 3. Child Behavior Disorders--therapy. 4. Child Development Disorders--therapy. 5. Behavior Therapy--methods. WS 350.6 H823b 1993]
RJ496.B7H67 1993
618.92'8--dc20
DNLM/DLC
for Library of Congress 93-41064
CIP

Opinions expressed in this book are those of the author and do not necessarily reflect the opinions or official policy of the National Institute on Drug Abuse, the National Institutes of Health, or any other part of the U.S. Department of Health and Human Services. The author's contributions to this book were made in his private capacity, and the book was neither endorsed nor supported by the federal government. The author wrote the book in his former capacity as a faculty member of the Department of Psychiatry of the University of Maryland Medical School. Correspondence concerning this book should be sent to the author at 5903 Lone Oak Drive, Bethesda, Maryland 20814.

ISBN 0-306-44438-0

A Division of Plenum Publishing Corporation
233 Spring Street, New York, N.Y. 10013

Printed in the United States of America

TO MY WIFE MARY, AND OUR CHILDREN—
NEILL, FRANK, AND JOHN

Preface

Over the last decade, interest in brain–behavior relationships has increased tremendously. In addition to the remarkable cross-cultural validity of neuropsychological research findings, the successful applications of neuropsychological assessment methods in schools has contributed to this trend. Considerable evidence suggests that the study of brain–behavior relationships is of great relevance to the practice of psychology with children.

An important focus of this trend has been an effort to integrate neuropsychology with learning theory. Within the last 10 years, a new specialty that combines brain–behavior relationships with behavior therapy methods has been evolving. This area of research and clinical interest should prove valuable to psychologists and educators involved in behavior-oriented interventions with brain-impaired children. In this book, the term *brain impaired* denotes children with traumatic brain injuries, specific developmental disorders (e.g., academic skill disorders, language and speech disorders, and motor skill disorders), attention-deficit hyperactivity disorders, undifferentiated attention-deficit disorders, and other organic mental disorders associated with physical disorders or conditions whose etiology is unknown.

The purpose of this volume is to describe this new area of interest and to examine the underlying clinical and research knowledge bases. Such a volume is urgently needed at this time, since the further progress of behavioral neuropsychology and the integration of neuropsychology and behavior therapy will depend on the availability of adequate reference works in this field. The book includes chapters on (1) an introduction to human neuropsychology; (2) a basic review of brain–behavior relationships; (3) assessment issues; (4) treatment planning; (5) treatment procedures; (6) treatment outcome issues; (7) single-subject research design; and (8) neuropsychological and behavioral case studies. Readers are not expected to be experts in neuropsychology but should be familiar with basic principles of behavioral psychology. The book is clinically oriented, making use of case studies and suggestions for further reading.

The book is deliberately brief to facilitate circulation to a wide, multidisciplinary audience. In addition to child neuropsychologists and pediatric neurologists, other professionals involved in the care and treatment of these children—such as clinical child psychologists, applied developmental psychologists, child psychiatrists, special educators, counselors, social workers, and learning-disability specialists—will find this volume pertinent to many issues they wish to address. Also, graduate students in all of the above fields of study will likely find this book of interest.

Acknowledgments

A number of people contributed to the present volume, directly or indirectly. Lawrence Hartlage, Cecil R. Reynolds, and Robert W. Elliot once again helped out as true friends; I owe them a great deal for their support and encouragement. I also appreciate the contributions of William G. Miller, coauthor of several of the chapters; however, the final responsibility for Chapters 2–5 and 7 rests with me. Tony Puente first suggested to me that I should write this book. Eliot Werner, my editor at Plenum, was unbelievably understanding of my mood changes and provided me with continued support and very sound advice. Terri Harold typed the manuscript with great speed and did wonders with what I gave her. My wife, Mary, and children, Neill, Frank, and John, were, as always, supportive and understanding of my endeavors.

Contents

1

Introduction to Behavioral Interventions with Brain-Damaged Children

Neuropsychology is a young, dynamic and growing field with multiple clinical applications. The number of practitioners of human neuropsychology has greatly increased, and many professional journals are now available in this field. While in the past most research literature and clinical reports focused on the adult population, there has been, over the past two decades, a growing interest in the special and unique problems of brain-injured children. Many factors have fueled this interest. Among others, the increasingly technologically complex culture in the United States requires an increasingly literate and educated population. As a result, the need for a well-educated work force has demanded an increased ability in reading, arithmetic, and writing. Neuropsychology is clearly present in the public schools and is most prominent in the area of learning disabilities. Also, the continuing success in the health care area in increasing the survival rate of infants and young children with neuropsychological deficits has presented the United States with a new population of individuals with compromised mental functioning, but with great and urgent educational and social needs. In addition, fetal alcohol syndrome and the possible neuropsychological deficits of "cocaine babies" are the contributions of the drug abuse problem to child clinical neuropsychology. State and federal government mandates require schools to develop and maintain programs for these handicapped children. For example, a new federal law, the reauthorization bill for PL 94-142, defines traumatic brain injury (TBI) as a new category for eligibility for special-education services. These multiple developments make applied neuropsychology with children the most dynamic and rapidly expanding area in neuropsychology.

As Hynd and Obrzut (1986) noted that, as the number of children who have survived previously fatal diseases, traumatic incidents, and neonatal crises increases, so must the services provided for these patients increase. Indeed, they pointed out that most authorities agree that the prevalence of various handicapping conditions for children is between 10% and 16% in the current population of the United States. They suggested that it is reasonable to predict and project that the incidence rate for various neurobehavioral and learning disorders will increase significantly in the next several decades. If this is true, an even greater number of children diagnosed as learning-disabled, as developmentally disabled, or as suffering from attentional disorders will require specialized neuropsychological and behavioral services.

The purpose of this book is to explore the clinical and research dimensions of behavioral neuropsychology and their relationship to the brain-damaged child. The aim is to describe an applied approach to the assessment and treatment of children primarily with attention-deficit–hyperactivity disorder (ADHD) and specific developmental disorders (i.e., academic skills, language and speech, and motor skills). Also, some attention is given to children with TBI and other developmental disorders. The following chapters provide an introductory overview of an assessment procedure and a behavioral treatment process that appears to be effective, especially in the treatment of ADHD but also with many other handicapping conditions.

By way of introduction, it might be noted that the first exploration of the interface of neurology and learning can be confidently attributed to the important work of John Hughings Jackson, the famous English neurologist who began these efforts in 1872 (Gaddes, 1981). Moreover, it should be well recognized that many current concepts of learning disabilities can be traced to Jackson's pioneering investigations, which began to elucidate the very complex and sophisticated relationships between mental functioning and brain structure (Horton & Wedding, 1984).

DEFINING BEHAVIORAL NEUROPSYCHOLOGY

As Meier (1974) defined it, "neuropsychology is the scientific study of brain and behavior relationships." Neuropsychological performance may be influenced by both organic and environmental variables (Horton & Puente, 1990). In recent years, the interest in mind–brain relationships has increased explosively. This interest has been encouraged by impressive demonstrations of the cross-cultural validity of neuropsychological data (Luria, 1966; Reitan & Davison, 1974) and very successful demonstrations of the practical value of neuropsychological data in the schools (Hynd & Orbrzut, 1986). A concurrent development in the practice of neuropsychology with children has been the explosive growth of behavior therapy and behavior modification technology (Masters, Burish, Hollon, & Rimm, 1987). Since the success of token economies (Kazdin, 1978) has spread far and wide, there has been considerable interest in behavior modification techniques and behavior therapy strategies by the school-based, institutional, and private-practice providers of psychological services to children. A natural development of these two concurrent trends would appear to be a blend of child clinical neuropsychology and child behavior therapy. It might be expected that such a development would be of significant value to educators, psychologists, neuropsychologists, child psychiatrists, pediatricians, and pediatric neurologists who treat children with a variety of neuropsychologically related difficulties.

Such a blend of behaviorism and neuropsychology has been developed under the rubric *behavioral neuropsychology,* a term first used in 1978 when a special-interest group with that title was founded at the annual meeting of the Association for Advancement of Behavior Therapy (AABT). Over the past years, a definition of behavioral neuropsychology has achieved some general acceptance among the members of the special-interest group, and indeed among a somewhat larger public. The definition is as follows:

> Behavioral neuropsychology may be defined as the application of behavior therapy techniques to problems of organically impaired individuals while using a neuropsychological assessment intervention perspective. This treatment modality suggests the inclusion of data from neuropsycho-

> logical assessment strategies would be helpful in the formulation of hypotheses regarding antecedent conditions (external or internal) for observed phenomena of psychopathology. That is, a neuropsychological perspective will significantly enhance the ability of the behavior therapist to make accurate discriminations as to the etiology of patient behaviors. Moreover, the formulation of a cogent plan of therapeutic intervention and a skillful implementation could, in certain cases, be facilitated by analysis of behavior deficits implicating impairment of higher cortical functioning. (Horton, 1979, p. 20)

While this definition might seem somewhat arbitrary and indeed makes assumptions regarding neuropsychology and behavior therapy that might be considered controversial (Hynd, 1981), nonetheless it is proposed as at least a working statement, one that has the advantage of providing at least a measure of conceptual clarity. A detailed examination of the various conceptual facets of behavioral neuropsychology both is beyond the scope of this chapter and also may be found in other references (Horton & Puente, 1986; Horton & Wedding, 1984). There are important issues, with respect to traditional behaviorism, inferred variables in radical behaviorism, and also contemporary behavioral thought, most particularly with respect to behavioral assessment techniques. At this point, we shall examine various organic and environmental variables that have particular reference to behavioral interventions with brain-injured children. A brief discussion of some selected relevant aspects of developmental psychology will lead the way.

LESSONS OF DEVELOPMENTAL PSYCHOLOGY

Developmental psychology might be seen as a study of age-related cognitive, emotional, and behavioral intraindividual developmental changes (Baltes, Reese, & Nesselroade, 1977). Development, at least in the minds of some workers in this area, involves at least two interacting systems. These include both organic and environmental variables. The organic variables are generally biological in nature, such as maturation, and the environmental variables are often seen as related to learning. As is well known, development is, to a degree, age-related. Erik Erikson, Maria Montessori, Jean Piaget, and A. R. Luria, among others, have conceptualized development in terms of a variety of psychosocial neurodevelopmental tasks. It might be suggested that most could agree, at least on one level, that childhood includes infancy, toddlerhood, early childhood, childhood, and, in some ways, adolescence. As noted by Horton and Puente (1990), theoretical categorizations of development might include, in addition to cognitive, emotional, and behavioral processes, also physical development, social development, personality structure adaption, and age-related memory changes.

While previous theories may have contributed to a misperception that development is entirely age-related, it would probably be fair to say that these conceptions are somewhat superficial. Contemporary views of development and developmental psychology are more in keeping with an emphasis upon the role of an individual as a partner and participant in the developmental process (Baltes, 1983). Simply put, the behavior of a child or an adult may interact with his or her biological system and environment in a somewhat reciprocal fashion (Featherman & Learner, 1985). To take but one example, a child who refuses to wear a seat belt is contributing to the likelihood that he or she will have a traumatic brain injury. Similarly, being tall and either handsome or beautiful can significantly affect the likelihood of social approval by peers. To recap, multiple factors may affect one's developmental status throughout childhood, and indeed beyond childhood. These multiple factors can interact in a wide variety of ways, creating multiple directional influences upon individuals.

NEUROPSYCHOLOGICAL FACTORS

In terms of providing the setting for the discussion that will follow, some brief comments will be devoted to the concepts of *brain damage* and *organicity.*

Brain Damage

A useful distinction is that between brain damage and cerebral dysfunction. Brain damage suggests structural injury to brain tissue. Put another way, this usually implies a brain lesion or a pathological alteration of the brain. Thanks to modern neurodiagnostic imaging methods, such as magnetic resonance imagery

(MRI) in many cases structural brain lesions may be readily identified. Nonetheless, it might be well noted that, in certain cases, changes in brain physiology are not reflected in structural modification, and thus additional work on correlating changes in brain physiology and neuropsychological testing results remains to be done. For example, while virtually all child neuropsychologists and pediatric neurologists would agree that a brain tumor or open head injury would be likely to result in structural brain lesions, there are multiple neurotoxic conditions that could produce neuropsychological deficits without obvious structural changes to the brain that would be apparent on visual inspection of the child (Hartman, 1988).

Often, the term *cerebral dysfunction* is used in situations where functional changes are clear, but structural changes cannot be verified. It might be noted that, in some cases, identification of alterations in brain morphology may merely await more careful and meticulous inspection and advances in brain imagery and computer technology. For example, the work of Hynd and Semrud-Clikeman (1989) has demonstrated that the results of computerized-tomography (CT) and MRI studies suggest that, in the brains of dyslexic persons, there is increased incidence of symmetry in the region of the planum temporale and parieto-occipital cortex that may be associated with language delay and with handedness. Furthermore, a related study that directly assessed brain morphology in developmental dyslexia and ADHD (Hynd, Semrud-Clikeman, Lorys, Novey, & Eliopulos, 1990) demonstrated specific deviations in the patterns of normal brain asymmetry and clinical diagnoses and academic achievement and psychiatric codiagnoses.

Organicity

In the classic volume by Reitan and Davison, entitled *Clinical Neuropsychology: Current Status and Appraisal,* which was published in 1974, there was considerable treatment of the concept of organicity. Davison (1974) gave the description as follows:

> The concept includes the assumption that any and all kinds of brain damage lead to similar behavioral effects and that behavioral differences among the brain damaged are due primarily to severity of damage and to premorbid personality characteristics. (p. 14)

It might be noted that, historically, the concept of *organicity* originated during the equipotentiality–localization debates in the early part of this century. As is well known, important neurological scientists, such as Paul Broca, demonstrated a relationship between behavioral functions and particular areas of the human brain. For example, Broca, in April 1861, presented at the meeting of the Paris Anthropological Society the brain of a patient who had been unable to speak when he was alive. After the patient died, his brain was available for inspection, and it was readily apparent that there was a lesion in the posterior third portion of the inferior frontal convolution of the left hemisphere. Broca was able to demonstrate that the patient's aphasia had been caused by neither a loss of memory nor motor dysfunction; rather, the aphasia was attributable to the brain lesion. Broca postulated that the articulated speech that arose from a specific brain area was missing in this patient, whose brain was examined after his death.

Similarly, Karl Wernicke, in 1874, demonstrated a clinical case of a patient who during his lifetime, had had a deficit in speech comprehension, and after his death his brain was found to have a lesion in the posterior third portion of the superior temporal gyrus of the left hemisphere. Again, careful observations had demonstrated that the patient had not had any motor speech difficulties, and therefore a center for the images of speech as distinct from motor speech abilities was postulated. Somewhat antithetical to this notion that specific areas of the brain were associated with specific higher mental functions was an opposing group of scientists who stressed the "equipotentiality" point of view. One of the major figures in this area was Marie J. P. Flourens (Luria, 1966). Generally, he was able to demonstrate experimental evidence that contradicts the localization position. Flourens theorized that the loss of function was more dependent on the amount of brain tissue impaired than on the specific location of the lesion. Considerable support of the equipotentiality movement was gained through the work of Kurk Goldstein, who worked with brain-injured veterans of World War I. His work appeared to suggest that concrete thinking is often associated with the brain-injured person's cognitive processes, and there was, in Goldstein's words, "the loss of the abstract attitude." Unfortunately, however, both the localization and the equipotential conceptualizations of higher mental processes have, over time, proved to be inadequate to account for the full range of neurocognitive abilities.

The more contemporary viewpoint is a somewhat integrationist's solution that owes a great deal to the previously mentioned Hughings Jackson and A. R. Luria, the famous Russian neurologist-neuropsychologist. As these views will be discussed later, they will only be very briefly noted here. Jackson was, of course, famous for his study of epileptic fits on a localized basis. For example, specific motor seizures, even to this day, are known as *Jacksonian*. Jackson postulated that human behavioral functions have a complex vertical organization. That is, functions are represented on multiple levels. Luria further developed Jackson's views and saw the human brain as composed of distinct blocks, with each section serving separate and distinct basic functions. Essentially, Luria saw higher cognitive processes as involving certain sections and multiple units at various points in time to produce the performance of any specific behavior, as noted by Horton and Wedding (1984):

> Essentially, Luria thought that every complex form of behavior depended on the joint operation of several faculties located in different areas of the brain. Disturbance of any one of a number of faculties will change behavior in different ways. But, in another way, this means that no single behavior is localized in a specific brain area, and that each behavior is the result of a specific combination of separate brain areas. (p. 30)

In the wake of these thoughts, it might be suggested that organicity is a somewhat dated concept. As noted further by Horton and Wedding (1984),

> to understand brain damage as existing on a single dimension is as realistic and useful as the assertion that human beings vary on the dimension of height. To be sure, the assertion is true in a general sense, and, in special situations, could be quite useful (e.g., college basketball). But, in many circumstances there would be a need for additional data with regard to sources of variation. (p. 12)

In spite of the limitations of the concept of organicity, there remains a trend in terms of diagnostic practices to retain the organic perspective. While organicity can be seen in various subtypes of mental disorders, nonetheless, considerable work needs to be done on the diagnostic classification of brain-injured children. In a later section, there is further discussion of various diagnostic issues with respect to organic subtypes. At this point, however, attention is addressed to the important issues related to neurological development.

NEUROLOGICAL DEVELOPMENT ISSUES

As mentioned earlier, an important consideration is the way in which developmental changes may be related to neurological functioning in children. One way to approach some of these issues is to consider the theoretical ideas of Luria (1966, 1973). Luria, who worked throughout his life to develop the cultural historical model of Lev Vygotsky with respect to higher cortical functioning, considered childhood a natural laboratory for understanding human neurocognitive processes. He saw childhood as a situation in which higher cognitive processes are refined over time (Horton, 1987). Indeed, one of the reasons that Luria was little interested in normative data on neuropsychological assessment devices was that he had collected extensive research data on at what age and in which developmental sequence of childhood certain neurocognitive functions arose. Using these internal mental norms based on the assessment of large numbers of normal and abnormal children, Luria was able to evaluate the neuropsychological functioning of children without recourse to tables of normal values (Horton, 1987).

Nonetheless, it should be clearly noted that there are great differences in adult cerebral organization and the cerebral organization of children (Rourke, Fisk, & Strang, 1989). The brains of children, in terms of localization of function, are both less well studied and considerably more difficult to understand than adult brains (Horton & Puente, 1989). For example, there is a much greater degree of variability in the expression of human neuropsychological abilities by a child's cerebral hemispheres. There are multiple reasons for this variability. Among other issues, it should be noted that children are in the process of neurocognitive development and are subject to little-understood growth spurts, developmental stages, and developmental lags. In addition, as noted by Hynd and Willis (1988), there are other issues with respect to medical problems that may be related to learning or development and to behavior difficulties, indirectly related to physical illness, and to behavioral problems that may be the result of disease or injury which can complicate the picture with respect to neuropsychological functioning in a child. Indeed, children might be seen as in the process of acquiring academic and adaptation to daily living skills, and given the aforementioned little-understood growth spurts, developmental stages, and developmental lags, it is quite difficult to accurately determine age-appropriate neuropsychological abilities. Moreover, it might be noted that, while researchers have been studying the neuropsychology of adults for a number of decades, only in relatively recent times have considerable data been available regarding the neuropsychology of childhood (Horton & Puente, 1990).

As can be seen by the foregoing, the problem of collecting appropriate normative neuropsychological data on children is well recognized (Hartlage, 1986; Horton & Puente, 1989). Normative data on neuropsychological tests for adults, of course, are inappropriate for application with children (Horton & Wedding, 1984). Additional issues relate to the great influence of environmental and organic variables on neuropsychological development, and to the fact that specific neuropsychological deficits may be expressed differently at particular developmental stages. As mentioned before, Vygotsky's cultural historical theory, which greatly influenced Luria (Horton, 1987), suggested that cultural, historical, and social influences were vitally important to the ability of various brain areas to shape observed neuropsychological performances in many areas of adaptation to daily living and in specific academic skills. For example, one way in which historical influences may be reflected in neuropsychological performance is in age-related socialization.

In terms of academic skills, it is very clear that there must be an opportunity to learn to read, spell, write, and do arithmetic. Individuals who have never been exposed to formal educational experiences certainly cannot be expected to read and write. Similarly, children must have an adequate opportunity to acquire academic skills before the inability to perform specific skills in reading, writing, arithmetic, and spelling might be considered a neuropsychological deficit. While this concept may be somewhat abstract, one way of understanding it is to consider the distinction between hardware and software in computer programming (Horton & Puente, 1989). The biological substrate might be considered the hardware, and the specific cultural influences and intellectual technology might be considered the software. It might be well noted that the inability of a particular computer to perform certain tasks may often be linked to deficiencies in the software.

Perhaps the most widely used paradigm in American neuropsychology for considering neuropsychological differences would be hemispheric lateralization of function. It is well known that the cerebral hemispheres serve specialized behavioral functions (Horton & Wedding, 1984). As has been amply portrayed in the scientific and popular literature, the left hemisphere is specialized for language functioning, and the right hemisphere is specialized for visual perceptual and manipulatory activities. And indeed, it has been known for some years that there are morphological differences between the cerebral hemispheres (Geschwind & Levitsky, 1968), nonetheless important more recent research by Hynd and his colleagues (Hynd & Willis 1988; Hynd *et al.*, 1990) has demonstrated evidence of deviations in brain morphology and behavioral correlates of developmental dyslexia and ADHD.

While the finding of an incidence of symmetry, or reversed asymmetry unique to dyslexia, is an important finding, nonetheless it must be noted that how hemispheric lateralization changes vary in terms of developmental stages is still very poorly understood (Bryden & Saxby, 1985). Much additional work must be done with respect to understanding higher developmental neurocognitive changes throughout childhood (Hartlage, 1986). It might be noted that Arthur L. Benton, in a chapter surveying the neuropsychology of childhood in the classic Reitan and Davison text (1974), remarked that the area was a "mare's nest." These words were quite true when written and indeed are still quite accurate. They are especially germane to the question of how neuropsychological deficits interact with specific neurocognitive developmental stages. Truly, this is an area in which much additional work needs to be done.

The difficulty was amply demonstrated by a classic study on brain-injured children by Teuber and Rudel (1962). In this extraordinary piece of work, they followed groups of brain-injured children over a 10-year period to determine the effects of early brain damage on neuropsychological abilities. Teuber and Rudel had thought that three possibilities with respect to the interaction of brain injury with developmental stages might occur: First, there might be a progressive recovering over time, somewhat similar to what could be expected with respect to traumatic brain injury in adults; second, there could be the constant, stable impairment over time that one might expect after the removal of a tumor or after a stroke after the period of recovery has elapsed in adults; or third, in a pattern possibly unique to children, there would be no discernible deficit at first, but over time, as different neurocognitive structures became activated in their developmental sequence, then specific neuropsychological deficits would arise.

Teuber and Rudel's results, although interesting, were dismaying for those who must provide clinical neuropsychological and behavioral treatment services to brain-injured children. Teuber and Rudel found that all three patterns were displayed by brain-injured children, depending on the task involved. Thus, it would appear that early brain injury may be a bewilderingly complex phenomenon. The normal developmental sequence of the task and the task under study, among other factors, plays a role in determining actual neurobehavioral performance. One possibility is that different groups of neurological structures at different phases in the developmental process subsume similar behavioral performances (Horton & Puente, 1989).

DIAGNOSTIC ISSUES

It is well recognized that the primary focus of the psychologist in clinical settings was initially on assessment issues. Similarly, the neuropsychologist, when first entering the neurology and neurosurgery ward, was primarily regarded as a diagnostician. As is well known, in the period following World War II, neurological diagnostic procedures in some cases carried the risk of mortality. The advantage of the neuropsychological exam was that it was a noninvasive procedure which carried no risk of death by an elderly, frail patient. Ralph M. Reitan, who founded his neuropsychology laboratory at the Department of Neurology at the Indiana University Medical Center, and Arthur L. Benton, who established his neuropsychological laboratory at the University of Iowa Medical Center, were both exemplars of this assessment tradition. Indeed, the primary thrust of their work at that time was related to assessment. Reitan, of course, developed the Halstead-Reitan Neuropsychological Test Battery, a coordinated comprehensive battery of neuropsychological instruments intended for the differential diagnosis of neuropathology such as strokes, brain tumors, and head trauma. In contrast to Retian's work, Benton developed a series of single tests focused on particular neurological syndromes. Perhaps the best single example of the many neuropsychological tests devised by Benton is the widely used Benton Visual Retention Test.

In some ways, current approaches to child neuropsychological assessment mirror the different approaches taken by Reitan and Benton. Neuropsychologists may prefer either to utilize a fixed-battery approach as pioneered by Reitan or to opt for an individualized or patient-centered approach as advocated by Benton. A third option is a flexible-battery approach, which attempts to combine the best features of both approaches. In choosing an approach, there are a number of important considerations with respect to the selection and interpretation of neuropsychological tests in a child population. These include psychometric considerations (i.e., validity, reliability, and appropriate age norms); referral questions; practicality; ease of use; acceptability to parents, teachers, and children; and, in some states, legal requirements for special education and other services, among others. In many situations, traditional educational and psychological tests are used in addition to neuropsychological tests in neuropsychological assessments of children.

Regarding the selection of one approach over another, the issue is moot. There are good reasons to select any of the three options. In this book, however, the focus is on a fixed-battery approach. The rationale for this choice is that a flexible or individualized approach requires a greater degree of interpretive acumen than can be gain from an introductory text such as this one. In short, it is considered best first to learn the basics, and then, as greater experience is gained, more difficult decisions regarding neuropsychological test selection and interpretation can be made with a degree of confidence.

It should be clearly recognized that neuropsychological testing results are often relied upon by others to made decisions that have important consequences. Every effort should be made to ensure accurate results from neuropsychological testing. In recent years, however, there has been considerable change in the primary role of the neuropsychologist. Because of the advent of the CT scanner and marvels of neuroimaging such as the MRI, there has been less need for specific diagnostic studies in many cases of suspected neuropathology. In keeping with the spirit of these changing times, of course, Ralph M. Reitan (Reitan & Wolfson, 1988) has developed a series of tasks for the rehabilitation of brain functioning known as *REHABIT* (1988), and Arthur L. Benton has, with others, (Meier, Benton & Diller, 1987) edited a book on neurological rehabilitation (1987). Even given the above, however, a significant role remains with respect to tracking behavioral correlates of neuropathology and integrating neuropsychological data with behavioral treatment planning. One of the issues in this endeavor relates to the diagnostic classification of organic mental disorders.

Organic Mental Syndromes and Disorders as Defined by the DSM-III-R

The standard classification of mental disorders used by the World Health Organization is the International Classification for Diseases (Worth Health Organization, 1992), which is currently in its ninth edition. In the United States, the American Psychiatric Association both developed and has successfully revised on a number of occasions the *Diagnostic and Statistical Manual* (DSM), which provides for psychiatric and psychological diagnoses of mental syndromes and disorders. Given the unsettled nature and many controversies regarding mental disorders, of course, the *Diagnostic and Statistical Manual* is truly a work in progress and is subject to ongoing revisions.

The major trend in the diagnosis of mental disorders has been successive revision and increasing specification. The first system of classification, which was published in 1962, had two categories of brain damage: acute and chronic. The second edition, which was published in 1966, added the variable of psychotic or nonpsychotic to the previous two categories of acute or chronic organic brain syndrome. In the third edition, or DSM-III, which was published in 1980, there was a greater specification of the number of types of organic mental disorder, as well as a welcome distinction between syndrome and etiology. In addition, the DSM-III was sensitive to developmental issues, as it identified particular groups of disorders that usually arise in infancy, childhood, or adolescence.

Also, the DSM-III utilized a multiaxial system which separated clinical syndrome, personality type or specific development disorder, and medical problems into successive groups. Problems often found in children with reading, spelling, handwriting, and math, among others, were included as specific developmental disorders. This multiaxial system has a considerable advantage over the earlier systems. Syndromes may be diagnosed based on behavioral evidence without requiring a specific etiological factor, whereas a disorder may directly implicate a specific neuropathology. With respect to behavioral interventions with children, there are a number of sections of the current *Diagnostic and Statistical Manual* (DSM-III-R; *American Psychiatric Association,* 1987) that are of particular importance.

In this section, particular attention will be devoted to the organic disorders. As currently constituted in the DSM-III-R, the organic mental syndromes are listed under six major categories: delirium and dementia; amnestic syndrome and organic hallucinosis; organic delusional syndrome, organic mood syndrome, and organic anxiety syndrome; organic personality syndrome; intoxication and withdrawal; and organic mental syndrome not otherwise specified. Global mental impairment is usually characteristic of delirium and dementia as organic mental syndromes. Generally speaking, delirium is characterized by a clouded consciousness or disorders of attention that are generally attributed to a transient condition; whereas, in dementia, the global mental impairment is in the presence of an unclouded consciousness. With children, there is often an issue with respect to whether a child is mentally retarded or demented. Perhaps the best way to draw the line between these two conditions is to appreciate the fact that dementia, a condition rarely diagnosed in children, is the lack of previously acquired mental abilities. Moreover, a diagnosis of mental retardation is an Axis II disorder, and there must also be an onset before the age of 18. The implications, of course, are that persons of age 19 and older cannot be appropriately diagnosed as having mental retardation, unless there was an onset before the age of 18.

As earlier noted, all of the diagnoses of organic mental disorders are applicable to children, even though in many individuals' minds they are most often associated with adults. In amnestic syndrome, there is selective impairment of cognitive ability. *Amnestic syndrome* refers to impairment of memory. While the DSM-III-R includes impairment of both short-term memory and long-term memory, the history and sense of the amnestic syndrome has been one that has focused primarily on the impairment of short-term memory. In organic hallucinosis, the hallucinations are the primary feature and should be preeminent above any other feature. Organic delusional syndrome, organic mood disorder, and organic anxiety disorder are syndromes in which disorders resembling various functional difficulties arise from organic causes. Simply put, organic delusional disorder, in some ways, resembles aspects of schizophrenia, organic mood disorder may resemble an affective disorder, and organic anxiety disorder may mimic an anxiety disorder. The crucial aspect of making these diagnoses is the existence or lack of evidence from the history, physical examination, or laboratory tests of a specific organic factor or factors which may be judged to be etiologically related to the organic mental disorder. The question is: Is there or is there not evidence of an organic component?

Organic personality syndrome refers to a persistent personality disturbance involving affective instability, aggression, impaired social judgment, marked apathy, and suspiciousness. It is worth recalling that this category first came into being for the purpose of accommodating patients with frontal lobe impairment. It is noteworthy that the diagnosis of organic personality syndrome should not be given to a child or adolescent if the clinical picture is limited to features that characterize ADHD. Similarly, there must be evidence from the history, physical examination, or laboratory tests of a specific organic factor or factors that can be judged to be etiologically related to the persistent personality disturbance.

Intoxication and withdrawal syndromes are, of course, related to substance abuse disorders. These disorders are causally related either to failing to take in or to taking in a psychoactive substance.

The last category, organic mental syndromes not otherwise specified, is essentially a "wastebasket" category for organic mental syndromes that fail to meet the criteria for the aforementioned categories.

At this time, it should be clearly understood that it is possible for an individual to have multiple organic mental syndromes. For example, a person can have an organic personality disorder and an intoxication syndrome at the same time. Indeed, the extent and variety of combinations and permutations possible is limited only by the total number of organic mental syndromes available.

The newest version of the American Psychiatric Association's *Diagnostic and Statistical Manual* (DSM-IV) is currently in progress. With respect to organic disorders, the current status suggests a possible elimination of the term *organic* and a reformulation of the organic disorders syndrome (Frances, Pincus, Widiger, Davis, & First, 1990). Essentially, dementia, delirium, and amnestic disorder would remain together in a section that could be titled "Cognitive Impairment Disorders," but the other currently listed disorders, such as those devoted to mood and anxiety and personality would be renamed "Secondary" or "Drug-Induced" and would be listed in the pertinent sections containing their descriptive phenomenology. Whether or not this reformulation will actually be accepted is a question only the future and the American Psychiatric Association work group can answer.

DEVELOPMENTALLY LINKED DISORDERS

In the DSM-III-R classification scheme, there is a series of disorders which are described as usually first evident in infancy, childhood, or adolescence. These include quite a number of conditions. With respect to Axis I disorders, which are primarily clinical syndromes, these include the disruptive behavior disorders, such as ADHD; anxiety disorders of childhood or adolescence; eating disorders; gender identity disorders; tic disorders; elimination disorders; sleep disorders not otherwise classified; and a "wastebasket" category of other disorders of infancy, childhood, or adolescence.

Also, there is a group of developmental disorders that are coded on Axis II. These developmental disorders include mental retardation; pervasive developmental disorders, such as autistic disorder; and specific developmental disorders (i.e., academic skills disorders, language and speech disorders, motor skills disorder, and specific developmental disorders not otherwise specified). Axis II usually refers to some relatively enduring conditions that are not in quite the same category as the clinical syndromes listed on Axis I. Developmental disorders and personality disorders both reside on Axis II.

In terms of this discussion, there is a degree of selectivity. With respect to the Axis I disorders, only the categories of disruptive behavior disorders and other disorders of infancy, childhood, and adolescence are broached. Within these categories, the primary focus in the disruptive behavior disorders is on ADHD and, the category of undifferentiated attention-deficit disorder. (Similarly, a degree of selectivity is exercised with the developmental disorders, but that will be explained later.)

ADHD is a particularly interesting disorder. Essentially, ADHD refers to children who have difficulties in motor activity and paying attention. For example, the child may be distracted by extraneous stimuli, may blurt out answers to questions before they have been completed, may have difficulty following through on instructions, may have problems sustaining attention on tasks or play activities, or may shift from one uncompleted activity to another. While in the DSM-III, ADHD was seen as a syndrome distinct from attention-deficit disorder without hyperactivity, the two were virtually combined in the DSM-III-R, and the disorder in the essentially "wastebasket" category of other disorders of infancy, childhood, or adolescence of undifferentiated attention-deficit disorder was left as a category to be elucidated later.

There appears to be some evidence that the DSM-V work group (Frances *et al.*, 1990) is considering the possibility of, again, subdividing this category into attention-deficit disorder with and attention-deficit disorder without hyperactivity. There is a growing body of literature (Barkley, DuPaul, & McMurray, 1990; Hynd, Lorys-Vernon, Semrud-Clikeman, Nieves, Huettner, & Leahey, 1993) which strongly suggests that these two types of attention-deficit disorder are separate and distinct childhood disorders rather than subtypes of a common attention deficit. Again, what will happen can be determined only by the future and the DSM-IV work group. With respect to the developmental disorders earlier mentioned, the specific developmental disorders will be the major conditions subject to further discussion, as mental retardation, pervasive developmental disorders, and other developmental disorders are less frequently encountered by the child neuropsychologist.

The category of specific developmental disorders, includes academic skills disorders, language and speech disorders, and motor skills disorders. Of these three the academic skills disorders have received the greatest attention in the child neuropsychology literature. Indeed, of these academic skills disorders (which, of course, include developmental arithmetic disorder, developmental expressive writing disorder, and developmental reading disorder), the category developmental reading disorder has received the greatest amount of attention. The specific criteria for developmental reading disorder are rather straightforward: reading achievement, as measured by a standardized, individually administered test that is markedly below the expected level, given what would be reasonable expectations of the person's intellectual capacity as determined by an individually administered IQ test and the person's level of educational experience. The difficulty with reading achievement would also be expected to interfere significantly with academic achievement or activities of daily living, which would require reading skills such as perusing a newspaper. A developmental reading disorder, or course, could not be due to a deficit in vision or hearing. As noted earlier, Hynd and his colleagues (1990) have demonstrated some interesting relationships with respect to brain morphology and developmental dyslexia, which both are exciting and will require replication.

It might be noted that, in cases of childhood disorders, a necessary but hardly sufficient condition for diagnosis would be the use of appropriately age-corrected normative data for the neuropsychological tests used (Hartlage, 1986; Reynolds, 1984). An appropriate diagnostic process also requires an appreciation of the neurocognitive changes which may be manifested at particular neuropsychological phases of development (Hartlage, 1986). Moreover, a sensitivity to the distinction between behavioral and neurological factors, in terms of their influences on neuropsychological performance, is needed.

EVOLVING DIRECTIONS IN CHILD NEUROPSYCHOLOGY

Clinical Practice

In clinical practice, an important issue is to understand the role and function of the various specialties that deal with children. A number of major specialties are briefly considered here: pediatric neurology, pediatric psychiatry, clinical child psychology, and school psychology.

Pediatric Neurology

It is perhaps fair to say that pediatric neurology, like general clinical neurology, has moved away from a focus on higher cortical functioning and toward an emphasis on the peripheral nervous system. While there are certainly behavioral neurologists in practice, the impression that is gained is that the majority of these deal with adults, and there are relatively few pediatric neurologists who are particularly attuned to behavioral functioning. There are, of course, some notable exceptions to this general statement, and the work of these few individuals has been of tremendous importance to the field of child neuropsychology. Still, it might be said that most pediatric neurologists are considerably more comfortable testing reflexes than when they are required to assess reading. It might be hoped that, in the future, with increasingly precise neurological procedures for imaging a developing brain, there will be multiple opportunities for fruitful and positive collaborations with pediatric neurologists, both by neuropsychologists and by behavior therapists.

Pediatric Psychiatry

It is of great interest that perhaps the majority of children diagnosed with attention-deficit disorder end up in the offices of child psychiatrists rather than pediatric neurologists. Clearly, in the last 30 years, there has been increasing interest on the part of child psychiatrists in the value of neuropsychological testing. Certainly, there is tremendous promise in terms of opportunities for neuropsychologists and behavior therapists to work closely with child psychiatrists to develop new and better assessment tools and more effective treatment programs for children with brain impairment. The unique training experiences and expertise of the child psychiatrist would be of inestimable value, particularly in the area of psychopharmacological interventions.

Clinical Child Psychology

Although clinical child psychology has some areas in common with clinical child neuropsychology (as could be expected because clinical child psychology is the parent discipline of clinical child neuropsychology), these do appear to be clear distinctions, to be sure. Generally speaking, and this may be a gross oversimplification, the focus of clinical child psychology has been more on functional problems of an emotional nature. By contrast, efforts in clinical child neuropsychology have been primarily devoted to disorders that usually have both neurocognitive and behavioral references. Future years may see an increasing diversity between these two important fields of child study.

School Psychology

Perhaps the single area in which there has been the greatest interest in the neuropsychological assessment of children has been school psychology (Reynolds, 1981). Indeed, the work of Hartlage, Hynd, and Reynolds, among others, has been quite exemplary in establishing the role of the neuropsychologist in the school psychology area. Quite clearly, in many cases, some of the best child neuropsychologists are those who have been prepared in school psychology programs. Moreover, in addition to focusing on children who have classic academic skills problems such as in reading, mathematics, and writing, some additional attention has been focused in school psychology on the problems of attention-deficit disorder, both with and without hyperactivity, and also on the neuropsychological assessment of children with various syndromes of mental retardation. It might be noted that, truly, the birth of clinical psychology was based upon the need of the Paris school system to determine which children were mental defectives and which were not. it is important to note that school psychologists have been dealing with brain-damaged children for decades but have been hampered by state and federal laws which have, in many cases, forced these children into categories which do *not* address their difficulties and deficits.

Professional Issues

There have been a number of professional issues of great importance. These include guidelines for education and training, as well as licensure and certification.

Education and Training

A task force of the International Neuropsychological Society (INS), chaired by Manfred J. Meier, has made major contributions to the development of models for educating and training neuropsychologists (Meier, 1981). The guidelines, however, are fairly generic, and additional work is needed to develop curricular and practicum experiences in the treatment of brain-injured children.

Certification and Licensure

In the majority of the states and provinces of the United States and Canada, the practice of child neuropsychology falls under a generic licensure of psychology. Interestingly, there has not been a specific licensure with respect to child neuropsychology. By contrast, the practice of school psychology in all jurisdictions is seen as requiring separate licensure or certification. With regard to credentialing, two boards have been established. The American Board of Clinical Neuropsychology (ABCN) has been initiated through the American Board of Professional Psychology (ABPP) and has instituted certification procedures for obtaining a diplomate in clinical neuropsychology. Also, the American Board of Professional Neuropsychology (ABPN) has been initiated, and that board offers a diplomate in professional neuropsychology. While both boards appear to be robust and vital, one fact which is true of both is that neither one has devoted specific attention to the special needs of brain-injured children as distinct from those of adults. One would hope that, in the coming years, energy, time, and resources will be devoted to better addressing these concerns.

Research Issues

This section is devoted to a consideration of new concepts, new technologies, and new populations.

New Concepts

In recent years, the concept of *subcortical brain damage* has become increasingly emphasized. As noted by Hynd and Willis in their 1988 book, *Pediatric Neuropsychology,* there are multiple interconnections between the cortical and subcortical structures. It might be fair to say that, in the past, there has been a relative neglect of the area of subcortical brain damage. In children, these areas may be of tremendous importance, and further research should devote particular attention to them (Swift, Dyker, & Durant, 1984). Also, new neuropsychological taxonomies or classifications systems, based on sophisticated statistical methods and mathematical models, will increase (Rourke, 1991).

Moreover, in rehabilitation and behavior management, there are emerging concepts with respect to the role of attentional processes in rehabilitation and to the necessity of having metacognitive models of impaired processes. The work of Mateer and her coworkers (Sohlberg & Mateer, 1989) in cognitive rehabilitation might be seen as particularly well developed.

New Technologies

The single most exciting area in terms of working with brain-injured children is the correlation of various neuropsychological tests with a number of newly emerging mental imaging procedures. The work of Hynd and his colleagues (1990, 1993), previously mentioned in this chapter, using MRI to identify brain morphology correlates in developmental dyslexia and ADHD, is an outstanding example of how this approach can be of potentially outstanding value. In addition, however, one might expect the areas of brain mapping and regional cerebral blood flow to be explored in the future. The potential value of establishing objective behavioral correlates of actual brain functioning in "real time" would be extraordinary.

New Populations

Relatively little work has been done on the assessment and treatment of children who have been exposed to such potentially neurotoxic substances as lead, solvents, metals, drugs, pesticides, and alcohol (Hartman, 1988). Much additional work will be required to deal with the problems of these children. Another area of interest will be children whose mothers took cocaine prior to their birth. A number of antidotal reports suggest that these children may be impaired in a variety of behavioral and cognitive skills, and little has been done to plan for their care. In addition, other medical disorders, such as diabetes, cancer, and asthma, are currently being investigated with neuropsychological measures, and their neurological correlates are being identified. While the field is certainly not without controversy, there is a significant likelihood that increasing numbers of these children will require specialized services. In addition, there have been *very* few studies on children which utilize longitudinal research designs. The sort of information such research can provide on neurocognitive developmental processes is desperately needed to effectively plan treatment services.

SUMMARY

Clinical neuropsychology is a relatively young field. The subarea of clinical child neuropsychology can be seen as burgeoning today. Child neuropsychology has been recognized as a necessity in most medical schools and in professional preparation programs in clinical child, and school psychology. Child neuropsychology is also clearly established in the public schools and, while most identified with the areas of ADHD and specific developmental disorders, also deals with a variety of handicapping conditions. An important future focus for clinical child neuropsychology will be attempts to blend it with behavior therapy techniques.

In the preceding sections, some efforts were devoted to conceptualizing the notion of behavioral neuropsychology, and to outlining some of the difficulties faced by brain-injured children. In addition, there were efforts to briefly mention some of the organic and developmental categories of the DSM-III-R, and to describe briefly some considered modifications for the DSM-IV. In addition, a number of clinical, professional, and research issues were addressed. The hope and expectation are that this chapter will set the stage for a thoughtful consideration of many of these issues.

REFERENCES

American Psychiatric Association. (1987). *Diagnostic and statistical manual of mental disorders* (3rd ed., rev.; DSM-III-R). Washington, DC: Author.

Baltes, P. B. (1983). Life-span developmental psychology: Observations on history and theory revisited. In P. B. Baltes (Ed.), *Developmental psychology: Historical and philosophical perspectives* (pp. 79–111). Hillsdale, NJ: Erlbaum.

Baltes, P. B., Reese, H. W., & Nesselroade, J. R. (1977). *Lifespan developmental psychology: Introduction to research methods.* Monterey, CA: Brooks/Cole.

Barkley, R. A., DuPaul, G. J., & McMurray, M. B. (1990). Comprehensive evaluation of Attention Deficit Disorder with and without Hyperactivity as defined by research criteria. *Journal of Consulting and Clinical Psychology, 58,* 775–789.

Bryden, M. P., & Saxby, L. (1985). Developmental aspects of cerebral lateralization. In J. E. Obrzut & G. W. Hynd (Eds.), *Child neuropsychology,* Vol. 1 (pp. 78–94). Orlando, FL: Academic Press.

Davison, L. A. (1974). Introduction. In R. M. Reitan & L. A. Davison (Eds.), *Clinical neuropsychology: Current status and applications* (pp. 1–18). New York: Wiley.

Featherman, D. L., & Learner, R. M. (1985). Ontogenesis and sociogenesis: Problematics for theory and research about development and socialization across the lifespan. *American Sociological Review, 50*(5), 659–676.

Frances, A., Pincus, H. A., Widiger, T. A., Davis, W. W., & First, M. B. (1990). DSM-IV: Work in progress. *American Journal of Psychiatry, 147,* 1439–1448.

Gaddes, W. H. (1981). Neuropsychology, fact or mythology, educational help or hindrance? *School Psychology Review, 10*(3), 322–330.

Geschwind, N., & Levitsky, W. (1968). Human brain: Left-right asymmetries in temporal speech region. *Science, 1961,* 186–187.

Hartlage, L. C. (1986). Pediatric neuropsychology. In D. Wedding, A. M. Horton, Jr., & J. S. Webster (Eds.), *The neuropsychology handbook* (pp. 441–455). New York: Springer.

Hartman, D. E. (1988). *Neuropsychological toxicology.* New York: Pergamon Press.

Horton, A. M., Jr. (1979). Behavioral neuropsychology: Rationale and research. *Clinical Neuropsychology, 1,* 20–23.

Horton, A. M., Jr. (1987). Luria's contributions in clinical and behavioral neuropsychology. *Neuropsychology, 1*(2), 39–44.

Horton, A. M., Jr., & Puente, A. E. (1986). Behavioral neuropsychology with children. In G. Hynd & J. Obrzut (Eds.), *Child neuropsychology: Clinical practice,* Vol. 2 (pp. 299–316). Orlando, FL: Academic Press.

Horton, A. M., Jr., & Puente, A. E. (1989). Neuropsychological considerations. In M. Hersen (Ed.), *Innovations in child behavior therapy* (pp. 105–133). New York: Springer.

Horton, A. M., Jr., & Puente, A. E. (1990). Life-span neuropsychology: An overview. In A. M. Horton, Jr. (Ed.), *Neuropsychology across the life-span* (pp. 1–15). New York: Springer.

Horton, A. M., Jr., & Wedding, D. (1984). *Clinical and behavioral neuropsychology.* New York: Praeger.

Hynd, G. W. (1981). Rebuttal to the critical commentary on neuropsychology in the schools. *School Psychology Review, 10*(3), 367–372.

Hynd, G. W., & Obrzut, J. E. (1986). Clinical child neuropsychology: Issues and perspectives. In G. W. Hynd & J. Obrzut (Eds.), *Child neuropsychology: Clinical practice,* Vol. 2 (pp. 3–14). Orlando, FL: Academic Press.

Hynd, G. W., & Semrud-Clikeman, M. (1989). Dyslexia and brain morphology. *Psychological Bulletin, 106,* 447–482.

Hynd, G. W., & Willis, W. G. (1988). *Pediatric neuropsychology.* Orlando, FL: Grune & Stratton.

Hynd, G. W., Semrud-Clikeman, M., Lorys, A. R., Novey, E. S., & Eliopulos, D. (1990). Brain morphology in developmental dyslexia and Attention Deficit Disorder/Hyperactivity. *Archives of Neurology, 47,* 919–926.

Hynd, G. W., Lorys-Vernon, A. R., Semrud-Clikeman, M., Nieves, N., Huettner, M. I. S., & Leahey, B. B. (1993). Attention Deficit Disorder without Hyperactivity (ADD/WO): A distinct behavioral and neurocognitive syndrome. *Journal of Child Neurology,* in press.

Jackson, J. H. (1958). *Selected writings of John Hughings Jackson,* J. Taylor (Ed.). New York: Basic Books.

Kazdin, A. E. (1978). *History of behavior modification: Experimental foundations of contemporary research.* Baltimore: University Park Press.

Luria, A. R. (1966). *Higher cortical functions in man.* New York: Basic Books.

Luria, A. R. (1973). *The working brain.* New York: Basic Books.

Masters, J. C., Burish, T. G., Hollon, S. D., & Rimm, D. C. (1987). *Behavior therapy: Techniques and empirical findings* (3rd ed.). New York: Academic Press.

Meier, M. J. (1974). Some challenges for clinical neuropsychology. In R. M. Reitan & L. A. Davison (Eds.), *Clinical neuropsychology: Current status and application* (pp. 289–323). New York: Wiley.

Meier, M. J. (Ed.). (1981). Report of the International Neuropsychological Task Force on Education, Accreditation, and Credentialing. *INS Bulletin,* September, 5–10.

Meier, M. J., Benton, A., & Diller, L. (1987). *Neuropsychological rehabilitation.* New York: Guilford Press.

Reitan, R. M., & Davison, L. A. (Eds.). (1974). *Clinical neuropsychology: Current status and application.* New York: Wiley.

Reitan, R. M., & Wolfson, D. (1988). *Traumatic brain injury.* Vol. II. *Recovery and rehabilitation.* Tucson AZ: Neuropsychology Press.

Reynolds, C. R. (1981). Neuropsychological assessment in habilitation of learning: Considerations and the search for the aptitude treatment interaction. *School Psychology Review, 10,* 342–349.

Reynolds, C. R. (1984). Critical measurement issues in learning disabilities. *Journal of Special Education, 18,* 451–476.

Rourke, B. P. (1991). Human neuropsychology in the 1990's. *Archives of Clinical Neuropsychology. 6,* 1–14.

Rourke, B. P., Fisk, J. L., & Strang, J. D. (1986). *Neuropsychological assessment of children: A treatment-oriented approach.* New York: Guilford Press.

Sohlberg, M. M., & Mateer, C. A. (1989). *Introduction to cognitive rehabilitation: Theory and practice.* New York: Guilford Press.

Swift, A. V., Dyken, P. P., & Durant, R. H. (1984). Psychological follow-up in childhood dementia: A longitudinal study of subacute sclerosing pan encephalitis. *Journal of Pediatric Psychology, 9*, 469–483.

Teuber, H. L., & Rudel, R. G. (1962). Behavior after cerebral lesions in children and adults. *Developmental Medicine and Child Neurology, 4*, 3–20.

World Health Organization (1992). *ICD-10*. Geneva, Switzerland: WHO.

2

Brain–Behavior Relationships

with WILLIAM G. MILLER

This chapter presents a brief description of developmental brain–behavior relationships. Special attention is given to developmental neuroanatomy and to hemispheric lateralization of function, but the material herein is not intended as a standard review of neuroanatomy. Many neurological textbooks adequately address this subject (Brodal, 1969; Nauta & Feintag, 1986; Reitan & Wolfson, 1985). Moreover, the cellular substructure of the childhood nervous system is not discussed in any detail. As noted by Horton and Wedding (1984):

> This is no way suggests that the cytoarchitectonic layers of the cortex are not suitable subjects for neuropsychological study or that particular cortical neurons may be ignored, but rather reflects the essentially primitive state of contemporary neuropsychological knowledge. (p. 47)

MORPHOLOGY OF THE CENTRAL NERVOUS SYSTEM

In this section, we examine the gross anatomy of the human brain and introduce the general morphology of the central nervous system. Second, a discussion of the development of various structures of the neocortex is presented.

The major subdivisions of the central nervous system are the spinal cord and the brain. The spinal cord serves to transmit sensory impulses to the brain and to conduct motor nerve impulses from the brain to the muscles to produce motoric behavior. The spinal cord is divided into segments (i.e., cervical, thoracic, lumbar, and sacral), which refer to attachment groups of nerves. Although the spinal cord is of crucial importance with respect to relaying sensory information and motor instructions, the brain itself tends to hold greater interest for most neuropsychologists. The brain can be divided into three major sections: the hindbrain, the midbrain, and the forebrain.

Hindbrain

The hindbrain is made up of major areas which include the medulla oblongata, the pons, and the cerebellum. The medulla oblongata is the first neural structure above the foramen magnum (i.e., the opening in the cranial cavity which allows the brain and spinal cord to be connected) and controls respiration, blood pressure, and heartbeat. The pons, the enlarged, bulging section of the brain stem just above the medulla, serves as a communication channel to forebrain areas and includes commissural fibers which connect the two hemispheres of the cerebellum. Behind the pons, the cerebellum adjoins the brain stem. The cerebellum, composed of two separate hemispheres, regulates motor control and coordination and works with the pons to regulate motor impulses in response to postural and muscle movement.

Midbrain

The midbrain is the intermediate zone between the hindbrain and the forebrain. It is situated where the brain stem merges with the thalamus and the hypothalamus. This area appears to be important for perceptual processing.

The reticular activating system (RAS) lies in the midbrain and the upper section of the hindbrain. Its purpose is the control of attention processes. The RAS regulates cortical tone and directs the organism's attention to incoming stimuli. In cases of injury to the RAS, the person experiences disorders of consciousness and with severe injury may lapse into coma.

Forebrain

The forebrain and its amazing abilities serve to separate humans from other primates. It is not possible to overstate its importance in neuropsychology. A number of unique and highly specialized structures are located in the forebrain, including the thalamus, hypothalamus, limbic system, basal ganglia, and cerebral cortex.

Thalamus

The thalamus is located near the center of the brain immediately above the limbic system and, in terms of evolution, is a particularly old brain structure. Indeed, in less advanced forms of life, the thalamus is the largest structure in the brain. The thalamus is composed of twin hemispheres, each underlying its respective cerebral hemisphere.

The function of the thalamus is that of a computer center for the brain. Specific sensory nerves relay vital information to the appropriate cerebral sensory area. Some authors (e.g., Horton & Wedding, 1984) have postulated that the thalamus is the most important structure for the perception of certain sensations. The thalamus also controls the brain's electrical activity, so that it is crucial to effective information processing. Brain lesions involving the thalamus are associated with memory, attention, and concentration problems.

Hypothalamus

Located above the roof of the mouth, the hypothalamus is a complicated structure and controls a number of vitally important life-support systems, including body temperature, blood pressure, sleeping, eating, drinking, and sexual activity. Lesions in the hypothalamus can cause disruptions in all of these functions and can cause emotional problems.

Limbic System

Closely connected to the hypothalamus is the so-called limbic system, which includes the amygdala, cingulate cortex, hippocampus, and septal area. The limbic system is interconnected by nerve pathways to multiple other areas of the nervous system and, in particular, to the frontal cortex. There is much to be learned concerning the precise roles of each of the limbic system components. At present, we know some things about the hippocampal area and the amygdala.

The hippocampal area is associated with memory disorders, particularly declarative memory for facts. This type of memory must be differentiated from procedural memory for skills, which seems to be located in the cerebellum. When the left hippocampus is damaged, the person is unable to acquire new long-term verbal memories (Russell & Espir, 1961). Impairment of the right hypocampal gyrus precludes the development of long-term nonverbal memories (Milner, 1971).

the amygdala, with some role in memory formations (Mishkin, 1978), is identified also with the expression of aggressive behavior. As in much brain–behavior research, this conclusion is based on the absence of aggressive behavior when the amygdala is surgically removed.

Basal Ganglia

The basal ganglia lie deep within the cerebral hemispheres. As in the limbic system, there are a number of subdivisions: the putamen, the globus pallidus, and the caudate nucleus. These structures, with the cerebral cortex and the midbrain, form the extrapyramidal motor system. The basal ganglia play a role in the production of movement and in the automatic integration of movement in concert with other components of the extrapyramidal system. In order to better understand the functions of the extrapyramidal system, it might be helpful to recall that the classic neurological condition known as *Parkinson's disease* represents an impairment of the extrapyramidal system.

Cerebral Cortex

The unique development and enlargement of the cerebral cortex over millions of years have been central to the distinction between human beings and other primates. In appearance, the cerebral cortex or neocortex is divided into two separate hemispheres that look like two underinflated gray rugby footballs. In right-handed human beings, in the majority of cases, the left cerebral hemisphere appears a bit larger than the right hemisphere. Standard practice refers to the larger of the two cerebral hemispheres as the *dominant hemisphere* and to the smaller hemisphere as the *nondominant hemisphere*.

There are a number of distinguishing physical features of the cerebral hemispheres. They are separated by the longitudinal cerebral commissures, and the surface of the hemispheres is convoluted by little hills and valleys technically, and respectively, called *gyri* and *sulci.* Two very deep and wide sulci form the major landmarks of the brain. The central sulcus, or fissure of Rolando, which lies in the middle of each cerebral hemisphere, separates the frontal and parietal lobes. The lateral cerebral fissure, or fissure of Sylvius, arises in the base of the brain and separates the frontal and temporal lobes in the front and the temporal and parietal lobes in the back.

The areas of the cerebral hemispheres are further subdivided into eight sections. The most common American approach is to look at the frontal, temporal, parietal, and occipial lobes within each cerebral hemisphere. As noted above, the frontal and parietal lobes are separated by the central sulcus, and the frontal and temporal lobes are separated by the lateral cerebral fissure. The parietal and occipital lobes are not anatomically separated, but a much smaller fissure, the parietal occipital fissure, is used to indicate where the parietal lobe ends and the occipital lobe begins.

The structure holding the two cerebral hemispheres together is the corpus callosum. It is a band of white fibers connecting the homotopic areas of the two cerebral hemispheres. The corpus callosum allows for direct communication between the two cerebral hemispheres. Split-brain patients, are those whose corpus callosum has been severed.

The actual surface of the cerebral hemispheres has been mapped out by a number of anatomists. The most popular framework is that of Korbinian Brodmann (Nauta & Feintag, 1986). This scheme has given numbers to specific cortical areas. For example, the primary areas for somatic sensory projection are 1, 2, and 3 and lie just behind the central sulcus (i.e., in the parietal lobes). these specific areas must be intact to enable the child to report tactile perceptions (touch). Similarly, there are primary areas for audition (area 41 in the temporal lobes) and for vision (area 17 in the occipital lobes). If these latter brain areas are severely damaged, the child is unable to hear sounds or to see objects. Brodmann's map of the cerebral cortex conforms remarkably closely with these functional areas, but other behavioral correlates are less exactly localized.

It would be well at this juncture to comment on some important differences between child and adult cerebral organization and localization of function. A child's brain, in terms of localization of functions, has been less well studied and is inherently more difficult to understand than the adult's brain. There is a greater degree of variation in the expression of human abilities subserved by a child's cerebral hemispheres. Children, by definition, are in the process of developing and are prone to various poorly understood growth spurts and to so-called developmental lags or delays. Further, children are acquiring their basic academic and daily living skills. It is difficult to know, with an absolute degree of certainty, how far along it is reasonable to expect a given child to be in terms of any number of abilities.

By contrast, adult brains are somewhat easier to understand. Although adults do age, their neuropsychological abilities are relatively stable from ages 16 to 45 years, and the rate of change after age 45 is fairly slow. This is in marked contrast to the more rapid developmental pace of children's brains. Also, the neuropsychology of adults has been the object of disciplined inquiry and study for several decades. Unfortunately, and by contrast, considerably fewer data are available on the neuropsychology of children. Because of the greater attention devoted to the neuropsychology of adults, and because of the relatively less complex nature of the task, it is somewhat easier to postulate specific brain–behavior correlates in adults. Even Luria's brilliant contribution, discussed in the next section, is based primarily on work with adult patients.

LURIA'S MODEL OF BRAIN FUNCTIONING

Luria (1966), the famous Russian neuroscientist, proposed a conceptual model for the organization of higher mental processes and the behavioral correlates of specific brain areas. He postulated three major brain blocks. (1) the brain stem structures; (2) the cerebral cortex posterior to the central sulcus; and (3) the cerebral cortex anterior to the central sulcus. Each major block makes a specific contribution to human cognition.

The Three Major Brain Blocks

The brain stem structures (Block I) are responsible for the tone and energy level of the cerebral cortex. Just as the electrical supply to a personal computer must be stable and constant in order for the arithmetic and logic unit to work, so the brain stem structures must support the mental activity of the cerebral cortex. The second major block functions in a different manner. The posterior cerebral cortex (Block II) subserves the perceptions of the senses by receiving, organizing, and retraining visual, auditory, and tactual stimuli. Block III completes the conceptual model. The anterior cerebral cortex is responsible for emitting motor responses, formulating intentions, planning, and evaluating behaviors.

Luria (1966) postulated further that the second and third blocks of the cerebral cortex are divided into primary, secondary and tertiary areas. The second block (i.e., the posterior cerebral cortex) is used here as an example to illustrate Luria's postulation. Essentially, the primary areas perform very basic functions of sensory input of visual, auditory, or tactual stimuli. The secondary areas perform more elaborate perceptions of the nature of the stimuli. For example, the primary area would alert a child whether or not she or he has been touched, but a secondary area could enhance the stimulus and inform the child whether an X or an O has been drawn on the skin. Tertiary areas would combine two or more secondary areas to subserve complex mental activities such as handwriting. In other words, information from different senses is combined to perform a higher level human behavior.

Functional Systems

Luria (1990) proposed that different areas of the brain combine into functional systems. Specific sections of the brain in each of the three blocks combine to produce behavioral performance. Functional systems could be created also by using different routes in the brain but yield the same ultimate behavioral outcome. A simple example would be that reading can be taught by either linguistic analysis or sight reading (Horton & Wedding, 1984). Abilities postulated to reside in the temporal lobes are most important in linguistic analysis, but the crucial skill of sight reading is performed by abilities postulated to reside in the occipital lobes. As stated, the behavioral outcome is the same, but the combination of brain areas responsible for production may vary quite markedly.

Neuropsychological Developmental Stages

In addition to postulating the different roles played by separate brain areas, Luria (1980) suggested that the higher cortical functions were developed in conjunction with environmental stimuli in different stages. To a degree, this hypothesis refers to Luria's work on Vygotsky's cultural historical theory (Horton, 1987). It is obvious that highly complex functional systems are not available in a toddler. Luria (1980) averred that cultural-historical-social influences upon children as they grow up are important in shaping the contributions of the available brain areas. Thus, the development of higher cortical functions, such as language, intentional memory, and abstract thought, is the product of both the development of neuroanatomical structures and the cultural, historical, and social environmental stimuli experienced by the child.

Luria (1980) proposed five stages in the development of higher cortical functions and intentional mental activity. The stages are based on his conceptualization of the three basic blocks of the brain. the *first stage,* beginning in the first year of life, is devoted to the development of the reticular activitating system (RAS). These subcortical structures are contained in the first block. The *second stage* overlaps with the first stage to a significant degree. In this stage, the primary sensory areas for vision, hearing, and tactual perception and the primary motor areas for gross motor movement come into play. For the most part, this stage is programmed by neurological structures (i.e., hardware), rather than environmental influence (i.e., software; Luria, 1980). As later stages emerge, these primary areas become integrated into more complex neuropsychological patterns. The *third stage* focuses on the single-modality–secondary-association areas of the brain. This stage moves the toddler into the preschool realm. The child is able to recognize and reproduce words, shapes, and movement. For the most part, different modalities of learning are accessed separately.

The task of intermodality sensory integration is begun in earnest in the *fourth stage* of Luria's paradigm of neuropsychological development. At about the time of first or second grade, the tertiary areas of the parietal lobes become active. As mentioned earlier, the tertiary parietal lobe is the area where the temporal, parietal, and occipital lobes meet and merge. Thus, the integration of the three major sensory input channels becomes a reality. At this stage, of course, cultural-historical-social influences are crucial in shaping the child's development as the task of assuming the culture's collected wisdom (e.g., reading, writing, and arithmetic) begins.

The *fifth stage* of Luria's conceptualization (1980) of neuropsychological development concerns the prefrontal lobes of the cerebral cortex. Although the fourth stage in Luria's paradigm is activated at about the time a child begins elementary school, the fifth stage becomes activated during adolescence or later. The prefrontal lobes, of course, are crucial for the development of the abilities of planning, execution of plans, evaluation of complex human behavior, critical judgment, and concept formation (Struss & Benson, 1984).

Luria's conceptualization (1980) of neuropsychological development suggests two additional significant points. First, it implies that there are qualitative differences between children at different stages of neuropsychological development. Children may utilize different neurological structures to perform different behaviors or tasks at different ages. There is an interaction between the child's stage of neuropsychological development and the kinds of behavioral tasks the child can perform competently. Second, Luria's conceptualization (1980) suggests that children could use different functional systems to perform the same task. Although the final behavioral performance may be the same, the combination of brain areas utilized could vary. This concept has important implications for the retraining of brain-injured children. It provides a rationale for a remediation approach which concentrates on developing functional competence by reorganizing the neural pathways that combine to produce the final behavior. Remediation will be discussed in later chapters, but for the moment, we turn our attention to the issue of asymmetry of the cerebral hemispheres.

HEMISPHERIC LATERALIZATION OF FUNCTION

Cerebral asymmetry refers to the morphological differences between the two cerebral hemispheres. It is fair to say, the two hemispheres are not identical but are very similar. In most right-handed individuals, the left cerebral hemisphere is slightly larger than the right cerebral hemisphere (Connolly, 1950). The usual explanation for this size disparity is the special role that the left cerebral hemisphere plays in language (Geschwind & Levitsky, 1968). It is assumed by many that those areas dealing with spoken language and written symbols for communication have become enlarged as oral communication, reading, and writing have become more important to the survival of the human race. Of particular interest to the clinical child neuropsychologist are reports that autopsy examinations of children with documented reading problems reveal that the right cerebral hemisphere is slightly larger than the left cerebral hemisphere (Hynd et al., 1986). These data have been interpreted by some workers in the field of child neuropsychology as suggesting a neuroanatomical basis for dyslexia.

The term *contralateral control* refers to the organization of the human nervous system at the level of the cerebral hemisphere. The cerebral hemisphere on one side of the brain controls the sensory and motor functions of the opposite side of the body. Thus, the right cerebral hemisphere controls visual, auditory, and tactile sensations and gross motor functions on the left side of the body, and vice versa. The sensory abilities are not 100% under contralateral control. Auditory perceptions, for example, are 80% under contralateral control and 20% under ipsalateral, or same-side, control.

Hemispheric Abilities

The cerebral hemispheres are somewhat specialized in the behavioral functions to which they contribute. Although some clinical understanding of these unique abilities of the cerebral hemispheres was attained by the famous English neurologist Hughlings Jackson in the 1870s, they were generally accepted by neuroscientists only after the findings of the split-brain research of Sperry (1961) had been widely circulated. Sperry conducted a series of experiments with patients who had had the connections between the two cerebral hemispheres surgically removed. These patients had a history of severe intractable epilepsy, and one method of treatment is to surgically sever the fibers connecting the two cerebral hemispheres. This treatment involves the corpus callosum, the main set of interhemispheric fibers, but may include severing the anterior commissure and the hippocampal commissure, two sets of secondary interhemispheric fibers. As a result of this neurosurgical procedure, the patients were less troubled by seizures. A secondary effect, however, was that the two cerebral hemispheres were disconnected and functioned somewhat independently (Golden, 1978; Horton & Wedding, 1984).

As observed by Nebes (1974):

> In contrast to earlier studies of patients with unilateral brain damage where there are great difficulties in controlling for multiple confounding variables, in the commissurotomy patients the two cerebral hemispheres are relatively intact and available for separate testing, allowing comparison within a single person of the two sides of the brain on a given task. (p. 1)

Although there is some agreement that each of the two cerebral hemisphere mediate different behavioral functions, there is less agreement regarding the developmental stage at which various behavioral functions are subserved by various brain structures (Dean, 1985). Some researchers have proposed that young children do not have behavioral functions subserved by the frontal lobes. Other researchers dispute this conclusion.

Bryden and Saxby (1985) postulated that hemispheric lateralization of functions begins early in life. By age 3, over 90% of children demonstrate superior left-hemispheric language-processing abilities. After age 3, research has failed to find major developmental differences between the left hemisphere's superior abilities with language or the right hemisphere's superior skill in reading body language (Bryden & Saxby, 1985; Saxby & Bryden, 1984, 1985). Interestingly, the development of a lateralized preference for handedness and footedness follows a similar age-related pattern. Preference for the right hand in the majority of children appears by age 2 (Bryden & Saxby, 1985), whereas preference for the right foot is developed in most cases by age 5 (Porac & Coren, 1981). There are some indications that abnormal hemispheric lateralization could be related to reading difficulties (Corballis, 1982).

The following overview of the localization of cerebral function, by necessity, is based upon adult neuropsychology data. We hope to provide some perspective on the brain–behavior relationships toward which children are progressing. However, it is prudent to remember that cerebral lateralization is relative rather than absolute (Corballis, 1982).

Left-Hemisphere Functions

The left cerebral hemisphere is usually thought of as specialized for language and speech. The abilities suggested include understanding and producing speech, reading, writing, arithmetic, and other uses of symbols for communication purposes.

Right-Hemispherec Functions

The right cerebral hemisphere is usually thought of as specialized for visuospatial and perceptual motor skills. These abilities include orienting in space, drawing geometric patterns, recognizing faces, and discriminating nonverbal material (Golden, 1978). Also, processing of emotional data appears to be subserved by the right hemisphere (Saxby & Bryden, 1984).

SPECIFIC FUNCTIONS OF CEREBRAL LOBES

There is a considerable body of clinical and research literature regarding the behavioral correlates of lesions in specific cerebral lobes. Again, most of this literature has been developed from the adult population. Although a lesion in any area is correlated with a behavioral deficit, this does not suggest that the lesion is causally related to the specific behavioral deficit. It is more likely that the relationship is quite subtle and complex.

Frontal Lobes

The frontal lobes are responsible for the planning, execution, and evaluation of motor behavior. Many of the abilities subserved by the frontal lobes include goal-directed behavior, time-span judgment, and intentional memory. In addition, some affective changes may be associated with frontal lobe impairments.

Left Frontal Lobe

The left frontal lobe is particularly involved in the production of speech. It includes Broca's area, which is intimately connected with motor speech. Unique behavioral deficits include impaired word fluency, inability to regulate external behavior by complex internal speech rules, and difficulties with verbal memory.

Right Frontal Lobe

The right frontal lobe seems particularly involved with the ability to sing. Problems in motor-visual-spatial integration (Teuber, 1963) and maze learning (Corkin, 1965) are also common with lesions in this area.

Temporal Lobes

The temporal lobes are concerned with the perception, analysis, and evaluation of auditory stimuli (Luria, 1966). The temporal lobes are also important participants in the neuropsychological structures subserving memory functions, including the reception and analysis of verbal and nonverbal stimuli. The entry of the verbal or nonverbal material into long-term memory, however, depends on the action of the hippocampus and other structures of the limbic system (Nauta, 1964).

Left Temporal Lobe

The left temporal lobe is involved in the auditory perception of verbal stimuli such as the sounds of letters, words, and numbers. Impairment of the left temporal lobe can result in difficulties in the analysis and integration of auditory language (Luria, 1966). Resulting problems in phonic analysis can impair reading, writing, and spelling skills, as the decoding of language phonemes is an integral part of these processes (Golden, 1978). The left temporal lobe is involved also in verbal short-term memory (Milner, 1958).

Right Temporal Lobe

The right temporal lobe is involved in the auditory perception of nonverbal stimuli such as rhythm and pitch. Impairment of the right temporal lobe can render a person unable to comprehend music. Nonverbal memory is associated also with this lobe (Meier & French, 1965).

Parietal Lobes

The parietal lobes mediate tactile and kinesthetic perception. Lesions in the parietal lobes produce problems in accurately appreciating tactile stimuli, for example, an inability to recognize objects by tactile sensitivity and an inability to integrate tactile information and kinesthetic input (Golden, 1978). Another area of deficit suggested by Luria (1966) is an inability to consider multiple aspects of an object at the same time. A variety of difficulties with skilled voluntary motor movements are thought to result from parietal lobe impairment (Horton & Wedding, 1984).

Left Parietal Lobe

The left parietal lobe is of great importance in verbal information processing because of its central position between the temporal and occipital lobes. The trilobe region (i.e., temporal, parietal, and occipital) is responsible for facilitating communication, and for coordinating and integrating information from visual, auditory, and tactile sensory modalities (Golden, 1978). For example, problems in speech and writing can be produced by a failure of the complex perceptual-motor feedback loop. The person is unable to correct subtle errors because the person is unaware of the problems owing to a lack of precise sensory input. Lesions in the parietal-temporal-occipital region can produce difficulties in reading, arithmetic, writing, naming, color labeling, and spelling. It is worth noting that verbal memory deficits associated with the left parietal lobe are usually difficulties in organizing verbal material (Luria, 1973).

Right Parietal Lobe

The right parietal lobe is associated with the combining of diverse visual, auditory, and tactile information into non-language-related wholes. For example, the perception of faces and the drawing of spatially accurate figures are thought to be dependent upon the right parietal lobe. Arithmetic operations in which numbers must maintain a place value also can be impaired. The most common symptoms of impairment, however, relate to dressing difficulties and to problems in attending to the left side of one's body. This last problem can include a denial of the left of the visual field (Lezak, 1976).

Occipital Lobes

Visual functions are mediated by the occipital lobes. The occipital lobe in each cerebral hemisphere perceives the contralateral visual field.

Left Occipital Lobe

The left occipital lobe is important in the visual discrimination and analysis of language-related visual forms such as letters, words, and numbers. Problems can include an inability to integrate visual stimuli into a coherent whole or to comprehend multiple aspects of a visual form (Luria, 1966). Such visual problems can contribute to difficulties with reading, writing, and arithmetic (Lezak, 1976).

Right Occipital Lobe

The right occipital lobe is responsible for the visual perception of nonverbal forms. Impairment of this lobe will produce difficulties in the visual recognition and differentiation of forms and unfamiliar patterns (Golden, 1978; Lezak, 1976). Problems in differentiating color hues, as opposed to verbally labeling the colors, is also likely to be a result of right-occipital-lobe lesions (Scotti & Spinner, 1970).

RECOVERY OF FUNCTION AFTER CHILDHOOD CEREBRAL TRAUMA

Brain "plasticity" is an important issue to address prior to considering the research evidence on recovery of function. The possible role of the environment in brain development is of great theoretical and practical interest (Horton & Wedding, 1984). Research on infrahumans has demonstrated that proper environmental stimulation can modify the central nervous system. Perhaps the most important of a number of earlier studies was conducted by Rosenzweig and his colleagues. Rosenzweig (1980) reared animals in either an enriched environment or an impoverished condition. The results were that the experimental manipulation affected the actual weight of the animals' cortex. Other research demonstrated positive changes in neurochemistry in the enriched condition (Rosenzweig, 1980). Also, research has confirmed that brain size and function can be modified by environmental experience (Rosenzweig, 1980). Also, there are suggestions that brains are most sensitive to the effects of differential experiencing during the earliest years of life (Rosenzweig, 1980).

At least on an animal level, there is evidence that the animals reared in the enriched environment are better able to adapt to their natural circumstance (Diamond, 1988; Rosenzweig, 1980).

NEUROPSYCHOLOGICAL RECOVERY

The "Kennard principle," often mentioned in discussions of brain damage in childhood (Rudel, 1978), proposed that, if one sustained a brain injury, it was best to have it earlier in life. Early brain injuries were assumed to be less disruptive of behavioral function. Rourke, Bakker, Fisk, and Strang (1983), however, pointed out that there is evidence incompatible with the Kennard principle. They suggested that the effects of early brain damage are multidetermined by such factors as the type of insult, the location of the lesion, the extent of the brain damage, and the developmental course of the insult. This is not, of course, to suggest that the age at which a lesion occurs does not have an effect, but to stress the tremendous number of factors which warrant thoughtful consideration (Rosenzweig, 1980).

As mentioned earlier, children who sustain brain injury have somewhat different results than do adults. Teuber, in a classic paper (Teuber & Rudel, 1962), illustrated many unique aspects of recovery of function by brain-damaged children. This research study utilized brain-damaged adults and children with age-appropriate controls and was continued for 10 years to assess the effects of early brain damage on new learning. The brain-damaged children were followed from age 5 to age 15.

Three possible developmental patterns of neuropsychological deficit were postulated. First, there could be initial impairment of behavior abilities following brain injury in a child, but the child would show a progressive pattern of recovery over time. Second, there would be impairment of behavioral abilities following early brain injury in a child, and this impairment would be constant as the child grew up. Third, there would *not* be discernible impairment of behavioral abilities following early brain injury in a child, but as the brain-injured child aged, behavioral deficits would arise. In the third instance, it appears that there is a delayed onset of the impairment in the child's abilities. As could be expected, brain-damaged children and brain-damaged adults did not demonstrate the same set of patterns over a number of tasks (Teuber & Rudel, 1962), but brain-damaged children displayed all three patterns, depending on the task assessed.

This classic research study demonstrates why child neuropsychology is so difficult to master. The effects of early brain damage are quite complex. They can depend upon *both* the task under study and the normal developmental sequence of that task, among other factors. It is possible that similar behavioral performances are accomplished by a different group of neurological structures at different phases of the developmental process.

NEUROPSYCHOLOGICAL PATTERNS

One of the most difficult aspects of child neuropsychology relates to the third pattern suggested by Teuber and Rudel (1962). The fact that certain tasks can become better predictors of brain damage as the brain-damaged child grows up suggests that some abilities emerge only in a developmental sequence. It suggests also that prior to a certain age, predictions about abilities that will emerge at that age would be rash. Bolter and Long (1985), in discussing this delayed onset of behavioral impairment, suggested:

> One possible explanation is that the lesioned area is either functionally immature or not utilized at the time of the insult. When the function assumes dependency on the damaged neural region at a specific point in developmental maturation, the weakness in the system becomes apparent through the appearance of a functional deficit. This supposition does appear consistent with our knowledge regarding the development of the central nervous system (CNS).

Perhaps more than anything else, this decade-long research study of Teuber and Rudel (1962) illustrates the need to consider neuropsychological deficits in brain-injured children within the context of the child's developmental age. A second important implication is the need for neuropsychological assessment batteries for children to include a broad range of human abilities (Bolter & Long, 1985).

THE SPECIAL CASE OF HEAD INJURY IN CHILDREN

At this point, attention will be devoted to the recovery of behavioral functions after head injury in children. Pediatric head injury has received some research attention, but there are few comprehensive studies (Klonoff, Crockett, & Clark, 1984). Perhaps the best designed series of investigations of head injuries in children were done by a multidisciplinary group of researchers at the University of British Columbia (Klonoff & Low, 1974; Klonoff & Paris, 1974; Klonoff, Low, & Clark, 1977). The University of British Columbia research is a model for others in this area. The studies included a large number of head-injured children, examined by a neurologist, a neurosurgeon, a neuropsychologist, and a psychiatrist on an extensive set of demographic, educational, and health-related variables. Such a data set is warranted, as head injuries are the most common neurological problem in the pediatric age group, and head injuries result in 15% of deaths in the 15- to 24-year-old age group (Klonoff, Crockett, & Clark, 1984).

Some of the very interesting findings related to the neuropsychological course of recovery after injury. The subjects were followed for five years and were divided into younger (ages 3–8) and older (ages 9–15) groups. There was a parallel pattern of recovery for both groups, with the most marked improvement taking place in the first two years postinjury. However, there was evidence of significant improvements up to five years after head injury. Moreover, the older head-injured children had a degree of residual neuropsychological impairment five years postinjury (Klonoff, Crockett, & Clark, 1984).

Some selected findings regarding the effects of head injury in children are

1. Boys are more likely than girls to suffer a head injury.
2. Lifestyle variables (congested residential area, lower income housing, marital instability, and lower occupational status of father) are related to the rate of head injury.
3. After head injury, younger children exhibit irritability and personality changes, whereas older children demonstrate headaches, dizzy spells, impaired memory functioning, and problems in learning (Klonoff, Crockett, & Clark, 1984).

Intellectual variables are of particular interest in head-injured children. Inspection of IQ data (i.e., Stanford-Binet Intelligence Scale data for children under 5 years old and age-appropriate Wechsler Intelligence Scale data for children ages 5–9) reveals that the scores of the brain-injured children were significantly lower than those of the normal control subjects during the entire five-year study, and that the most marked differences were at the initial assessment and at the one-year-later assessment. Also, the IQ variable recovered more rapidly than the neuropsychological variable, a finding suggesting that different domains of adaptive ability were being measured. As a whole, the results strongly indicate that IQ is influenced by brain injury and that it would be foolhearty to utilize IQ as a matching variable with control subjects (Klonoff, Crockett, & Clark, 1984).

The prediction of neurological sequelae of childhood brain trauma is important in child management. In the British Columbia research it was found that full-scale IQ at the initial testing session was the best single predictor of neurological sequelae. Other predictors included period of unconsciousness, posttraumatic amnesia, EEG rating, neurological rating, gestation period, retrograde amnesia, and age (Klonoff, Crockett, & Clark, 1984). Residual neuropsychological status after five years was best predicted by initial full-scale IQ, period of unconsciousness, and posttraumatic amnesia (Klonoff, Crockett, & Clark, 1984).

It is clear from the foregoing results that the IQ variable is of particular significance in studies of head-injured children. As noted before, children and adults are different neuropsychological populations, and attempts to blindly extrapolate findings from one population to the other are uninformed at best.

SUMMARY

This chapter presented a number of aspects of brain–behavior relationships. These included the morphology of the central nervous system: the basic structural aspects of the hindbrain, midbrain, forebrain, and various structures such as the thalamus, hypothalamus, limbic system, basal ganglia, and cerebral cortex. In addition, Luria's model of brain function was briefly covered, that is, the three major brain blocks that work as units as an integrated whole, the various functional systems through which the brain works, and Luria's model of neuropsychological developmental stages. In addition, attention was devoted to the hemispheric lateralization of functioning. This discussion included looking at hemispheric abilities, such as left-hemisphere functions and right-hemisphere functions, and also devoting attention to specific functions of the cerebral lobes of the brain: the frontal lobes, temporal lobes, parietal lobes, and occipital lobes. In addition, the recovery of function after childhood cerebral trauma was discussed, including the general principles of neuropsychological recovery and some possible patterns of neuropsychological recovery. Special attention was devoted to the topic of head injury in children.

REFERENCES

Bolter, J. F., & Long, C. J. (1985). Methodological issues in research in developmental neuropsychology. In L. C. Hartlage & C. F. Telzrow (Eds.), *Neuropsychology of individual differences* (pp. 41–60). New York: Plenum Press.

Brodal, A. (1969). *Neurological anatomy* (2nd ed.). New York: Oxford University Press.

Bryden, M. P., & Saxby, L. (1985). Developmental aspects of cerebral lateralization. In J. E. Obrzvt & G. W. Hynd (Eds.), *Child neuropsychology: Vol. 1. Therapy and research.* (pp. 73–94). Orlando, FL: Academic Press.

Connolly, C. J. (1950). *External morphology of the primate brain.* Springfield, IL: Thomas.

Corballis, M. C. (1982). The origins and evolution of human laterality. In R. N. Malatesha & L. C. Hartlage (Eds.), *Neuropsychology and cognition,* Vol. 9, (pp. 1–35). Boston: Martinus Nijhoff.

Corkin, S. (1965). Tactually-guided maze learning in man: Effects of unilateral cortical excisions and bilateral hippocampus lesions. *Neuropsychologia, 3,* 339–351.

Dean, R. S. (1985). Foundation and rationale for neuropsychological base of individual difference. In L. C. Hartlage & C. F. Telzrow (Eds.), *Neuropsychology of individual difference.* (pp. 7–40). New York: Plenum Press.

Geschwind, N., & Levitsky, W. (1948). Human brain left-right asymmetries in temporal speech region. *Science, 161,* 186–187.

Golden, C. J. (1978). *Diagnostic and rehabilitation in clinical neuropsychology.* Springfield, IL: Thomas.

Horton, A. M., Jr. (1987). Luria's contributions to clinical and behavioral neuropsychology. *Neuropsychology, 1*(2), 39–44.

Horton, A. M., Jr., & Wedding, D. (1984). *Introduction to clinical and behavioral neuropsychology.* New York: Praeger.

Hynd, G. W., Obrzut, J. E., Hayes, F., & Becker, M. G. (1986). Neuropsychology of childhood learning disabilities. In D. Wedding, A. M. Horton, Jr., & J. Webster (Eds.), *The neuropsychology handbook* (pp. 456–488). New York: Springer.

Klonoff, H., & Low, M. (1974). Disordered brain function in young children and early adolescents: Neuropsychological and electroencephalographic correlates. In R. N. Reitan & L. A. Davison (Eds.), *Clinical neuropsychology: Current status and application* (pp. 121–178). New York: Wiley.

Klonoff, H., & Paris, R. (1974). Immediate, short-term and residual effects of acute head injuries in children: Neuropsychological and neurological correlates. In R. M. Reitan & L. A. Davison (Eds.), *Clinical neuropsychology: Current status and application* (pp. 179–210). New York: Wiley.

Klonoff, H., Low, M. D., & Clark, C. (1977). Head injuries in children: A prospective five year follow-up. *Journal of Neurology, Neurosurgery and Psychiatry, 40,* 1211–1219.

Klonoff, H., Crockett, D. F., & Clark, C. (1984). Head trauma in children. In R. Tarter & G. Goldstein (Eds.), *Advances in clinical neuropsychology* (pp. 139–157). New York: Plenum Press.

Lezak, M. D. (1976). *Neuropsychological assessment.* New York: Oxford University Press.

Luria, A. R. (1966). *Higher cortical function in man.* B. Haigh, Trans. New York: Basic Books.

Luria, A. R. (1973). *The working brain.* New York: Basic Books.

Luria, A. R. (1980). *Higher cortical functions.* New York: Basic Books.

Meier, M. J., & French, L. A. (1965). Some personality correlates of unilateral and bilateral EEG abnormalities in psychomotor epileptics. *Journal of Clinical Psychology, 21,* 3–9.

Milner, B. (1958). Psychological defects produced by temporal lobe excision. *Association for Research in Nervous and Mental Diseases, 36,* 244–257.

Milner, B. (1971). Interhemispheric differences and psychological processes. *British Medical Bulletin, 27,* 272–277.

Mishkin, M. (1978). Memory in monkeys severely impaired by combined but not separate removal of amygdala and hippocampus. *Nature, 273,* 297–298.

Nauta, W. J. H. (1964). Some brain structure and functions related to memory. *Neuroscience Research Progress Bulletin, 2,* 1–20.

Nauta, W. J. H., & Feintag, M. (1986). *Fundamental neuroanatomy.* New York: W. H. Freeman.

Nebes, R. W. (1974). Hemispheric specialization in commissurotomized man. *Psychological Bulletin, 81,* 1–14.

Porac, C., & Coren, S. (1981). *Lateral performances and human behavior.* New York: Springer-Verlag.

Reitan, R. M., & Wolfson, D. (1986). The Halstead-Reitan Neuropsychological

Test Battery. In D. Wedding, A. M. Horton, Jr., & J. Webster (Eds.), *The neuropsychology handbook* (pp. 134–160). New York: Springer.

Rosenzweig, M. R. (1980). Animal models for effects of brain lesions and for rehabilitation. In D. C. Stein, J. J. Rosen, & N. Butters (Eds.), *Plasticity and recovery of function in the central nervous system.* New York: Academic Press.

Rourke, B. P., Bakker, D. J., Fisk, J. L., & Strang, J. D. (1983). *Child neuropsychology.* New York: Guilford Press.

Rudel, R. G. (1978). Neuroplasticity: Implications for development and education. In J. S. Chall & A. F. Minsky (Eds.), *Education and the brain.* Chicago: University of Chicago Press.

Russell, E. W., & Espir, M. L. E. (1961). *Traumatic aphasia.* London: Oxford University Press.

Saxby, L., & Bryden, M. P. (1984). Left-ear superiority in children processing auditory emotional material. *Developmental Psychology, 20,* 72–80.

Saxby, L., & Bryden, M. P. (1985). Left visual field advantage in children for processing visual emotional stimuli. *Developmental Psychology, 20,* 253–261.

Scotti, G., & Spinner, H. (1970). Color imperception in unilateral hemispheric patients. *Journal of Neurology, Neurosurgery and Psychiatry, 33,* 22–41.

Sperry, R. W. (1961). Cerebral organization and behavior. *Science, 133,* 1949.

Struss, D. T., & Benson, D. F. (1984). Neuropsychological studies of the frontal lobes. *Psychological Bulletin, 95*(1), 23–38.

Teuber, H. L. (1963). Space perception and its disturbances after brain injury in man. *Neuropsychologia, 1,* 47–53.

Teuber, H. L., & Rudel, R. G. (1962). Behavior after brain lesions in children and adults. *Developmental Medicine and Child Neurology, 4,* 3–20.

3

Comprehensive Assessment

with WILLIAM G. MILLER

A comprehensive assessment must evaluate the social, emotional, and neuropsychological (brain–behavior) factors that impinge on a child's development. Assessment is a process of describing the child's abilities, characteristics, and interactions. Diagnosis, on the other hand, involves using data from an assessment to classify the child relative to preexisting categories. For example, part of a comprehensive assessment may entail giving a child an intelligence test such as the Wechsler Intelligence Scale for Children—Revised (WISC-R) and deriving an intelligence quotient (IQ) of 100. By contrast, diagnosis entails determining that this IQ score places the child in the average range of measured intelligence relative to his or her age-peers.

Effective treatment planning rests upon the appropriate assessment and diagnosis of a brain-injured child's problem. This chapter presents an overview of selected assessment methods. The usual assessment procedures utilized in clinical child neuropsychology include interviews, behavior rating scales, direct observation, and psychometric testing. As might be expected, given the focus of this book on brain-injured children, a major concentration is on neuropsychological testing. The specific assessment procedures to be covered here are interview assessment, direct observation, behavior ratings, and major neuropsychological-psychological test procedures for children, such as the age-appropriate extensions of the Halstead-Reitan Neuropsychological Battery (HRNB), the Luria-Nebraska Neuropsychological Battery

—Children's Revision (LNNB-CR), and the Kaufman Assessment Battery for Children (K-ABC).

INTERVIEW ASSESSMENT

The interview is the most widely used form of assessment in clinical child psychology. Given its wide usage and the many books devoted entirely to interviewing adults (e.g., Sullivan's classic *The Psychiatric Interview,* 1954, and Benjamin's *The Helping Interview,* 1969), specific interviewing skills such as using open versus closed formats and empathic responding are not covered here. The different aspects of child versus parent interviewing, however, are mentioned. It is appropriate to comment at this point on the special value of the interview in clinical child neuropsychology.

In clinical child neuropsychology, paramount attention is focused upon neuropsychological testing procedures. The majority of articles in research journals publishing papers pertaining to child neuropsychology are based on neuropsychological testing. In terms of research interest, little attention has been devoted to interviewing in clinical child neuropsychology. This is an unfortunate situation, as the clinical use of the interview is invaluable in assessment when used in conjunction with child neuropsychological testing. The careful use of the interview enables the examiner to obtain the perspective of the persons who are suffering from a problem. More important than the information gained is how the child and the parents view the problem. This viewpoint is most easily obtained by speaking directly with these individuals.

Child Interviewing

As noted by Kendell and Braswell (1985), few children refer themselves for assessment. However, it is a truism that children can tell a unique version of the truth. How the child views a problem and sometimes, more important, what areas the child does not see as a problem can be invaluable information to use in designing an intervention.

Information can be elicited in a number of ways. One of the simplest methods is for the examiner to speak to the child and request information (Karoly, 1977). Another method with very young children, is to use puppets like those in DUSO kits (Dinkmeyer, 1973).

Another issue pertains to the sorts of information gathered. In addition to the chief complaints or problems as perceived by the child, other important information includes school subjects liked and disliked; relationships with parents, peers, and siblings; and sports and leisuretime activities enjoyed (e.g., television programs preferred). A sometimes helpful device is to ask the child what he or she would wish for if given three wishes. The nonspecific and fantasy aspect of this request enables the child to project his or her own desires onto this task.

It is worth recalling that the famous neurologist and neuropsychologist A. R. Luria (1966) always performed a "preliminary conversation" before conducting any neuropsychological testing. He asserted that this conversation served to guide his thinking in the assessment process.

Parent Interviewing

Usually, the parent (most often the mother) is the person who brings the child to the examiner. It is important to interview the parent in order that the child's problems can be precisely described in terms of specific behaviors, antecedent conditions, and behavioral consequences (Kendell & Braswell, 1985).

Many specific content areas should be examined. In addition to the current complaint or problem, relevant areas include emotional functioning, social relations, health history, educational history, school adjustment, intellectual abilities, leisuretime activities, family history of psychiatric and medical illness, family educational attainment, and family vocational pursuits, among others.

One possible means of dealing with the need for comprehensive coverage in a short amount of time is to use written questionnaires supplemented by a verbal discussion concerning the answers to the questions. This approach allows the parents to have written records of their answers in their own handwriting. Often, this written record can be very helpful in a later parent conference if there are questions about who disclosed what information.

Moreover, it is of particular interest to correlate the data obtained from the parent with the child's responses to similar questions. This process will often reveal interesting facets of the parent–child relationship.

DIRECT OBSERVATION

In introducing the section on direct observation, it is appropriate to distinguish between direct observation of behavior and the use of behavioral rating scales. Direct observation involves observation of the child in the home, in the school, or in other natural environments. In behavior modification, operant conditioning, or applied behavior analysis circles, direct observation has been the primary means of gathering data. By contrast, behavioral ratings are judgments made by a teacher or a parent who has had considerable experience with the child based on a number of preset criteria or standards.

The clinical differences between the two methods lies in the amount of personal judgment allowed the observer or the rater. In direct observation, the inferences of the observer are intentionally kept to a bare minimum. In many cases, there is an organized series of target behaviors for the observer to code. Often, there are precise, objective definitions for each specific behavior of interest. The intent is to provide a record of behavior that is minimally influenced by the characteristics of the observer. On the other hand, persons making behavioral ratings often work with imprecise criteria (e.g., impulsivity), and they are expected to make decisions based on their total experience with the child.

Direct observation has certain advantages and disadvantages. On the positive side, when observation is done within a comprehensive system which includes cognitive, affective, and behavioral categories, an explicit flowchart for selecting categories, and careful attention to reliability issues (Kazdin, 1975), direct observation produces the most potentially objective data source. Information is likely to be contaminated minimally by biases or the preconceptions of others. Some groups of operantly oriented behavior therapists are very reluctant to accept any other category of data (Hall, 1971).

On the negative side, however, obtaining these high-quality data is very expensive in terms of the time and effort expended. Direct observation requires recruiting of the observers. In addition, these observers must often be extensively trained in a complex coding classification. This training can take considerable time and effort. Special considerations must be taken to ensure that the observational data are reliable (Mash & Terdal, 1981). Also, many difficulties can be encountered when entering natural environments such as homes, schools, playgrounds, and shopping malls.

The development of various observational systems has received a great deal of attention. Observational instruments for recording classroom behaviors, for example, have been published in a variety of books (Sattler, 1988). One observational system used frequently in child behavior therapy is the Behavioral Coding System developed at the University of Oregon (Patterson, Ray, Shaw, & Cobb, 1969).

An alternate procedure to the use of trained observers, of course, is to utilize persons in the child's natural environment, such as peers, teachers, siblings, or parents. The obvious problems to be solved are preexisting biases and the need to assess the reliability of the observational data produced.

BEHAVIOR RATING SCALES

In contrast to direct observation, behavior rating scales provide an economical means, in terms of time and effort, of obtaining data on the child's behavior. Also, the rating scale can communicate the point of view of the person completing the rating scale. Clinically, it is not uncommon for children to present problems in one setting (e.g., school) but not in another (e.g., home). Although rating scales require a judgment by the rater, scale items can be developed which have varying levels of specificity. In one case, general dimensions could be rated, but in another case, more specific factors could be assessed. Two widely used rating scales are briefly described here to provide an appreciation of these instruments: the Child Behavior Checklist (Achenbach, 1978) and the Conners Teachers Rating Scale (Conners, 1969).

Child Behavior Checklist

One version of the Child Behavior Checklist (CBCL) is appropriate for children from ages 4 to 16. Another version of the CBCL, not included in this discussion, covers ages 2–3 yrs. The CBCL is composed of 113 child behaviors which can be checked off on a 0- to 2-point scale (0 = never, 1 = sometimes, 2 = frequently) by parents or parent surrogates. Various scales assess the child's abilities in educational, social, and leisuretime activities. Age- and sex-normative data are available for children ages 4–5, 6–11, and 12–16. The major strength of the CBCL is its use as a means of descriptive classification (Kendall & Braswell, 1985); it has evolved over a 20-year period (Achenbach & Edelbrock, 1983).

Conners Teacher Rating Scale

The Conners Teacher Rating Scale and its parent version are the scales most commonly used in assessing hyperactivity (Conners, 1969). The teacher rating scale has 39 items (two parent versions have 93 items and 48 items), but a short form of 10 items is available for the assessment of hyperactivity. Each item has a 0- to 3-point scale. The Conners scale has become the standard measure for selecting hyperactive children for research studies (Barkley, 1981). Although the wide acceptance of the Conners rating scales for the assessment of hyperactive children is grafitying, a weakness of the scales is that, except for the finding that anxious, hyperactive children are less responsive to stimulant medication (Barkley, 1977), the scales appear to be of little value for treatment planning (Kendell & Braswell, 1985).

NEUROPSYCHOLOGICAL TESTING

In this section, attention will be devoted to neuropsychological testing. Because of the limitations of space, the primary focus will be on wide-ranging standardized fixed neuropsychological test batteries. It is acknowledged that many other neuropsychologically related single tests have venerable histories in the field of clinical child neuropsychology. Nonetheless, our focus is on fixed child neuropsychological test batteries. This decision is based on the assumption that the multitest nature of these child neuropsychological test batteries is more appropriate for the description of multifaceted patterns of strengths and weaknesses exhibited by brain-impaired children. The specific child psychological-neuropsychological test batteries selected for attention are (1) the Halstead-Reitan Neuropsychological Batteries for Children; (2) the Luria-Nebraska Neuropsychological Battery—Children's Revision; and (3) the Kaufman Assessment Battery for Children.

The option of supplementing these child neuropsychological tests is, of course, open to the individual clinician. The author, in his clinical work with brain-impaired children, often supplements these fixed child neuropsychological test batteries with other instruments as suggested by the specific parameters of the referral problem and the unique aspects of the child's educational, medical, neurological, and social history.

Halstead-Reitan Neuropsychological Test Batteries

The Halstead-Reitan Neuropsychological Test Batteries for Children are the downward age extension of the popular Halstead-Reitan Neuropsychological Battery for Adults (Reitan & Davison, 1974). Often, the Halstead-Reitan Neuropsychological Batteries for Children and Adults are incorrectly referred to. The exact terminology for the adult test battery is the Halstead-Neuropsychological Battery (Reitan & Davison, 1974). There are two separate neuropsychological test batteries for children derived from the work of Ward Halstead and Ralph Reitan. The two batteries cover the 9–14 age range and the 5–8 age range. The older children's battery is correctly termed the Halstead Neuropsychological Test Battery for Children (Reitan & Davison, 1974). Children older than 14 can usually be assessed with the adult battery. The younger (5–8) children's battery is correctly termed the Reitan-Indiana Neuropsychological Battery for Children (Reitan & Davison, 1974). At present, there is not a downward extension below age 5 (Selz, 1981).

Brief History of the Halstead–Reitan Neuropsychological Batteries

At this point, it is appropriate to devote some attention to the history of the Halstead–Reitan neuropsychological test batteries for children. As noted elsewhere (Horton & Miller, 1985), Ward Halstead was excited about further clarifying the concept of *intelligence*. Halstead's special interest was "biological intelligence," which he defined as intelligence dependent upon the organic integrity of the cerebral cortex (Halstead, 1947). He contrasted "biological intelligence" with "psychometric intelligence," which he defined as what psychometric intelligence tests (e.g., the Stanford-Binet) of that period the (1930s) measured. To operationalize his concept of biological intelligence, Halstead studied persons with brain lesions and attempted to devise a battery of psychological tests which would demonstrate neuropsychological deficits. Ralph M. Reitan, a doctoral student of Halstead, saw the clinical applications of the test battery (Horton, Wedding, & Phay, 1981).

Reitan made a number of original contributions to Halstead's pioneering work. He modified and added to Halstead's test battery and developed the two aforementioned neuropsychological test batteries for older and younger children. The Halstead and the Reitan test batteries for children have a number of characteristics in common (Selz, 1981). First, the batteries examine a wide range of neuropsychological abilities. Second, the test batteries are capable of reflecting both the general and the specific effects of brain injury. Third, the test batteries are organized in such a manner that multiple methods of inference, not just levels of performance, can be utilized (Reitan, 1967). Thus, in the final analysis, Reitan revised or developed all three test batteries by starting with Halstead's original measures and by adding or creating new tests.

Halstead Neuropsychological Test Battery for Children

The Halstead Neuropsychological Test Battery for Children is primarily a downward extension of the adult version of the Halstead-Reitan Neuropsychological Test Battery. The battery is composed of the following tests.

The *Category Test* was devised to assess concept formation and abstract reasoning. The child inspects a series of 168 slides and selects a response option between 1 and 4 for each slide. On the basis of feedback indicating correct and incorrect answers, the child is to deduce the correct principle by which the slides are organized.

The *Tactual Performance Test* (TPT) was devised to assess nonvisual tactile form discrimination, tactile-based psychomotor problem solving, and incidental memory. The child is blindfolded and placed before a formboard, a modification of the Sequin–Goddard formboard, with wooden blocks in front of him or her. The shapes of the blocks are the same as the spaces in the formboard. The examiner runs the child's hand over the board to give him or her an idea of the dimensions. The child's task is to fit the blocks into the board using only tactile cues. The child does this three times. First, he or she uses the preferred hand; second, he or she uses the nonpreferred hand; and on the third trial, both hands can be used. After the three trials, the board is taken away, the child's blindfold is removed, and the child is requested to draw the formboard with the shapes in their proper location. The three scores derived from the test are time, memory, and localization.

The *Seashore Rhythm Test* and the *Speech Sounds Perception Test* are both measures of auditory skills. The rhythm test was devised to assess different rhythmic sequences. It is sensitive also to attentional deficits. The Speech Sounds perception Test was devised to assess the ability to discriminate speech sounds. On the rhythm test, the stimuli are 30 pairs of rhythmic beats and the response option required is for the child to write *S* for same or *D* for different. On the speech perception test, the stimuli are 60 tape-recorded nonsense words. The child responds by underlining the one word of the four printed alternatives that matches the tape-recorded stimulus.

The *Finger Tapping Test* was devised to assess motor speed. The child taps a special mechanical apparatus first with the preferred and later with the nonpreferred index finger for five 10-second trials for each hand. The score is the average number of taps in a 10-second period, recorded separately for each hand.

The *Tactile Finger Recognition Test*, the *Finger Tip–Number Writing Perception Test*, and the *Tactile Form Recognition Test* are measures of tactile discrimination. The format varies from identifying a finger touched, a number written on a finger tip, or a plastic shape (i.e., cross, circle, square, or triangle) placed in the palm of the child's hand. The score is the number of errors for each hand.

The *Aphasia Screening Test* is a measure of language skills. Areas assessed include reading, spelling, articulating, naming, basic arithmetic, comprehending, writing, and the copying of shapes. Items are at a low level of difficulty.

The *Grip Strength Test* is a measure of motor strength. The child grips a hand dynamometer for alternating trials with each hand. The score is the average of the two trials for each hand.

The *Trail Making Test* is a measure of visual search and cognitive flexibility. The test consists of two parts (A and B). Each part consists of circles arranged on a sheet of paper. Part A has numbers in each circle. The task is to connect the numbers in order. Part B has numbers and letters, and the task is to alternately connect the numbers and the letters in sequence. Scores are the number of seconds required to finish each part.

The *Lateral Dominance Examination* is a test of lateral preference. It consists of tasks requiring the child to demonstrate the use of the right or left hand, eye, or foot.

For more detail on the above tests and on the instructions for administration, the reader is referred to Reitan and Wolfson's excellent text (1985).

Reitan-Indiana Neuropsychological Test Battery for Children

The Reitan-Indiana Neuropsychological Test Battery for Children contains a number of tests from the Halstead Neuropsychological Test Battery for Children that were simplified for younger children (ages 5–8). These tests include the Category Test; the Tactual Performance Test; the Finger Tapping Test, the Aphasia Screening Test, the Tactile, Auditory and Visual Imperception Test; the Tactile Finger Recognition Test; the Finger Tip–Symbol Writing Recognition Test (i.e., *X* and *O* rather than numbers); the Tactile Form Recognition Test; the Strength of Grip Test; and the Lateral Dominance Examination.

Reitan, realizing the need for additional assessment instruments to use with this younger age range, developed six new test procedures. The *Color Form Test*, the *Progressive Figures Test*, and the *Matching Pictures Test* were developed to measure conceptual ability and mental flexibility. On the Color Form Test, geometric shapes of different colors are arranged on a sheet of paper. Similarly to Part B of the Trail Making Test, the task is to alternately connect colors and shapes. The Progressive Figures Test is an extension of the Color Form Test. On a sheet of paper, various geometric shapes are within other geometric shapes. The task is to connect similar geometric figures. For example, the child might start on a large square with a small circle inside and then move to a large circle. The Matching Pictures Test is a simple matching-to-sample task.

The *Target Test* and the *Individual Performance Test* measure the perception and reproduction of visual-spatial abilities. On the Target Test, the stimulus material is a large sheet with nine dots. The child is given an answer sheet with the same nine dots in any array. The examiner touches the dots on the large sheet in a sequence, and the child is to reproduce the examiner's sequence on the answer sheet. The Individual Performance Test is composed of the following four subtests: Matching V's, Star, Matching Figures, and Concentric Squares. On the Matching V's subtest, the task is to match *V*'s on blocks with *V*'s on a strip of cardboard. On the Star subtest, the task is to draw a star made up of two overlapping triangles. On the Matching Figures subtest, the task is to match figures on blocks and figures on a strip of cardboard. On the Concentric Squares subtest, the task is to draw a figure made up of three concentric squares.

The sixth test, the *Marching Test,* was developed to assess motor coordination skills. The test has two sections. On the first section, the stimulus material consists of a sheet of paper with two sets of circles connected by two lines. The task is to mark each circle with a crayon in sequence. On the second section, the task is to "march" up the two sets of circles and touch the circles with index fingers, modeling the examiner in sequence.

As might be expected, these neuropsychological test batteries are quite extensive and require a considerable amount of time to administer. Also, the age-appropriate Wechsler Intelligence Scale is often given in conjunction with the Halstead Neuropsychological Test Battery for Children and the Reitan-Indiana Neuropsychological Test Battery for Children. Again, for more detail, the reader is referred to the text by Reitan and Wolfson (1985). In the next section, we mention briefly Reitan's methods of interpretation of the batteries.

Methods of Inference

Perhap one of the foremost methodological achievements of Reitan was the development of multiple methods for inferring brain damage from the neuropsychological test scores of children and adults (Reitan, 1967). Using multiple methods of inference, Reitan was able to cross-validate his clinical hypotheses within the context of a single individual's test protocol. Reitan's cross-checking of his own conclusions is a feature which contributed greatly to the acceptance of clinical neuropsychology by the scientific community. His adaptation of neurological diagnostic techniques and the elaboration of his own approach evolved into four methods of inference: (1) the level of performance; (2) the pattern of performance; (3) the pathognomonic signs; and (4) the comparative efficiency of the two sides of the body (right–left differences). The methods of inference are described below.

Level of performance refers to a child's performance relative to his or her normative group. Simply put, is a child superior, average, or below average relative to age-peers? Level-of-performance measures are the way that psychological tests are usually interpreted. However, there are problems with using such measures as the only data for neuropsychological assessment. Simply put, level-of-performance indicators are not sensitive enough to serve as the only data in making inferences regarding individual children.

Pattern of performance refers to a configuration of test scores. For example, a child may do poorly on measures of verbal concept formation but may do very well on the Tactual Performance Test. Such a pattern has been found in some individuals with a history of antisocial acts (Horton & Wedding, 1984).

Pathognomonic signs refers to errors that are rarely, if ever, made by anyone with an intact, normal brain. For example, the inability to perceive a light touch on the hand or on both hands is highly abnormal.

Comparative efficiency of the two sides of the body refers to using one side of the body as a control for the other. This is potentially the richest source of hypotheses regarding subtle cerebral dysfunction. Measures of motor and sensory ability are usually administered to both sides of the body, and it is possible to have one side of the body serve as a bench mark for the other side of the body. On motor tasks, normal expectations are that the dominant side (i.e., the right side in the majority of cases) will be 10% better than the nondominant side. Therefore, a lack of the expected difference or more than the expected difference is a valid cause for questioning why this condition arose.

Reitan's clinical interpretation of the neuropsychological batteries is based on the combined use of these four methods of inference (Reitan & Wolfson, 1985). In the next section, we review some of the research findings relevant to these batteries of tests.

Research Studies

The majority of the research studies conducted by Reitan, his co-workers, and his doctoral students have focused upon separating brain-injured from normal children. A less-studied area is learning problems believed to be neuropsychologically based.

With respect to determination of brain damage in older children (aged 9–14), there is ample evidence that the Halstead Neuropsychological Test Battery for Children is quite effective. Research (Klonoff & Low, 1974) has reported a hit rate of 85% (i.e., 90% in normals and 80% in brain-damaged children) with the use of multivariate statistical techniques. This result confirmed other research (Boll, 1974; Boll & Reitan, 1970; Reed, Reitan, & Klove, 1965) which had demonstrated significant statistical differences.

In terms of particular test measures, the results for children are different from what would be expected for adults. The age-appropriate Wechsler scales were the most sensitive discriminators of brain impairment for children in the 9–14 age range. Other than the Wechsler scales, the Trail Making Test, the Finger Tapping Test, and the Speech Sounds Perception Test were most effective (Boll, 1974).

On the Reitan-Indiana Neuropsychological Test Battery for Children (RINTBC), significant differences were found between brain-damaged and normal children in the 5–8 age range. Researchers (Klonoff, Robinson, & Thompson, 1969) found hit rates ranging from 80% (i.e., for 5-year-olds) to 96% (i.e., for 8-year-olds). A further study by Klonoff and Low (1974) found comparable results (i.e., 80% hit rates in normal children and 75% in brain-damaged children). In yet another study, Reitan (1974) demonstrated significant differences on almost every measure on the neuropsychological test battery.

In terms of individual measures on the RINTBC, there are some similarities with the older children (age 9–14). Once again, the age-appropriate Wechsler scale proved the most effective means of predicting group membership. When the Wechsler scales are not considered, the most sensitive measures on the neuropsychological test battery were the Tactile Form Recognition Test, the Tactile Finger Recognition Test, the Progressive Figures Test, and the Marching Test (Reitan, 1974).

It is noteworthy that measures of problem solving (i.e., the Trail Making Test and the Progressive Figures Test) and of motor speed skills (the Finger Tapping Test and the Marching Test) are important in both age groups, but that the younger group has tactile perception measures (the Tactile Form Recognition Test and the Tactile Finger Recognition Test) as the most sensitive measures, whereas the older age group has auditory perception measures (Speech Sounds Perception Test) as the most sensitive (Boll, 1974; Reitan, 1974). This finding could reflect the increasing development and importance of language ability as the child matures.

In terms of learning problems which are neuropsychologically based, Selz and Reitan (1979) were able to discriminate learning-disabled, brain-damaged, and normal children in the 9–14 age range at a 73% hit rate by using a set of interpretive rules based on the aforementioned four methods of inference.

In conclusion, it should be clear that the child neuropsychological batteries developed and expanded by Reitan from the adult neuropsychological battery devised by Halstead are an important contribution to the field of clinical child neuropsychology. These batteries are able to distinguish brain-damaged from normal children at statistically significant levels of accuracy, and thus, they make an important contribution to the assessment of the neuropsychological status of children.

Luria-Nebraska Neuropsychological Battery—Children's Revision

The Luria-Nebraska Neuropsychological Battery—Children's Revision (LNNB-CR) is a downward extension of the adult version of the Luria-Nebraska Neuropsychological Battery (LNNB) (Golden, Purisch, & Hammeke, 1979). The LNNB-CR is designed for children in the age range of 8–12 years. Older children can be assessed with the adult LNNB. At present, there is not an LNNB version appropriate for children under age 8. There have been some reports, however, that a life-span Luria-Nebraska Neuropsychological Examination (Golden, 1986) is under development and will be appropriate for age 2 to the very elderly.

History of the Luria-Nebraska Neuropsychological Battery

The LNNB-CR is based on the work of the famous Soviet neurologist and neuropsychologist Alexander Romanovich Luria. Interestingly, Luria based his work on Lev Vygotsky's cultural-historical theory (Horton & Miller, 1985). Luria, working with Vygotsky and others in Moscow, attempted to explicate the relationship of language and thought by studying how thought processes are different in children at different ages. Luria was able to demonstrate that, as children develop language, they develop cognitive abilities. Later, because of political pressures, Luria was forced to work with brain-injured war veterans, and he developed further his neuropsychological assessment procedures. Luria's procedures retained a developmental slant, however, as he adapted many of the techniques that were first developed to assess the relationship between language and cognition in young children (Horton, 1987). The focus on language in Luria's work with children is reflected in the fact that Luria's primary statement on neuropsychological assessment procedures in *Higher Cortical Functions in Man* (1966) is replete with language-based techniques.

The LNNB entered the field of American neuropsychology via an interesting route. In the early 1970s, Anne-Lise Christensen visited Luria in Russia and decided to produce a written record of Luria's assessment procedures. At that time, there was no written record beyond a section in *Higher Cortical Functions in Man* (1966). Christensen published a book, a manual, and test cards collectively titled *Luria's Neuropsychological Investigation* (1975). This work was reviewed in *Contemporary Psychology* by Ralph M. Reitan (1976), who noted the need for standardization and validation before Luria's procedures could be accepted as valid and reliable. This review caught the attention of Charles J. Golden, who was then at the University of South Dakota. Golden, a graduate of the University of Hawaii who had been trained in the use of the Halstead-Reitan Neuropsychological Test Battery at Hawaii State Hospital, made a decision to carry out Reitan's suggestion.

Thus, Golden decided to standardize the administration and scoring of *Luria's Neuropsychological Investigation* (Christensen, 1975) and to validate its worth as a neuropsychological test battery. Golden and his doctoral students started a series of research studies which produced an experimental version entitled the Luria-

South Dakota Neuropsychological Battery. This version was revised, based on field testing, and, after a job change by Golden, became known as the Luria-Nebraska Neuropsychological Battery (Golden *et al.*, 1979).

The LNNB was quite controversial when it was first introduced (Adams, 1980; Delis & Kaplan, 1981), but criticisms were answered (Golden, 1980; Golden, Ariel, McKay, Wilkening, Wolf, & MacInnes, 1982; Golden, Ariel, Moses, Wilkening, McKay, & MacInnes, 1981a), and numerous research reviewers have demonstrated the value of the LNNB in adult clinical neuropsychology (Golden, Hammeke, & Purish, 1980; Horton & Wedding, 1984; Moses & Golden, 1980).

As a result of the eventual success and the general acceptance of the LNNB as an assessment tool in clinical neuropsychology for adults, Golden began the work of extending the LNNB downward for the assessment of children. Golden again utilized graduate students to aid in this work. At the University of Nebraska Medical Center, Golden's students were postdoctoral fellows, including Greta Wilkening, Richard Berg, and Robert Leark, all of whom contributed greatly to the LNNB-CR.

Luria-Nebraska Neuropsychological Battery—Children's Revision

The LNNB-CR is made up of 149 separate items arranged in 11 clinical scales. The items and scale organization, just as in the LNNB, are directly drawn from Luria's descriptions of his testing procedures in *Higher Cortical Functions in Man* (1966) and in Christensen's *Luria's Neuropsychological Investigation* (1975). The scales are titled as follows: Motor, Rhythm, Tactile, Visual, Receptive Speech, Expressive Speech, Writing, Reading, Arithmetic, Memory, and Intellectual Processes.

The *Motor* scale includes items assessing motor speed, coordination, imitation, and construction skills. It is the longest single scale on the LNNB-CR (Golden, 1987). As in all of the LNNB-CR scales, the items tap a variety of skills in a single content area. The *Rhythm* scale assesses the child's ability to appreciate and produce musical sounds. These items require tonal discrimination, singing songs, and reproducing rhythmic patterns. The *Tactile* scale deals with aspects of tactile perception. Specific items include finger localization, two-point discrimination, and stereognostic skills. The *Visual* scale assesses a variety of visual skills, including the visual identification of objects, pictures, and shaded figures and the mental rotation of figures. The *Receptive Speech* scale deals with the comprehension of spoken language, including analyzing, phonemes, understanding simple instructions, and carrying out visual-verbal instructions. The *Expressive Speech* scale evaluates the child's ability to produce oral language, such as repeating words and sentences, automatic speech, naming objects, and speaking in response to stimuli. The *Writing* scale measures spelling and motor writing skills. The items include analysis of words, spelling, and writing from both visual and oral stimuli. The *Reading* scale includes letter and word recognition and paragraph reading. The *Arithmetic* scale measures simple math skills, such as number recognition, number comparison, and elementary math calculations. The *Memory* scale covers verbal and nonverbal skills, including word-list learning, visual memory, verbal memory with homogeneous or heterogeneous interference, paragraph remembering, and visual-verbal paired associates. The *Intellectual Processes* scale was intended to assess general intelligence. Item content covers many skills similar to those on the Wechsler Intelligence Scale for Children—Revised (WISC-R), such as vocabulary, interpretation of pictures and stories, picture arrangement, comprehension of paragraphs, and solving simple arithmetic problems.

In addition to the clinical scales based on content domains established by Luria, Golden developed three summary scales for the LNNB-CR. Just as on the LNNB, the *Pathognomonic* scale is made up of the items which best discriminated normal from brain-injured children. The *Left Sensory-Motor* and the *Right Sensory-Motor* scales are used to lateralize brain damage in the sensorimotor region. The sensorimotor scales are made up of opposite-side Motor and Tactile scale items (Golden, 1987).

Technical Aspects

Just as with the LNNB, each item of the LNNB-CR is considered a separate test. Criteria for scoring include speed of response, number of responses, response latency, correctness of response, and learning ability. Responses are scaled on a 0–2 ordinal scale. Scores of 0 indicate a performance within normal limits; scores of 1 are borderline; and scores of 2 are viewed as performances suggesting brain damage (Golden, 1987).

One of the most interesting aspects of the LNNB-CR is its similarity in format to the Minnesota Multiphasic Personality Inventory (MMPI). Each item can be combined with others to devise new scales (McKay & Golden, 1979). Therefore, the development of new scales is limited only by creative imagination and empirical considerations. Moreover, the LNNB-CR scale scores can be transformed into *t*-score scales ($x = 50$, $SD = 10$). This feature facilitates comparison between scales and among scales (Golden, 1987).

Like the LNNB, the LNNB-CR has been the subject of a number of research investigations (Golden, 1987). These studies have demonstrated the value of the LNNB-CR in clinical child neuropsychology. In the following paragraphs, the results of some of these studies are mentioned briefly. The studies are discussed with respect to the differentation of brain-damaged and normal children, the ability of the LNNB-CR to distinguish learning-disabled children from other children, and the relationship of the LNNB-CR to other selected measures used in clinical child neuropsychology (e.g., the Halstead Neuropsychological Test Battery for Children and the Wechsler Intelligence Scale for Children—Revised).

Research Findings

Brain-Damaged versus Normal Children. The first studies of the LNNB-CR concentrated on the discrimination of brain-damaged children from normal children. As would seem obvious, this is the primary task of a clinical child neuropsychological battery and the acid test of its worth to the pediatric neurologist, the child psychiatrist, and the school psychologist. Greta N. Wilkening, who had worked with Golden to develop the LNNB-CR, enlisted the help of several colleagues to perform the initial validation study (Wilkening, Golden, MacInnes, Plaisted, & Hermann, 1981).

In this study, 76 brain-damaged children and 125 normal children were compared. The LNNB-CR had a hit rate of 82% (i.e, 91% normal children and 65% brain-damaged children). Similar studies by Gustavson, Golden, Leark, Wilkening, Hermann, and Plaisted, (1982) and Gustavson, Golden, Wilkening, Hermann, Plaisted, MacInnes, and Leark (1984) also found that the LNNB-

CR could differentiate brain-damaged children and normal children. In the Gustavson *et al.* (1984) study, the authors obtained a hit rate of 87% (i.e., 93% normal children and 78% brain-damaged children). These values were, of course, essentially the same as those obtained by Wilkening and colleagues in the initial study (1981).

Learning-Disabled versus Normal Children. Another important test of the LNNB-CR is its ability to identify learning-disabled children. A number of studies have addressed this issue. Nolan, Hammeke, and Barkley (1983) compared three groups, of 12 children each, with math disabilities, reading and spelling disabilities, and no disability based on scores on the Wide Range Achievement Test (WRAT). All children had WISC-R IQs of 80 or higher. The reading- and spelling-disabled group was significantly worse (had elevated scores) than the normal or math-disabled groups on the Expressive Speech, Writing, and Reading scales. Contrary to expectations there were no significant differences between the normal and the math-disabled groups.

Geary, Jennings, Schultz, and Alper (1984) also assessed the ability of the LNNB-CR to discriminate learning-disabled children from normal children. In this study, there were two groups, a learning-disabled group and a normal group, with 15 children in each group. The LNNB-CR had a hit rate of 93% (i.e., 100% percent for the learning-disabled children and 86.7% for the normal children). Geary and Gilger (1984) used a similar design with two groups of 17 children each. The groups were significantly different on the Expressive Speech, Writing, Reading, and Rhythm scales of the LNNB-CR.

In yet another study utilizing the same type of design as the two Geary studies, Teeter and Malsch (1984) also assessed the ability of the LNNB-CR to discriminate learning-disabled children from normal children. The LNNB-CB was able to produce a hit rate of 96% for the learning-disabled children and 93% for the normal children.

In another study on the discrimination of learning-disabled children from normal children with the LNNB-CR, Hyman (1984), found significant differences on all clinical scales.

Other studies of the LNNB-CR and learning-disabled children have investigated the issue of subtypes. Gilger and Geary (1985) classified three groups of children into subgroups based on differing WISC-R Verbal IQ (VIQ) and Performance IQ (PIQ) patterns (i.e., PIQ < VIQ and VIQ < PIQ) and also administered each child the LNNB-CR. Significant differences were found on the Receptive Speech and Expressive Speech scales. One possible criticism of the Gilger and Geary (1985) study, however, is that the number of learning-disabled children varied within each group, and they were mixed in with normal children.

In order to address these design flaws, Morgan and Brown (1988) constructed a study which again looked at WISC-R Verbal and Performance IQ pattern groups but included only learning-disabled children. Morgan and Brown closely matched the groups on age and WISC-R Full Scale IQ scores.

In contrast to the results of Gilger and Geary (1985), Morgan and Brown (1988) found no significant difference between the learning-disability-subtype groups. Their results question the ability of the LNNB-CR to distinguish various learning-disability subtypes when the WISC-R Full Scale IQ is controlled. A limitation of the Morgan and Brown study, however, is that the subtypes were based on WISC-R VIQ/PIQ score patterns. It may be that subtype groups based on academic skill abilities would show differences on the LNNB-CR (Morgan & Brown, 1988). Indeed, Nolan *et al.* (1983) were able to discriminate a reading/spelling-skills-impaired group from math-skills-impaired and normal groups with the LNNB-CR Expressive Speech, Writing, and Reading scales.

In conclusion, the current research on the LNNB-CR suggests that learning-disabled children can be distinguished from normal children. Whether or not subtypes of learning-disabled children can be discriminated by the LNNB-CR is unclear at this time but probably depends on the specific basis on which the subtypes are composed.

Attention-Deficit-Disordered versus Normal Children. There has been relatively little research on the discrimination of attention-deficit-disordered (ADD) children from normal children by means of the LNNB-CR. In one study, however, Schaughency, Lahey, Hynd, Stone, Piacentini, and Frick (1989) composed groups of children with ADD with hyperactivity (ADHD), children with ADD without hyperactivity (ADD), and a control group of children with internalizing disorders. All children in the group were administered the LNNB-CR. No significant differences among the group were found. The results suggest the LNNB-CR may not be sensitive to the neuropsychological dysfunction associated with ADD and ADHD (Schaughency *et al.*, 1989). This postulate, however, is based upon a single study, and it would be premature to conclude that there may be no value in assessing ADD or ADHD children with the LNNB-CR. These results are preliminary, and further research is warranted.

Relationship of the LNNB-CR to Other Neuropsychological Tests

An important issue to consider with the LNNB-CR is its concurrent validity with other neuropsychological measures. Two important measures warranting comparison are the Halstead Neuropsychological Battery for Children (HNBC) and the WISC-R.

Halstead Neuropsychological Battery for Children. With respect to the HNBC, two studies have administrated both the HNBC and the LNNB-CR to children. Tramontana, Sherrets, and Wolf (1983) found many correlations between LNNB-CR and HNBC scores. When standard criteria were used for brain damage, the two neuropsychological batteries had very similar hit rates (i.e., HBNC, 75%; LNNB-CR, 77%).

The second study comparing the HNBC and the LNNB-CR involved the administration of the batteries to epileptic children with epilepsy. Berg, Bolter, Ch'ien, Williams, Lancaster, and Cummins (1984) concluded that the two child neuropsychological batteries demonstrated agreement in 91% of the cases.

Wechsler Intelligence Scale for Children—Revised. A number of studies have examined the relationship between the WISC-R and the LNNB-CR. Wilkening *et al.* (1981) and Gustavson *et al.* (1982) found multiple correlations in the low 80s for summary measures. Gilger and Geary (1985) suggested that the LNNB-CR is more sensitive than the WISC-R to verbal deficits.

In terms of classification accuracy, Carr, Sweet, and Rossini, (1986) compared the WISC-R and the LNNB-CR in psychiatric and brain damaged groups of children. The WISC-R had a hit rate of 85% (i.e., 78% for psychiatric children and 91% for brain-damaged children), and the LNNB-CR had a hit rate of 81% (i.e., 84% for psychiatric children and 78% for brain-damaged children). These results suggest similar classification accuracy. A later study by Sweet, Carr, Rossini, and Kaspa (1986) suggests that, although the WISC-R and LNNB-CR are similar in classification accuracy, they provide different sets of information about the children assessed. Golden (1987) averred that the LNNB-CR and the WISC-R provide complementary information, and that the LNNB-CR has special value in pinpointing neuropsychological strengths and weaknesses.

The next section comments on an instrument that may also be considered a neuropsychological test: the Kaufman Assessment Battery for Children (K-ABC).

Kaufman Assessment Battery for Children

The K-ABC was more recently developed than the LNNB-CR, and in a very short period of time, it has generated a considerable body of research data.

History of the K-ABC

The K-ABC (Kaufman & Kaufman, 1983b) was developed by Alan S. Kaufman and Naden L. Kaufman for children ages 2½–12½ years. Alan Kaufman was a doctoral student of Robert L. Thorndike at Teachers College, Columbia University, and later worked at the Psychological Corporation in the development of the WISC-R and the McCarthy Scales. He is best known, however, for his book *Intelligence Testing with the WISC-R* (1979), the classic reference on the WISC-R. Naden L. Kaufman, Alan's spouse, worked with her husband on an earlier book on the McCarthy Scales (Kaufman & Kaufman, 1977) and has worked as a school psychologist.

In developing the K-ABC, the Kaufmans utilized recent research advances in the assessment of human mental abilities. The K-ABC is constructed on a paradigm of sequential and simultaneous information processing (Reynolds & Kamphaus, 1986). This theoretical base was gathered from research in neuropsychology (Luria, 1966), in cerebral specialization (Sperry, 1968), and in cognitive psychology (Neisser, 1967) which has been extant for a number of years. The dual-processing model of cognition relies on neuropsychological constructs.

Simultaneous and sequential processing are seen by the Kaufmans as separate mental abilities. Simultaneous processing requires the child to put diverse bits of information together at the same time to solve a problem. Spatial organizational abilities are often cited as an example of simultaneous processing. On the WISC-R, for example, the Block Design subtest would be a model for this cognitive skill. By contrast, sequential processing requires the child to put the bits of information in serial order in order to solve a problem. The bits of information are organized in a temporal or linear sequence. The difference between the two types of mental abilities is analogous to driving a car in heavy traffic (simultaneous) versus using a cookbook to bake a cake (sequential). The child's brain utilizes both types of information processing, but usually one or the other is used more frequently (Reynolds & Kamphaus, 1986).

Technical Aspects

In terms of test construction, the K-ABC is a model for others in the field of neuropsychology. The K-ABC has five global scales: Sequential Processing, Simultaneous Processing, Mental Processing Composite, Achievement, and Nonverbal. The *Sequential Processing* and *Simultaneous Processing* scales are measures of the constructs previously described. The *Mental Processing Composite Scale* is a summary scale which combines both sequential and simultaneous processing. The *Achievement Scale* is a measure of what the child has learned, and includes verbal skills (e.g., vocabulary) and school subjects, (e.g., reading, arithmetic, and riddles). The Achievement Scale can be considered a measure of the child's success in learning about the world thus far in one's life (Reynolds & Kamphaus, 1986). The *Nonverbal Scale* is a short form of the Mental Processing Composite Scale, which one can administer without using verbal instructions or requiring verbal responses (Kaufman & Kaufman, 1983b). The global scales are transformed into standard scores with a mean of 100 and a standard deviation of 15, as is done on the age-appropriate Wechsler scales (Kaufman & Kaufman, 1983a).

The K-ABC has a total of 16 subtests, but only certain ones are administered at any given age. The largest number, 13, is given to children aged 7 to 12½ years. The Sequential Processing Scale subtests reflect the core mental abilities assessed by the scale: *Magic Window* (identifying a picture after seeing part of the picture), *Face Recognition* (recognizing a photograph of a face seen before), *Gestalt Closure* (identifying an obscured object), *Triangles* (assembling triangles to match a model), *Matrix Analogies* (selecting a picture to complete a verbal model, *Spatial Memory* (recalling the location of pictures on a page), and *Photo Series* (arranging photographs in a meaningful order) (Reynolds & Kamphaus, 1986). The Achievement Scale subtests are *Expressive Vocabulary* (naming objects), *Faces and Places* (naming persons or places), *Arithmetic* (number manipulation or math concepts), *Riddles* (deductive reasoning), *Reading/Decoding* (reading words and letters), and *Reading/Understanding* (following written instructions).

In terms of other test measures used in child neuropsychology, the K-ABC is very well standardized. The K-ABC sample was matched on major demographic variables according to the 1980 U.S. Census figures and included 2,000 children (Kaufman & Kaufman, 1983a). However, Hispanic-Americans and low-educational-level blacks were underrepresented (Sattler, 1988).

Research Findings

In terms of usefulness for child neuropsychology, studies of the K-ABC have focused on specific applications. Telzrow, Redmond, and Zimmerman (1984) examined the relationship of the K-ABC to Border's subtypes of reading disability. They found a clear relationship on the K-ABC in line with theory predictions. In a separate study, Morris and Bigler (1985) examined the relationship of the K-ABC and children with left-hemisphere and right-hemisphere neuropsychological deficits. They demonstrated a clear relationship between the K-ABC simultaneous and sequential scales and lateralized neuropsychological impairment consistent with the theoretical predictions.

Another area of interest is the relationship of the K-ABC to more established measures in child neuropsychology, such as the WISC-R and the LNNB-CR. With respect to the WISC-R, well-designed studies (Kaufman & Kaufman, 1983a) have demonstrated a high correlation between the WISC-R Full Scale IQ and the K-ABC Mental Processing Composite.

With respect to comparison with the LNNB-CR, two studies (Leark, Snyder, Grove, & Golden, 1983; Snyder, Leark, Golden, Grove, & Allison, 1983) have explored this issue. In the Snyder *et al.* (1983) study, the pattern of correlation demonstrated considerable shared variance (i.e., .64) between the K-ABC Mental Processing Composite and the LNNB-CR Intellectual Processes Scale. The conclusion was that the K-ABC was consistent with Luria's theoretical paradigm and also provided additional information to that already obtained from the LNNB-CR. In the Leark *et al.* study (1983) these impressions were supported further. Once again, the LNNB-CR Intelligence Scales had the highest correlation with the K-ABC Mental Processing Composite. Additionally, similar high correlations of the LNNB-CR Pathognomic Scale with the Nonverbal, Achievement, and Sequential scales suggest that the K-ABC is sensitive to brain damage (Reynolds & Kamphaus, 1986).

In closing this section on the K-ABC, it is clear that more research is warranted on this test battery. At present, however, the K-ABC should not be the primary instrument for identifying the intellectual abilities of gifted, normal, mentally retarded, or learning-disabled children (Sattler, 1988).

Rather, the K-ABC may prove most useful for guiding tentative educational interventions with brain-damaged and learning-disabled children (Reynolds & Kamphaus, 1986). For example, in the *K-ABC Interpretive Manual* (Kaufman & Kaufman, 1983a), a model for utilizing the child's neuropsychological strengths to plan educational programs is presented. The K-ABC attempts to provide a framework for guiding a strengths model of remediation. Hartlage and Telzrow (1983) suggested that the development of compensatory skills based upon the child's neuropsychological strengths holds the greatest promise for remediating educationally troubled children suffering from structural brain damage and/or learning disabilities. The hope is that additional research will evaluate the validity of proposed instructional strategies based on K-ABC profiles and on the strengths model of neuropsychological intervention (Reynolds, 1981).

SUMMARY

This chapter focused on comprehensive assessment approaches in working with children. These are fairly varied. They include interview assessment, which can entail interviewing either the child or the parent. In addition, direct observation of the child's behavior is described as a procedure. Two, behavior rating scales were also covered: the Child Behavior Checklist and the Conner Teacher Rating Scales. Neuropsychological test batteries were also covered: the Halstead-Reitan Neuropsychological Test Battery for Children, the Reitan-Indiana Neuropsychological Test Battery for Children, and the Luria-Nebraska Neuropsychological Battery—Children's Revision. These test batteries were briefly described with respect to their history, technical aspects, and various research studies. In addition, we briefly reviewed the relationship of the Luria-Nebraska Neuropsychological Battery—Children's Revision to other neuropsychological tests: the Halstead Neuropsychological Battery for Children, the Wechsler Intelligence Scale for Children—Revised, and the Kaufmann Assessment Battery for Children. There was a brief discussion of the history of the Kaufmann Assessment Battery for Children and the technical aspects and research findings for that instrument.

At the time that this book was being completed, the WISC-III (Wechsler, 1991) had been published by the Psychological Corporation. Because the recency of this publication precludes the accumulation of sufficient research and clinical findings to fully evaluate this test, it is not treated here. What can be relatively clearly stated is that the WISC-III is, in many ways, virtually identical to the WISC-R (Wechsler, 1974). There have been a number of superficial changes and the norms have been updated, but with the exception of the addition of a new subtest, the Symbol Search subtest (Wechsler, 1991), there are few substantive changes. One particular area of concern, however, is that the factor structure of the WISC-III is currently in question (Little, 1992). Simply put, there are questions regarding the factor structure proposed for interpretation of the WISC-III, and until additional information is available, clinicians and researchers should be very careful in making interpretations.

REFERENCES

Achenbach, T. M. (1978). The Child Behavior Profile: 1. Boys aged 6–11. *Journal of Consulting and Clinical Psychology, 46*, 478–488.

Achenbach, T. M., & Edelbrock, C. (1983). *Manual of the Child Behavior Checklist and Revised Child Behavior Profile*. Burlington, VT: Thomas Achenbach.

Adams, K. (1980). In search of Luria's battery: A false start. *Journal of Consulting and Clinical Psychology, 48*, 511–516.

Barkley, R. (1977). A review of stimulant drug research with hyperactive children. *Journal of Child Psychology and Psychiatry, 18*, 137–165.

Barkley, R. A. (1981). *Hyperactive children: A handbook for diagnosis and treatment*. New York: Guilford Press.

Bender, L. A. (1938). *Visual Motor Gestalt Test and its clinical use*. American Orthopsychiatric Association Research Monograph, No. 3. New York: American Orthopsychiatric Association.

Benjamin, H. (1969). *The helping interview*. Boston: Houghton Mifflin.

Berg, R. A., Bolter, J. F., Ch'ien, L. T., Williams, S. J., Lancaster, W., & Cummins, J. (1984). Comparative diagnostic accuracy of the Halstead-Reitan and the Luria-Nebraska Neuropsychological Adult and Children's Batteries. *Clinical Neuropsychology, 6*(3), 200–204.

Boll, T. J. (1974). Psychological differentiation of patients with schizophrenia vs. lateralized cerebrovascular, neoplastic, or traumatic brain disease. *Journal of Abnormal Psychology, 83*, 456–458.

Boll, T. J., & Reitan, R. M. (1970, May). *Motor and sensory-perceptual deficits in brain-damaged children*. Paper presented at the meeting of the Midwestern Psychological Association, Cincinnati.

Carr, M. A., Sweet, J. J., & Rossini, E. (1986). Diagnostic validity of the Luria-Nebraska Neuropsychological Battery—Children's Revision. *Journal of Consulting and Clinical Psychology, 54*, 354–358.

Christensen, A. (1975). *Luria's neuropsychological investigation*. New York: Spectrum Press.

Conner, C. K. (1969). A teacher rating scale for use in drug studies with children. *American Journal of Psychiatry, 126*, 884.

Delis, D. D., & Kaplan, E. (1981). The assessment of aphasia with the Luria-Nebraska Neuropsychological Battery: A case critique. *Journal of Consulting and Clinical Psychology, 50*, 32–39.

Dinkmeyer, D. C. (1973). *Developing understanding of self and others (DUSO)*. Circle Pines, MN: American Guidance Services.

Geary, D. C., & Gilger, J. W. (1984). The Luria-Nebraska Neuropsychological Battery—Children's Revision: Comparison of learning disabled and normal children matched on full scale IQ. *Perceptual and Motor Skills, 58*, 115–118.

Geary, D. C., Jennings, S. M., Schultz, D. D., & Alper, T. G. (1984). The diagnostic accuracy of the Luria-Nebraska Neuropsychological Battery—Children's Revision for 9 to 12 year old learning disabled children. *School Psychology Review, 13*(3), 375–379.

Gilger, J. W., & Geary, D. C. (1985). Performance on the Luna-Nebraska Neuropsychological Test Battery–Children Revision. A comparison of children with and without significant WISC-R VIQ-PIQ discrepancies. *Journal of Clinical Psychology, 41*, 806–811.

Golden, C. J. (1980). In reply to Adams' "In search of Luria's battery: A false start." *Journal of Consulting and Clinical Psychology, 48*, 517–521.

Golden, C. J. (1986). *Lifespan Luria-Neuropsychological Investigation*. Workshop presented at the Annual Meeting of the National Academy of Neuropsychologists in Las Vegas, Nevada.

Golden, C. J. (1987). *The Luria-Nebraska Neuropsychology Battery—Children's Revision Manual*. Los Angeles: Western Psychological Services.

Golden, C. J., Purish, A. D., & Hammeke, T. (1979). *The Luria-Nebraska Neuropsychological Battery*. Omaha: University of Nebraska Press.

Golden, C. J., Hammeke, T., & Purisch, A. D. (1980). *The Luria-Nebraska Neuropsychological Battery: Manual* (rev.). Los Angeles: Western Psychological Services.

Golden, C. J., & Marvish, M. (1986). The Luria-Nebraska Neuropsychological Battery. In D. Wedding, A. M. Horton, Jr., & J. S. Webster (Eds.), *The neuropsychology handbook* (pp. 161–193). New York: Springer.

Gustavson, J. L., Golden, C. J., Leark, R. A., Wilkening, G. N., Hermann, B. P., & Plaisted, J. R. (1982). *The Luria-Nebraska Neuropsychological Battery—Children's Revision: Current research findings*. Paper presented at the meeting of the American Psychological Association, Washington, DC.

Gustavson, J. L., Golden, C. J., Wilkening, G. N., Hermann, B. P., Plaisted, J. R., MacInnes, W. D., & Leark, R. A. (1984). The Luria-Nebraska Neuropsychological Battery—Children's Revision: Validation with brain-damaged and normal children. *Journal of Psychoeducational Assessment, 2*, 199–208.

Hall, R. V. (1971). *Managing behavior/behavior modification: Basic principles*. Lawrence, KS: H & H Enterprises.

Halstead, W. C. (1947). *Brain and intelligence*. Chicago: University of Chicago Press.

Hartlage, L. C., & Telzrow, C. F. (1983). The neuropsychological basis of educational interventions. *Journals of Learning Disabilities, 16*, 521–528.

Horton, A. M., Jr. (1987). Luria's contributions to clinical and behavioral neuropsychology. *Neuropsychology, 1*(2), 39–44.

Horton, A. M., Jr., & Miller, W. G. (1985). Neuropsychology and behavior therapy. In M. Hersen & A. Bellack (Eds.), *Annual review of behavior modification* (pp. 1–55). New York: Academic Press.

Horton, A. M., Jr., & Wedding, D. (1984). *Introduction to clinical and behavioral neuropsychology*. New York: Praeger.

Horton, A. M., Jr., Wedding, D., & Phay, A. (1981). Current perspectives on assessment of and therapy for brain-damaged individuals. In C. J. Golden, S. S. Alcaparres, F. Striden, & B. Graber (Eds.), *Applied techniques in behavioral medicine*. New York: Grune & Stratton.

Hyman, L. M. (1984). An investigation of the neuropsychological characteristics of learning disabled children as measured by the Luria-Nebraska (Children). *Dissertation Abstracts International, 44*(11), 711OA.

Karoly, P. (1977). Behavioral self-management in children. In M. Hersen, L. Epstein, & P. Miller (Eds.), *Progress in behavior modification*. Vol. 5. New York: Academic Press.

Kaufman, A. (1974). *Intelligence testing with the WISC-R*. New York: Wiley.

Kaufman, A. S., & Kaufman, N. L. (1977). *Clinical evaluation of young children with the McCarthy Scale*. New York: Grune & Stratton.

Kaufman, A. S., & Kaufman, N. L. (1983a). *K-ABC interpretive manual*. Circle Pines, MN: American Guidance Service.

Kaufman, A. S., & Kaufman, N. L. (1983b). *Kaufman Assessment Battery for Children (K-ABC) administration and scoring manual*. Circle Pines, MN: American Guidance Service.

Kazdin, A. E. (1975). *Behavior modification in applied settings*. Homewood, IL: Dorsey Press.

Kendell, P. C., & Braswell, L. (1985). *Cognitive-behavioral therapy for impulsive children*. New York: Guilford Press.

Klonoff, H., & Low, M. D. (1974). Disordered brain function in young children and early adolescents: Neuropsychological and electroenchepalographic correlates. In R. M. Reitan & L. A. Davison (Eds.), *Clinical neuropsychology: Current status and application*. New York: Wiley.

Klonoff, H., Robinson, G. C., & Thompson, G. (1969). Acute and chronic brain syndromes in children: *Developmental Medicine and Child Neurology, 11*, 198–213.

Leark, R. A., Snyder, T., Grone, T., & Golden, C. J. (1983, August). *Comparison of the K-ABC to standardized neuropsychological batteries: Preliminary results*. Paper presented to the Annual Meeting of the American Psychological Association, Anaheim, CA.

Little, S. G. (1992). The WISC-III: Everything old is new again. *School Psychology Quarterly, 7*(2), 136–142.

Luria, A. R. (1966). *Higher cortical functions in man*. B. Haigh, Trans. New York: Basic Books.

Mash, E. J., & Terdal, L. (1981). Behavioral assessment of childhood disturbance. In E. J. Mash & L. G. Terdal (Eds.), *Behavioral assessment of childhood disorders*. New York: Guilford Press.

McKay, S., & Golden, C. J. (1979). Empirical derivation of neuropsychological scales for the lateralization of brain damage using the Luria-Nebraska Neuropsychological Test Battery. *Clinical Neuropsychology, 1*, 1–5.

Morgan, S. B., & Brown, T. L. (1988). Luria-Nebraska Neuropsychological Battery—Children's Revision: Concurrent validity with three learning disability subtypes. *Journal of Consulting and Clinical Psychology, 56*(37), 463–466.

Morris, J. M., & Bigler, E. (1985, January). *An investigation of the Kaufman Assessment Battery for Children (K-ABC) with neurologically impaired children*. Paper presented to the annual meeting of the International Neuropsychological Society, San Diego.

Moses, J. A., & Golden, C. J. (1980). Discrimination between schizophrenic and brain-damaged patients with the Luria-Nebraska Neuropsychological Test Battery. *International Journal of Neuroscience, 10,* 121–128.

Neisser, U. (1967). *Cognitive psychology.* New York: Appleton-Century-Crofts.

Nolan, D. R., Hammeke, T. A., & Barkley, R. A. (1983). A comparison of the patterns of the neuropsychological performance in two groups of learning disabled children. *Journal of Clinical Child Psychology, 12*(1), 22–27.

Patterson, G. R., Ray, R. S., Shaw, D. A., & Cobb, J. A. (1969). *Manual for coding of interactions* (rev.). New York: Microfiche.

Reed, H. B. C. Jr., Reitan, R. M., & Klove, H. (1965). The influences of cerebral lesions on psychological test performances of older children. *Journal of Consulting Psychology, 29,* 247–251.

Reitan, R. M. (1967). *Psychological effects of brain lesions in children.* Privately published mimeographed manuscript.

Reitan, R. M., (1974). Psychological effects of cerebral lesions in children of early school age. In R. M. Reitan & L. A. Davison (Eds.), *Clinical neuropsychology: Current status and application.* (pp. 53–90). New York: Wiley.

Reitan, R. M. (1976). Neuropsychology: The vulgarization that Luria always wanted. *Contemporary Psychology, 21,* 737–738.

Reitan, R. M., & Davison, L. A. (Eds.). (1974). *Clinical neuropsychology: Current status and application.* New York: Wiley.

Reitan, R. M., & Wolfson, O. (1985). *The Halstead-Reitan Neuropsychological Test Battery: Theory and clinical interpretation.* Tucson, AZ: Neuropsychology Press.

Reynolds, C. R. (1981). Neuropsychological assessment and the habilitation of learning: Considerations in the search for the aptitude x treatment interaction. *School Psychology Review, 10,* 343–349.

Reynolds, C. R., & Kamphaus, R. W. (1986). The Kaufman Assessment Battery for Children: Development, structure and application in neuropsychology. In D. Wedding, A. M. Horton, Jr., & J. S. Webster (Eds.), *The neuropsychology handbook* (pp. 194–216). New York: Springer.

Sattler, J. M. (1988). *Assessment of children's intelligence* (3rd ed.). Philadelphia: W. B. Saunders.

Schaughency, E. A., Lahey, B. B., Hynd, G. W., Stone, P. A., Piacentini, J. C., & Frick, P. J. (1989). Neuropsychological test performance and the Attention Deficit Disorders: Clinical utility of the Luria-Nebraska Neuropsychological Battery—Children's Revision. *Journal of Consulting and Clinical Psychology, 57*(11), 112–116.

Selz, M. (1981). Halstead-Reitan Neuropsychological Test Batteries for Children. In G. W. Hynd & J. E. Obrzut (Eds.), *Neuropsychological assessment and the school-age child* (pp. 195–235). New York: Grune & Stratton.

Selz, M., & Reitan, R. M. (1979). Rules of neuropsychological diagnosis: Classification of brain function in older children. *Journal of Consulting and Clinical Psychology, 47,* 258–264.

Snyder, T. J., Leark, R. A., Golden, C. J., Grove, T., & Allison, R. (1983, March). *Correlations of the K-ABC, WISC-R, and Luria-Nebraska Children's Battery for exceptional children.* Paper presented at the meeting of the National Association of School Psychologists, Detroit.

Sperry, R. W. (1968). Cerebral organizational behavior. *Science, 132,* 1949.

Sullivan, H. S. (1954). *The psychiatric interview.* New York: W. W. Norton.

Sweet, J. J., Carr, M. A., Rossini, E., & Kaspa, C. (1986). Relationship between the Luria-Nebraska Neuropsychological Battery—Children's Revision and the WISC-R: Further examination using Kaufman's factors. *International Journal of Clinical Neuropsychology, 8,* 177–180.

Teeter, P. A., & Malsch, K. (1984). *Predictive validity of the Luria-Nebraska Neuropsychological Battery with learning disabled children.* Paper presented at the meeting of the National Academy of Neuropsychologists, San Diego.

Telzrow, C., Redmond, C., & Zimmerman, B. (1984, October). *Dyslexic subtypes: A comparison of the Bannatyne, Boder and Kaufman models.* Paper presented at the annual meeting of the National Academy of Neuropsychologists, San Diego.

Tramontana, M. G., Sherrets, S. D., & Wolf, B. A. (1983). Comparability of the Luria-Nebraska and Halstead-Reitan Neuropsychological Batteries for older children. *Clinical Neuropsychology, 5,* 186–190.

Wechsler, D. (1974). *Wechsler Intelligence Scale for Children—Revised.* New York: Psychological Corporation.

Wechsler, D. (1991). *Wechsler Intelligence Scale for Children* (3rd ed.). San Antonio: Psychological Corporation.

Wilkening, G. N., Golden, C. J., MacInnes, W. D., Plaisted, J. R., & Hermann, B. (1981). *The Luria-Nebraska Neuropsychological Battery—Children's Revision: A preliminary report.* Paper presented at the meeting of the American Psychological Association, Los Angeles.

4

Treatment Planning

with WILLIAM G. MILLER

The focus of this chapter on treatment planning for the problems of children. First, there are a few defining comments about behavioral neuropsychology and neuropsychological profiles of children. Next, there is a discussion of recovery patterns of children who have suffered brain impairment. Then, there are comments regarding the use of behavioral treatment methods with brain-injured children.

The chapter is clinically oriented. There are, of course, cases where it would be possible to debate fine points, but the intent of the chapter is to communicate concepts and principles that readers can use in their practices. As a result, the focus is on the larger picture and major concepts. At this point, the discussion shifts to behavioral treatment methods with children.

One very important issue over the past few years has been the change in referral questions presented to the clinical neuropsychologist who deals with children. Less often is the referral question of diagnosis of brain damage presented, although that still comes from time to time. More often, the referral question is the issue of neuropsychological strengths and weaknesses and treatment recommendations. Positron emission tomography (PET) and various other imaging techniques have eliminated the easy diagnostic question ("Is the child brain-injured or not?") and as a result, there is a focus now on treatment.

Over the last 10 years, the author has developed behavioral neuropsychology, which is the application of behavioral therapy techniques to the problems of organically impaired individuals with the use of a neuropsychology perspective. This perspective suggests that the fields of neuropsychology and behavior therapy can be blended, with the inclusion of neuropsychological assessment data for planning behavioral treatment of children who may have some brain impairment (Horton, 1979).

TREATMENT PLANNING GUIDELINES

At this point, there will be a discussion of overall guidelines for planning treatment for children. This is a broad overall matrix for conceptualizing intervention strategies for children. Table 4.1 can be helpful for developing a framework to understand children with learning problems. It is simplistic, but there's an old saying: "Any idiot can make things complex; it takes a genius to make them simple."

In terms of overall framework, there are three basic subtypes: Type 1, Type II, and Type III, or left-hemisphere dysfunction, right-hemisphere dysfunction, and generalized cerebral dysfunction. The table follows the basic overall conceptualization in American neuropsychology of the two hemispheres of the brain.

As is well known, the left hemisphere is more language-oriented, and the right hemisphere more perceptual-motor-oriented. Most neuropsychologists would agree that various functions have been attributed to the left hemisphere, such as speech and language, and also that various functions have been attributed to the right hemisphere, such as spatial orientation and picture and pattern recognition.

Table 4.1 posits predictable patterns in children with learning problems: The Type 1 child will have a comparatively lower WISC-R Verbal than Performance IQ with consistently lower language ability, as opposed to a Type II child, who will have the opposite pattern of strengths and weaknesses. In the Type III child, no consistent patterns can be identified. Basically, there is a lowered language ability combined with consistently lowered perceptual-motor ability in a Type III.

Now, the question arises: What does this have to do with the treatment of the subtypes of learning-disabled children. Generally speaking, over the large number of studies that have been done, a

TABLE 4.1 Basic Neuropsychological Profiles for Children

	Type I child	Type II child	Type III child
Neuropsychological profile	Comparatively lower WISC-R Verbal than Performance IQ score with consistently lowered language ability (i.e., depressed ITPA and PPVT scores) relative to perceptual-motor skills (i.e., Bender-Gestalt or VMI)	Comparatively lower WISC-R Performance than Verbal IQ and consistently lowered perceptual-motor ability relative to language skills	No consistent pattern of WISC-R strength and weakness or clear superiority of either language or perceptual-motor abilities and skills
Neurological syndrome	Left-hemisphere dysfunction	Right-hemisphere dysfunction	Generalized cerebral dysfunction
Emotional correlates	Reserved, tentative, and uncertain of self-efficacy	Impulsive and uncritical of personal performance	Restless, irritable, and hyperactive
Educational intervention	Whole-word or look-say reading programs and perceptually oriented instructional modes	Linguistic and aural instruction modes	Extreme structure and special placement
Prognosis	Persistent problems during academic career (after third grade) but relatively good adjustment in nonacademic pursuits	Diffiiculty in early school grades (K–2) but tends to do better in later elementary grades (3–6) with generally successful academic career	Little ultimate academic success

large number of subtypes have been identified. Although space limitations preclude a discussion of these studies at this point, there is an overall generalization which covers many cases.

Simply put, there is usually a group of children who have language problems, a separate group of children with visual-spatial problems, and a residual group with both problems. The first two groups account for most of the cases, however. Much of this thinking is taken from the work of Eleana Broder (1973), who published some crucial insights into the learning problems of children. Broder was a pediatric neurologist at the University of California at Los Angeles. She was born in Mexico City and spent the early part of her life there, so she was truly the product of a bilingual education. This fact may have encouraged her various insights into Los Angeles area children with learning problems.

She conceptualized three subtypes of dyslexic children (Broder, 1973): (1) a dysphonic child, for whom the problem is primarily language difficulties; (2) a dysidectic subtype, who has a more visual-spatial problem; and (3) a mixed group that may have both sorts of problems. The dysphonic group is often more than half the children in a sample. By contrast, the dysidectic group of children and the mixed group of children are much less numerous. The percentages across the board suggest that the dysphonic groups are usually more than 60%; and the dysidectic group is usually a little more than 10% (up into the teens), but for the most part, the percentages were relatively consistent over four studies.

In terms of educational interventions, there are some overall strategies. For Type I, one might suggest using the strengths of the child in order to deal with the problems. There are two schools of thought in remediation. One is the "teach-to-the-deficit" school, which over the past 20 years has not been very successful (Hartlage & Telzraw, 1986). The second school of thought suggests, "Use the person's strengths to compensate for the deficits" (Horton & Wedding, 1984). There is a greater degree of research support for the second school of thought. Basically, with Type 1 children, the preferred approach involves using intact modalities, for example, using the child's visual-spatial abilities in a whole-word reading program. It is crucial to identify and use the strongest modality in order to compensate for various areas of deficit. For the Type II child a linguistic program or a phonics-based reading approach is suggested by Table 4.1, and for the Type III child, extreme structure in task assignment special placement in a special education class, or perhaps a multisensory approach like the tracing of letters or Montessori exercises is preferred.

The initial work in this area was done by Lawrence Hartlage (1975), previously of the Medical College of Georgia. In his classic study, Hartlage matched children with respect to strong modalities and preferred method of reading instruction and found a great deal of success with this educational intervention. Simply put, emphasizing the child's strengths was helpful in dealing with his or her deficits.

Emotional correlations are also included in the model. The Type I child tends to be more reserved and attentive; Type II tends to be more compulsive and critical; and Type III is restless, irritable, and hyperactive. In terms of the emotional correlates, one of the exciting things about Hartlage's (1975) conceptualization is that it provides an excellent model for organizing a wealth of data. The overall framework allows a clinician to ask, "What is this kid like?" "How closely does he or she match these types?" and "Where can I go in terms of some kind of rational intervention?"

The following illustration is offered as a personal story regarding the subtypes. A number of years ago, the author was working in a junior high school as a guidance counselor. There were eighth- and ninth-grade children, and the author attempted to assist students who were "problem children." School records were reviewed to pinpoint causes of academic problems. The results of this unpublished 1971 investigation showed that these children started having reading problems at the third-grade level, and after that, they had developed discipline problems. The remarkable aspect is that virtually every student with a behavioral problem had this pattern of beginning academic difficulties with reading in the third grade.

Hartlage's theory (1975), which, of course, was developed independently, explained what had happened. In his model, the Type I child has persistent academic problems after the third grade and then relatively good social adjustment. Interestingly, the child in the author's unpublished study who was the worst problem in the junior high school had been the starting guard on the basketball team. The child had extraordinary perceptual-motor abilities. Nonetheless, the child was also very difficult to deal with in the classroom. Until the third grade, the child could read or deal with language and school subjects on a sight-reading basis, but after third grade things became so complex and so difficult that he needed to have an auditory system to fall back on. It was as if (using an analogy from computer science) he was using a punch card system and in the third grade had to switch to discs. Although the child needed to switch to discs, he was still using punch cards, which are inefficient, and was falling farther and farther behind because he couldn't use the correct system. There is some basis in the literature for suggesting that this is a reasonable model.

In some cases in which the child is extremely intelligent, he or she can sight-read and be minimally academically successful. There are cases of dyslexics who have got through the educational system by hook or crook. Nelson Rockefeller, a former governor of the State of New York and vice president of the United States, was one who was able to get through Dartmouth College although he kept reversing letters. Bruce Jenner, the Olympic decathlon champion, and Pablo Picasso, the famous artist, also were dyslexic. A number of these individuals have achieved renown for doing things that did not involve reading well; their excellent skills in other areas therefore enabled them to be successful.

Type II children most often have difficulty in the early school grades but do better in the later school grades and have a generally successful academic career. By contrast, Type III children have few strengths to build on. Consequently, there are fewer options for remediation.

The greatest value of this model is in cases where the clinician is communicating to parents and teachers about a child and what the parent or teacher can do for the child. The model can be quickly explained in a one-hour parent–teacher conference. It is possible to provide a reasonable framework for the test results and point toward interventions for the child.

The crucial test of a neuropsychologist in dealing with school systems and children is whether or not it is possible to make an impact. One could be the world's greatest assessor and know exactly where a lesion is, but if the results cannot be explained so that parents and/or teachers can understand, and make changes in the child's environment, then there will be no impact on the child's life. It is important to recall that many parents of these children may have IQs that are not exceptional. The author remembers one gentleman in particular who fixed copying machines for a well-known corporation and about halfway through the conference said, "You know I was like this myself when I was in school." It is important to realize that parents are not always highly educated individuals who are going to be able to understand complex neuropsychological explanations. However, these parents are the people who will have an impact on the child's life. They are the people who will be there and who will make the crucial decisions about the child's life. If it is possible to communicate with them, then the child will have a chance of a better future.

At the same time, it should be admitted that there is always going to be some child who doesn't fit the model. In the real world, there aren't usually pure subtypes but combinations of various sorts. Clinical skills are to be utilized to adapt the model to the specific child.

RECOVERY PATTERNS IN CHILDREN

At this point, the discussion will focus on recovery patterns in children who have had a cerebral trauma. The focus, as before, will be on broad conceptualizations. From extrapolations of the developmental animal literature, one may expect a rather specific recovery pattern. Immature subjects generally show behavioral and neurological resiliency, and the more immature, the better. An old principle suggests that, if one is going to be brain-injured, it is best for it to happen early in life. This generalization, known as the *Kennard principle* has been severely questioned (Hartlage & Telzrow, 1986). Moreover, a great many data on infrahumans show that early intervention will probably influence outcome.

A conceptual framework of ability patterns will be outlined at this point. Simply put, it is suggested that there is a developmental sequence in the recovery of behavior functions. In a general, overall sense, recovery appears to duplicate a young child's development, which, of course, would interact with the sort of lesion, where the lesion is, and multiple other factors (Horton and Wedding, 1984). There are multiple qualifiers to this oversimplification, but generally speaking, children relearn motor skills first and then relearn speech, with complex cognition the last ability to return. Generally speaking, a distinct pattern of recovery can be seen in many cases.

In terms of common sequelae of brain injury in younger children, they are more likely to have emotional personality changes. Older children are more likely to encounter learning and memory problems as well as headaches and dizziness. These findings are taken from the work of researchers at the University of British Columbia who have done major longitudinal studies with childhood head injury (Klonoff, Crockett & Clark, 1984).

In terms of learning disabilities and head injuries, gender effects suggest that boys are more vulnerable. The odds are 4 to 1 that the clients with learning disabilities will be male rather than female. Males also have a higher predisposition to brain damage because of head injuries. Boys are more likely to have a head injury by a ratio of 12 to 7. The reasons are not clearly understood, but the demographic data are clear. In addition, the medical history may poorly predict the sequelae of a head injury, but environmental factors do significantly predict head injury. Moreover, children under 1 year old are most susceptible to sustaining a head injury. Also, accident-proneness is more frequent in boys. By contrast, no strong relationship has been found between medical history, developmental abnormalities, hyperactivity, brain damage, and predisposition to head injury.

To summarize, the client's medical history is a poor predictor, yet there is a significant relationship between the rate of head injury and the type of environment, such as a congested residential area, lower income housing, marital instability, and lower occupational status of the father. Environmental factors, to be blunt, have predictive value. As mentioned before, the behavioral sequelae in young children are personality changes, whereas older children experience memory and learning problems.

TREATMENT ISSUES

In the discussion of treatment issues, the particular framework that has been the most helpful is one developed by Lewinsohn (1977), who did significant empirical research with brain-injured persons and, with his graduate students, developed a model of remediation strategies (Lewinsohn, Danaher, & Kikel, 1977). His model (see Table 4.2) is divided into specific assessment and intervention phases. The first phase deals with normative

TABLE 4.2 Lewinsohn's Model

1.	General assessment of neuropsychological functioning
2.	Specific assessment of neuropsychological functioning
3.	Laboratory evaluation of intervention techniques
4.	*In vivo* application of intervention techniques

comparisons. In other words, comparing the individual with a relevant norm group by using standardized measures such as the child version of the Luria-Nebraska or the WISC-R serves to categorize the child in comparison with his or her peer group (i.e., Is he or she above or below the norm?).

In the next phase, the question is what the child's status is in terms of internal ability structure. Put another way, is the child more likely to be very poor in language and phonics skills yet quite good in visual-spatial abilities? The answer involves looking at internal individual comparisons to determine how the child actually does in the immediate environment. This is a behavioral assessment but with a neuropsychological perspective.

In the third phase, it is best to intervene first under somewhat controlled circumstances. After some treatment effectiveness is demonstrated, one can begin to move toward an intervention in the uncontrolled "real world." This set of steps is frequently lacking in contemporary treatment research and current thinking. It is important to recall that what works to initiate a change may not be what works to have the change generalized.

The fourth stage consists of initiating change in the natural situation and maintaining that change in the future. This process must be conceptualized in novel ways. Moreover, it may not be the ingredient necessary to maintain the change over time in an uncontrolled situation. This latter point is often overlooked in the treatment setting. What is wanted is for the child to get better in all situations over multiple times with all manner of persons.

At this point, some additional conceptual issues need to be mentioned. One is Bandura's concept of self-efficacy (1982). He suggested that the most powerful way to get persons to change their behavior is for them to believe they can do it. The most effective way to do this is to have them physically perform the action and be successful. For example, if someone has public speaking anxiety, the best way to alleviate this problem is to have the person speak repeatedly, and then her or his anxiety will decrease. In terms of treatment with children, the implication is that it is important to engage the child in active physical interventions rather than merely talking. This is not to say that supportive counseling may not be needed, but, as much as possible, the child should do things.

In terms of resources, it is very important when planning treatment to know what can be done in the actual situation. As mentioned before, it is not possible to plan a treatment program without taking into account the available resources. In a rural area, for example, there may not be resource teachers, reading teachers, special education classrooms, computers, pediatricians, and so on. Many decisions depend on what resources are available and what sorts of therapies can be allocated.

BEHAVIOR MANAGEMENT

Much of the research on cognitive-behavioral therapy seems to suggest that these interventions work best if a strong operant conditioning component is included in the treatment program (Horton & Wedding, 1984). One important key to success is to include a response-cost component in the child's treatment program (Horton & Wedding, 1984). *Response cost* is defined as making the response costly to the person making the response. The key with response cost is to take away something valued from somebody that he or she already has. Sometimes, it is necessary to provide the object or activity to clients first so one can then start taking it away. The classical example of response cost is finding someone for speeding. If one drives too fast, one has to pay the price of a traffic ticket (Horton & Wedding, 1984).

Response cost is an effective technique for reducing disruptive behavior very quickly. A particularly important point is that the emotional problems usually found with classical punishment techniques are eliminated. With response cost, there is less of a tendency to dislike the person or persons implementing the procedure than with the classical punishment procedures.

In treatment planning, it is suggested that an operant component is often needed. Cognitive-behavioral techniques may be helpful, but there should also be a component of operant conditioning. Also, it is important to realize that children with attention-deficit–

hyperactivity disorder (ADHD) have been found not to work best with simple positive reinforcement; rather, they do best with a combination of both positive reinforcement and response-cost contingencies. This finding comes from the work of Kendall, among others. Maintaining the use of these operant contingencies within the framework of cognitive therapies and self-instruction techniques can be very important. This approach is very helpful to keep in mind in planning a behavioral program, and it is a very successful way of working with children. Of course, it is still essential to do task analyses of the child's behavior, including collecting data and having data charts. As other texts adequately cover task analyses and data collection, these topics are not further discussed here.

TREATMENT RECOMMENDATIONS

There are a number of simple recommendations with respect to treatment strategies with children. First, with left-hemisphere brain injury, use visual and tactile modalities to communicate and simplify verbal communication while using adequate vocal volume. Also, teach in small steps and give frequent feedback. In addition, have the child paraphrase any verbal commands or oral instructions. This is important to make sure the child actually heard the request. Sometimes, a child develops secondary emotional problems based on learning difficulties because the child, through no fault of his or her own, does not hear or comprehend instructions and then is punished for noncompliance.

Second, for right-hemisphere brain injury, use verbal linguistic modalities and communicate clear vertical and horizontal visual reference points, especially if a lesson involves the child's doing seat work. For example, it is often important to give the child lined paper if he or she has difficulty with visual reference points. It is foolish to expect the child with visual-spatial problems to write on a piece of unlined white paper. It is best to give the child clear and distinct reference points in paper-and-pencil tasks.

Third, there are additional suggestions for dealing with attention and memory problems. Again, keep communication short and simple, and reduce distractions as much as possible. Also, it is important to use memory aids, such as written notes, 3 × 5 cards, and printed daily schedules, and to have the child repeat in his or her own words the verbal instructions given. In the future, personal computers may serve as backup memory systems. At present, however, 3 × 5 cards are cheap.

SUCCESSFUL TECHNIQUES

Some representative behavior-modification studies of children illustrate what sorts of techniques may be used. This is not a comprehensive review but an attempt to give a flavor of what sorts of things have been done thus far in using behavior modification with children who have brain injury. Effective techniques have included social reinforcement, stimulus control, social praise, tokens, overcorrection, and differential reinforcement (see Horton & Miller, 1985, for a review).

As an aside, one thing about childhood attention-deficit disorder (ADD) is that the literature is clear that, in some cases, stimulant drugs are helpful in reducing inattention. Unfortunately, the drugs don't by themselves motivate the child to do well in his or her schoolwork, whereas a token program or some kind of behavioral program can be quite effective in dealing with the child's academic deficiencies. Really these are two different things. The attention-deficit-disorder problem is often separate from problems with a developmental reading or math disorder. Therefore, it is important to do different things to address each separate problem.

With respect to behavioral interventions there is ample evidence that behavioral methods are very effective. With respect to the use of neuropsychological assessment and behavioral therapy methods, there are needs for many studies in the next few years, but at present, there has been considerable progress in blending behaviorism and neuropsychology.

CASE REPORT

A child was referred because of a suggestion of organic deficit in conventional psychological testing. The child was the third of three children and had two older sisters, aged 15 and 22. His father had died of alcoholism a year before the referral. The chief complaint was that the child could not control his behavior toward others. He was in special education but was allowed to go to school only 2½ hours per day. He was on Ritalin but was reported still to be very hyperactive. (There is a sizable percentage of children with ADD, as high as 40%, who fail to respond to stimulant drugs.) The child was reported to have a high-frequency hearing loss. Other problems were that he had been a blue baby (without enough oxygen at birth) and that he had had to have multiple stitches in his head after being mauled by a dog some years before the referral.

A previously psychological evaluation had found that his Peabody Individual Achievement Test standard scores were from 102 to 111 (i.e., well within normal limits). On the WISC-R, he earned a Verbal IQ of 107, a Performance IQ of 112, and a Full Scale IQ of 110. His scaled scores on the subtests, were unremarkable. The referring psychologist had also noted rotation of the Bender-Gestalt test designs, the reason that the child had been referred.

One thing needed before doing any neuropsychological testing is to get a picture of what the child is like and then to look at the testing in relationship to the child's interests and favored activities. Typically, a child neuropsychologist should ask, "What sorts of things do you like in school?" "What don't you like?" "What are your favorite sports and activities?" "What do you do in your leisure time?" and then "What are your three wishes (i.e., if there were three things you could have, what would you want)?" The reason for asking these questions is to get a framework of the child's interests, abilities, and how he or she sees himself or herself. If what is shown on testing doesn't match the child's self-report, then something may be wrong because these two things should match: What the child does in terms of interests, abilities, what he or she is good at, and what he or she is not good at should match the strengths and weaknesses of the neuropsychological testing closely. If the data do not make sense, they need to be investigated further. In actually dealing with children, one must first understand the child, then do the neuropsychological testing, and then see how the two fit together.

This child was particularly interesting because he had been playing and came to the testing session, dirty and sweaty, in a baseball cap. Few children come to an assessment session dirty and sweaty; rather, the parents usually take great care to have the child clean and odor-free. During the interview, the child was restless and distractible except when he talked about his father;

then he appeared quite sad. When asked about school, he said he disliked writing, math, and reading but liked spelling and gym. Regarding sports, he liked baseball, soccer, and racquetball. The most noteworthy thing was that the child was to be picked up to go to a baseball game just after the testing session because the coach had said, "We won't win without him."

His three wishes were a brand-new Chevy Toy Car a brand-new Mongoose bike, and a three-wheeler. His IQ values were relatively good, and his achievement level from the previous testing had both been quite adequate.

On the children's revision of the Luria-Nebraska, he had seven scales that were elevated above the critical level. This result suggested significant impairment of his neuropsychological abilities relative to his age-peers. The impaired scales included Writing, Receptive Language, Memory, Rhythm, and Motor. Nonetheless, his formal academic abilities, reading and arithmetic were within normal limits. It is important to realize this was not a classic learning-disabled child. Normal expectations would have been for a difference between the intellectual and the academic abilities. However, there were no deficiencies in this child's core academic abilities. Nonetheless, he was in special education and was allowed to go to school only 2½ hours per day.

Inspection of the 2-point error items revealed difficulties in performing complex verbal operations, short-term memory under conditions of interference, and difficulties with spatial relations. The results appeared consistent with a left-hemisphere focus. The diagnostic impressions were of an attention-deficit disorder with hyperactivity and a conduct disorder. It is worth mentioning that many researchers have suggested that there is an overlap between attention deficits and conduct disorder.

It was recommended that the child be considered for special class placement appropriate to his emotional needs. One thing that was difficult to express in this case was the issue that a child can be neuropsychologically-impaired even if he or she does not fit the standard definitions. If IQ level is average and actual achievement is below average, he or she fits the stereotyped learning-disabled-child model that most people envision for a child with problems in school. If a child is learning on an average level, however, it is difficult to diagnose him or her as a learning-disabled child. What is important to understand is that such a child would not qualify as a classic learning-disabled child, but that he or she could have been performing at an above-average level if it were not for the neuropsychological problems.

The set of recommendations suggested that this child's oral instructions be short, simple, and distinctly spoken to make sure that he comprehended. In the testing situation, he was a little bit distractible, and it was important in testing to repeatedly obtain his attention before delivering the various stimuli. Also, recommendations included having the child paraphrase oral instructions before assuming that he understood them. This approach would prevent people's giving the child oral instructions he did not understand and then his getting into an argument about who had told what to whom.

In addition, some cognitive-behavioral therapy techniques were suggested to encourage self control of his emotions and behavior. One of the major problems of this child was tantrums. Self-instruction was suggested to deal with this problem. He was relatively intelligent, so it was expected that he would be able to handle this sophisticated intervention. Also, it was suggested that the therapist generate a list of problem situations that the child could imagine himself in and role-play the situation with the child utilizing the self-instruction technique. This process would, of course, include modeling the various situations with multiple practice opportunities and therapist feedback to the child (Horton & Wedding, 1984).

A few brief points regarding behavioral strategies would be appropriate at this juncture. In the behavioral management of ADHD, the child often responds better to response cost (the loss of previously acquired reinforcers) and positive reinforcement than to positive reinforcement by itself. The best system is a mix of the two. Also, response cost is less likely to elicit emotional tantrums. Response cost is, therefore, a much more efficient way of decreasing maladaptive behaviors.

In addition, the frequency of reinforcement is important. For example, in the early token-economy research, children were given tokens several hundred times a day. Simply put, reinforcement, to be effective, has to be immediate and very frequent. The child is not going to wait until next week to get a reinforcement. After all, it is sometimes hard to get adults to wait a week for reinforcement.

Also, in this case, the mother's lack of parenting skills was a very significant problem. It was clear that she had a great need to learn effective parenting skills, and it was also clear that this task would require an exceptional amount of time and energy. At the time when the assessments took place, the child's manipulative strategy was to use tantrums to get his own way, and the strategy was working quite well.

Rex Forehand (Forehand & McMahon, 1981) of the University of Georgia has done some excellent work on child compliance. These are essentially methods for getting the child to do what the parent tells him or her to do. Forehand's group has developed an excellent system for using a room with a one-way mirror. A child psychologist stands behind a one-way mirror, and a hearing device is placed in the parent's ear while the parent works with the child. The psychologist instructs the parent through the hearing device in what to do in order to deal with the child and gives the parent real-time instructions. For example, the psychologist may say, "Don't say that; say this," or "Don't hit the child."

One of the interesting things found in the Forehand (1981) research concerned what he termed alpha versus beta commands. These are good versus bad or negative versus positive commands. The ratio of commands or interactions is often more negative than positive from the parent to the child in distressed parent–child relationship. It is best to have a ratio of 4 positive interactions to 1 negative interactions, in other words, to have four "Let's go get some ice cream" or "Gee, that's wonderful" interactions to one "I told you not to do that" interaction. It is important to have fun and good times with the child if you want the child to obey you.

Forehand's group found in its research that the parents who had problems with their children were those who did not have fun with them. They did not take the children out and did not spend significant amounts of time in playing games or in other sorts of leisuretime activities. It was important to point out that cycles of negative interaction drive out positive and affectionate interactions and further disrupt family systems. The parent and child will interact more positively if multiple positive interactions are planned and reinforced.

SUMMARY

The focus of this chapter was on treatment planning for the problems of children. The chapter dealt with a number of treatment-planning guidelines, including three basic subtypes based on the work of Lawrence Hartlage (1975). These subtypes were considered in terms of neurological correlates, suggested educational interventions, and prognosis. Also, there was a discussion of various recovery patterns of children who may have sustained a head injury. In the treatment issues section that followed, a framework developed by Peter Lewinsohn (1977) was discussed. His model is based on four phases: a normative assessment, a behavorial assessment, a laboratory or controlled intervention, and then intervention in the child's natural environment. Next, issues regarding behavior management were discussed, including some brief treatment recommendations. Based on the treatment-planning guidelines earlier discussed, specific recommendations were given. In addition, some suggestions were made regarding successful techniques to use with children, and a case report illustrated the use of these techniques was described.

REFERENCES

Bandura, A. (1982). Self-efficacy mechanism in human aging. *American Psychologist, 37,* 122–147.

Broder, E. (1973). Developmental dyslexia: A diagnostic approach based on three atypical reading–spelling patterns. *Developmental Medicine and Child Neurology, 15,* 663–687.

Forehand, R., & McMahon, R. J. (1981). *Helping the non-compliant child: A clinician's guide to parent training.* New York: Guilford Press.

Hartlage, L. C. (1975). Neuropsychological approaches to predicting outcome of remedial educational strategies for learning disabled children. *Pediatric Psychology, 3,* 23–28.

Hartlage, L. C., & Telzrow, C. (1986). *Neuropsychological assessment and treatment of children and adolescents.* Sarasota, FL: Professional Resource Exchange.

Horton, A. M., Jr. (1979). Behavioral neuropsychology: Rationale and research. *Clinical Neuropsychology, 1*(2), 20–23.

Horton, A. M., Jr., & Miller, W. G. (1985). Neuropsychology and behavior therapy. In M. Hersen & A. Bellack (Eds.), *Annual review of behavior modification* (pp. 1–55). New York: Academic Press.

Horton, A. M., Jr., & Wedding, D. (1984). *Introduction to clinical and behavioral neuropsychology.* New York: Praeger.

Klonoff, H., Crockett, D. P., & Clark, C. (1984). Head injury in children: A model for predicting course of recovery and progress. In R. E. Tarter & G. Goldstein (Eds.), *Advances in Clinical Neuropsychology* (Vol. 2, pp. 139–157). New York: Plenum Press.

Lewinsohn, P. M., Danaher, B. G., & Kikel, S. (1977). Visual imagery as a mnemonic aid in brain damaged persons. *Journal of Consulting and Clinical Psychology, 45,* 717–723.

5

Treatment Procedures

with WILLIAM G. MILLER

This chapter presents a brief overview of selected treatment procedures for brain-injured children. The procedures presented are, first, cognitive-behavioral methods and, second, operantly oriented or behavior modification methods. The cognitive-behavioral techniques require that the child have some ability to self-regulate his or her action. As noted by Horton and Barrett (1988), cognitive-behavioral techniques entail self-generated thought processes, whereas operantly oriented or behavior-modification methods more often rely on physical, tangible actions.

The techniques to be presented are (1) problem-solving approaches; (2) self-instructional training; and (3) behavior modification contingencies. Relaxation techniques and biofeedback methods, used primarily with adults, have been described adequately in many texts on behavioral medicine and are not described here.

The application of these treatment techniques involves multiple methods concurrently implemented. For the sake of simplicity of exposition, however, the techniques are described one by one. It should be understood that these descriptions of treatment techniques are quite brief and that more elaborate discussions are available in other texts. (See Gelfnard and Hartmann, 1984; Horton & Wedding, 1984; Kazdin, 1986.)

PROBLEM SOLVING

One way of conceptualizing problems in living is to relate them to inadequate problem-solving skills. D'Zurvilla and Goldfried (1971), in a classic paper, outlined the relevance of inadequate problem-solving skills to behavior modification. The authors defined a problem as a situation requiring coping responses in which the patient has no adequate response prepared. The patient must develop or select an effective response alternative by employing problem-solving skills.

There is a remarkable degree of agreement regarding the operations involved in effective problem solving (D'Zurvilla & Goldfried, 1971). Perhaps the reason for the unusual agreement is that the problem-solving method proposed is simply a variation of the "scientific method" proposed by Sir Francis Bacon (1561–1626) and still followed by scientists today. Goldfried and Davidson (1976) outlined five stages of problem solving process:

1. General orientation
2. Problem definition and formulation
3. Generation of alternatives
4. Decision making
5. Verification

Each step, however, need not be approached in a lockstep fashion. Rather, the various stages can be accessed in a flexible manner (Goldfried & Davison, 1976). The following discussion is a brief overview of each step.

General Orientation

Three premises underlie problem solving: (1) the belief that life is full of problems and that coping with problems is part of life; (2) the belief that one can control one's life and effectively cope with problem situations (Bandura, 1982); and (3) the inclination to reflect on various options versus the tendency to respond with only the first available response (Goldfried & Davison, 1976).

There is considerable research literature attesting to the value of expecting to be successful in coping with life problems (Glass & Singer, 1972). Additionally, there are a number of research studies suggesting the greater value of a reflective than of an impulsive cognitive tempo in problem-solving (Simon, 1960). Indeed, the classic research of Dollard and Miller (1950) suggests that the first step in complex reasoning tasks is to "stop and think."

Problem Definition and Formulation

In this stage of problem solving, there are two elements: (1) defining the situation and (2) formulating the problem (Goldfried & Davison, 1976). The value of defining a situation in operational terms is that it clarifies the important aspects of the situation (Skinner, 1953). Similarly, the formulation of a problem statement points out the actions needed to resolve the problem. Interestingly, this step is often one of the more difficult to take in designing a behavior modification program. It seems that the formulation of an effective problem statement would be more a matter of clinical skill or work of art than would appear at first.

Generation of Alternatives

The most important part of the problem-solving process is the generation of alternatives (Goldfried & Davison, 1976). The key to success in this stage is to generate as many possible alternative strategies as possible. The preferred method of obtaining these numerous, diverse options is "brainstorming" (Goldfried & Davison, 1976). This procedure involves generating multiple ideas but withholding initial judgments about the ideas, and then combining various ideas to produce better ideas. D'Zurvilla and Goldfried (1971) suggested that brainstorming is likely to produce better alternatives than attempting to generate only *good* options.

It is worth mentioning again that the stage of generating alternatives may alternate with the next stage, which is decision making. One can shift back and forth between these stages in order to facilitate the problem solving process.

Decision Making

In this stage, one selects a preferred strategy from the available generated alternatives. Previous work (D'Zurvilla & Goldfried, 1971) suggests that an important consideration is the "utility concept", which has two aspects: the prediction of the consequences of each choice and the prediction of the utility of the predicted consequences in effectively solving the specific problem.

An additional set of considerations involves making decisions on the basis of "strategies" or "tactics" (Goldfried & Davison,

1976). Simply put, strategies are "policy" or "value" questions. They are general courses of action and reflect value-level decisions. For example, whether or not to modify certain types of sexual behavior is a value decision.

By contrast, tactics are the specific ways of implementing a selected alternative option. Decisions at this level generally deal with "fact" or "executive" questions. For example, whether or not to use tokens or a report card system to monitor how children gain positive reinforcement is a "fact" issue.

Research in human information processing also is relevant to this discussion. In his book *Administrative Behavior* (1966), Nobel prize–winner Herbert Simon made the point that human cognitive abilities are finite. This statement implies that humans, in making decisions, often fail to make an optimal decision largely because of a lack of capacity to consider all possible alternatives. Humans tend to select the first alternative that "satisfies" (i.e., solves the problem in any degree). Simon postulated that human problem solving tends to accept less than ideal or suboptimal solutions. As noted earlier, the reason is the limited nature of human cognition.

Verification

In this stage, one matches the progress made with the expectation for improvement. Put another way, the results obtained are compared with the goals formulated. If the results are too incongruent with the standard for success, then one has to start the problem-solving process over again. By contrast, if the results obtained match or exceed the expected outcomes, then it is time to go on to other problems and/or activities. As noted earlier in the discussion of decision making, the original decision may not have been optimal. Ideal or perfect outcomes are probably unrealistic goals in the first place. This step, of course, is where one may wish to consider whether unrealistic goals are a secondary problem in themselves.

SELF-INSTRUCTIONAL TRAINING

As noted by Kendall and Braswell (1985):

> Self-instructions are self-directed statements that provide a thinking strategy for children with deficits in this area and serve as a guide for the child to follow through the process of problem-solving. (p. 119)

Phrased another way, the child learns to talk himself or herself through the problem. It is worth mentioning that the process of using language to guide behavior is quite compatible with A. R. Luria's research on the development of higher order mental abilities in children (Horton, 1987).

Self-Statement Types

There are usually considered to be five types of self-statements (Meichenbaum & Goodman, 1971). The first type of self-statement is the problem definition. The child decides the task to be performed, or "what to do." A second type of self-statement is the problem approach. With this self-statement, the child starts to deal with the various aspects of the problem. The child decides "what are the possibilities." The third type of self-statement deals with focusing attention. In brief, the child tells himself or herself to deal with the problem and to continue concentrating on relevant aspects, that is, to "think about what to do." A fourth type of self-statement is a self-reward statement. The child gives himself or herself a verbal pat on the back. The child says, "I did well," after finding a correct solution. The fifth type of self-statement is a coping self-statement. This type of self-statement is used to keep the child working on a solution to the problem after an initial solution has not worked out. The essence of the coping statement is that one error does not mean that the child's later efforts will not be ultimately successful. The coping self-statement is a sort of self-pep-talk. The child says, "Well, I goofed, and I will have to try again" (Kendall & Finch, 1979).

It is important to realize that the process of using self-instructional training takes both work and considerable practice and that the self-statements should be individualized for the specific child using them (Kendall & Braswell, 1985). The training of children in the use of self-statements requires a rather explicit set of steps. These steps are discussed next.

Self-Instructional Training Sequences

Meichenbaum and Goodman (1971) and Kendall (1977) have proposed five specific steps for self-instructional training. In the first step, the therapist talks out loud in modeling the appropriate use of self-statements to solve a problem. The child actively observes the therapist. The child is to learn the use of self-statements from this procedure.

During the second step, the child, in the presence of and under the observation of the therapist, uses verbal self-statements, spoken out loud, to solve the problem. The therapist can correct any inappropriate use of the self-statements at this stage.

In the third step, the therapist again models the use of self-statements to solve a problem but this time whispers the self-instructions. Gradually, the self-instructions are made less public and more nonverifiable. The child observes in the presence of the therapist and learns the use of self-instruction.

In the fourth step, the self-instructions are no longer spoken. The therapist uses covert self-instructions to solve the problem. The child, however, is still in the presence of the therapist and actively observed by the therapist for nonverbal signs of the covert self-instructions. The child learns that he or she can use self-instructions even if they are not overtly spoken.

Finally, during the fifth step, the child, in the presence of the therapist, uses covert self-instructions to solve the problem. At this stage, the only way (except for *in vivo* brain-imaging techniques) to verify if the child is using self-instruction is to ask the child directly or to observe for nonverbal cues of thinking.

It is worth recalling that these self-instructional steps are backed up by behavioral contingencies. That is, the child receives external incentives for the training. As stated by Kendall and Braswell (1985) in their book *Cognitive-Behavioral Therapy for Impulsive Children*.

> The behavioral contingency features of the cognitive-behavioral self-control therapy for children include (1) self-reward and social reward, (2) response cost, (3) self-evaluation, and (4) rewarded homework assignments. (p. 124)

BEHAVIOR CONTINGENCIES

The work on behavioral contingencies owes a great deal to the research of B. F. Skinner (1953). Skinner, a Harvard professor, formulated many crucial insights into behavior modification (Kazdin, 1978). He postulated two types of learning: operant and respondent. Essentially, operant learning is voluntary behavior, and respondent learning is involuntary behavior (that is, it is physiologically based). Although later thinking in behavior modification has been less enthusiastic about this arbitrary division of learning, the two factor model is one crucial aspect of learning theory that may stand the test of time. The specific point is that operant behavior is determined by its consequences (Kazdin, 1980, 1986). Stated somewhat differently, what comes soon after an action influences whether or not the same action will be repeated. For example, children receive praise and adults are given salary checks on a regular basis to reward their behavior of going to school or to work. Similarly, persons are often more careful about where they leave their cars after receiving a parking ticket. The basic principle is that what persons will or will not do in the future is influenced by what positive or negative consequences followed their behavior in the past.

From this basic principle that behavior is determined by its consequences flow many of the techniques of behavior modification and behavior therapy (Kazdin, 1975).

In order to change behavior the most important aspects are (1) to define target behaviors; (2) to assess the current level of the target behavior; and (3) to develop procedures for increasing and/or decreasing the target behavior. Each aspect is briefly discussed in the following section.

Defining the Target Behavior

The target behavior is the specific behavior selected for modification. Selection of the target behavior is the first and often the most important decision in designing a child behavior-modification plan. There are many subtle considerations in choosing the target behavior. For example, the target behavior must be not only objective, observable, and measurable but also describable in language that laypersons can understand.

Another important concept is *keystoning*. This means that the behavior selected for modification should be one that will have effects on other behaviors one might wish to increase or decrease. Put another way, you might have three possible behaviors you wish to influence (i.e., Behaviors A, B, and C). If you select Behavior A over Behaviors B and C, then increasing A will have beneficial effects on B and C. For example, a child may not speak positively to others but may bite and spit. If you choose as your target behavior the child's speaking positively to others, and if you are successful, it is likely that the child will bite and spit less often. Many times, these relationships between and among behaviors are not obvious, and deciding which target behavior to modify first requires ingenuity, imagination, and insight.

In order to choose the most appropriate target behavior, it is necessary to gather a good deal of information.

Behavioral Assessment

There are a number of ways to behaviorally assess the child. The most common way is to observe the child in the natural setting and see how her or his behaviors covary. This procedure can yield hypotheses that can be tested by empirical means.

Another strategy is to ask the child's significant others (e.g., parents, teachers, siblings, and playmates) about the child's problem behaviors. It is of course important to consider developmental factors in evaluating these self-reports. Also, it is helpful if some agreement can be found among multiple data sources. Various behavioral checklists and neuropsychological tests (see earlier chapters) are helpful in jogging the memory of significant others and in placing problems in the proper perspective regarding neuropsychological abilities.

Last, but not least, the examiner can talk to the child himself or herself. Although you are likely to get a different point of view from the child than from the parents regarding noncompliance problems, the child's perspective (assuming the child is verbal) can be invaluable in understanding how things came to the point where professional assistance was requested. Also, as noted earlier, it is important to understand the relationships between and among the child's behaviors, and who is in a better position than the child to report on those?

It is important to recall that all of these multiple data sources should be viewed through the ABC model, which refers to antecedents, behaviors, and consequences. Antecedents are actions, settings, behaviors, emotions, or cognitions that precede the behavior of interest and that may seem to signal the child to perform the behavior of interest. Item B, the behavior, is the behavior of interest. The consequence is whatever happens immediately after the behavior of interest. The consequences, item C, either positive or negative, will seem to increase or to decrease the behavior of interest. Also, it is important to realize that behaviors are often related to the child's perception of how things are rather than to objective reality. A child may take a certain action because he or she thinks that a particular consequence will be forthcoming. In fact, the action may be misguided, but it is important to realize that one strategy for changing the child's behavior may be to change the child's perception of reality or, at least, his or her expectations of the consequences of an action.

PROCEDURES FOR INCREASING A BEHAVIOR

At this point, some comments are provided on ways of increasing a behavior from either a low rate or no rate (i.e., zero behaviors). In order to address this area, one important distinction must be made, namely, the distinction between those children who do not know how to or cannot physically perform a behavior and those children who are able to perform the behavior and know what to do but are not motivated to perform the behavior.

Simply put, the first step in increasing a behavior is to determine if the reason the behavior is not more frequent is a problem of performance or of motivation. One rather dramatic and humorous example of the relevance of this point was a cartoon in the newsletter of Division 25 (Experimental Analysis of Behavior) of the American Psychological Association. In brief, the cartoon depicts a person attempting to teach a dog to fly by holding a bone above the dog's head. The frustrated animal eventually attacks the person. The moral of the story, of course, is to determine if the behavior deficit is one of performance or one of motivation.

Once this critical distinction has been made, the approach to increasing behavior focuses on either instructional activities or maximizing motivation. In some cases, both approaches are required. The next two sections of this chapter review briefly the strategies for increasing behavior by either instructional or motivational approaches.

Instructional Strategies

Instructional strategies include verbal instructions and modeling-based procedures, which are discussed briefly below.

Verbal Instruction

Although the use of verbal instruction is *not* the popular view of behavior modification, nonetheless, if simple lack of knowledge is the reason for a behavior deficit, then telling the child what to do in a simple, direct, specific manner is behavior modification. There are, of course, some special considerations in making the most of this strategy. Gelfand and Hartmann (1984) suggested the following steps:

1. Make sure you have the child's attention.
2. Be sure the child can physically do what you request.
3. Use language appropriate to the child's developmental level.
4. Repeat your instructions until either the child performs the behavior or it is clear that he or she is not motivated.

Some additional strategies are to break the behavior you wish the child to perform into very small steps and to verbally instruct the child in the completion of each small step. This technique has the caregiver prompt or cue each bit of behavior until the entire chain of desired behaviors is performed.

An example of how this might work is presented for a 5-year-old male child in a classroom situation:

"Jimmy" (wait until the child looks at you).

"Please pick up the pencil" (child picks up the pencil).

"Give the pencil to me" (if child fails to comply, repeat request).

"Give the pencil to me" (repeat until either the child complies or (after 5 requests) it is clear he is not going to comply).

The above example is oversimplified, but it illustrates the main points of verbal instruction technique.

Modeling

If simply telling the child what you wish done does not produce results, then the next logical step is to show him or her what to do (i.e., modeling). This technique was developed by Bandura (1969). In a classic experiment, Bandura demonstrated that children who were exposed to models of aggressive behavior toward a Bobo doll were in turn more aggressive. Research has demonstrated the value of modeling in the learning of complex verbal and nonverbal behavior (Bandura, 1969).

A variation of modeling is guided participation (Blanchard, 1979), that is, physically guiding the child's response after the child watches the model perform the behavior to be learned. Physical guiding and modeling can be done in various small steps that lead to the final behavior. For example, a child who has a fear of dogs might first view a film of someone petting a dog. Later steps might include watching the model touch a dog in the same room, touching the dog simultaneously with the model, and so on. It is important to realize that gradual steps of the final behavior should be used in modeling. Also, the child can use performance aids. These are devices or methods which allow the behavior to be performed more easily. In the example of the fear of dogs, the child might feel a greater sense of safety if the dog is small, if the dog is on a leash, if the dog is in a pen, if an adult is holding the dog, and so on.

In discussing modeling, Bandura (1969) identified four key elements:

1. The child must pay attention to the model's behavior.
2. The child must be asked to remember what the model did or said.
3. The child must be able to perform the physical and psychological skills necessary to replicate the model's performance.
4. The child must be motivated to perform the model's behavior.

A final point to be made is that the models used must be appropriate to the child's developmental level and to the child's individual characteristics. It is obvious that a 3-year-old boy will need different models than a 16-year-old girl.

Motivational Strategies

Motivational strategies are divided into those that rely on positive reinforcement and those that include contingency contracting. As noted earlier, motivational approaches assume that the child is physically and psychologically able to perform the desired behavior.

Positive Reinforcement

As most persons are aware, positive reinforcers are events following a behavior that cause the behavior to increase in rate, intensity, duration, or frequency. Positive reinforcers include a variety of events or items (Hall, 1971). Examples include the classic M & Ms, free time, access to computers or movies, special foods, having one's photo publicly posted, individual tutoring sessions, and multiple other activities.

One of the most important things to recall about reinforcers is that their effects depend upon the wants, needs, and desires of the child who is to be reinforced (Gelfand & Hartmann, 1984). Put another way, different children are likely to prefer different reinforcers. A reinforcer for one child may not reinforce the behavior of another child (Hall, 1971).

Moreover, reinforcers may vary in their value based upon the psychological and/or physiological state of the child to be reinforced. For example, a child who has just eaten a candy bar is likely to be less motivated to perform a behavior for an M & M then if the child had not had any candy for the previous week.

Many behavioral assessment techniques can be used to identify positive reinforcers to use in the modification of a child's behavior. To review, one can observe what activities the child engages in when given free time and the opportunity to make independent choices. The Premack principle (Premack, 1965) suggests that a more frequent behavior can serve as a reinforcer for a less frequent behavior. For example, if reading for an 8-year-old boy is a less frequent behavior than playing video games, then the opportunity to play video games can serve as a reinforcer for the child to spend additional time reading.

A second method of identifying reinforcers is to use a checklist. A specialized reinforcement survey schedule for children is the Reinforcer Identification List (Gelfand & Hartmann, 1984). Another approach, of course, if the child is developmentally advanced enough to use language, is simply to ask the child what he or she would like as a reinforcer. If none of these techniques identify promising positive reinforcers, then one might simply try a variety of reinforcers until one works (i.e., causes the target behavior to increase).

At this point, it is appropriate to comment on the distinction between primary and secondary reinforcers. Essentially, primary reinforcers are items, such as a favorite food, that satisfy basic needs. Secondary reinforcers are items, such as token chips or points on a chart, that keep score on the future delivery of primary reinforcers. Phrased somewhat differently, secondary reinforcers depend on primary reinforcers for their effectiveness. Often, practical reasons favor the use of secondary reinforcers over primary reinforcers. For example, it is much easier to mark points on a chart than it is to serve up an ice cream sundae or to show a movie.

A number of other considerations argue also for the use of secondary reinforcers. These considerations include satiation, frequency of administration, speed of administration, and control (Gelfand & Hartmann, 1984). *Satiation* refers to the child's becoming tired of the reinforcer. Secondary reinforcers can be backed up by a variety of primary reinforcers. All that is needed is to devise a proper rate of exchange. *Frequency of administration* refers to the fact that the positive reinforcers work best if delivered very frequently. For example, some token systems average 275 tokens per day per child. In order to give frequent reinforcers, it is often necessary to dispense them in very small units. This is one of the reasons that early behavior modifiers first used the M & M candy rather than a pound of chocolate. *Speed of administration* refers to the fact that reinforcers must be given as soon as possible after the target behavior has occurred. In terms of time, it is best if the reinforcement occurs within 30 seconds and preferably sooner. Last, the term *control* refers to the ability to be the sole source of the positive reinforcer, so that the child must deal with the behavior modifier in order to obtain the positive reinforcement.

Another important issue with positive reinforcement is that behavior must be shaped. That is, as discussed in the section on modeling, the target behavior must be broken down into very small steps, and small reinforcements must be used to reinforce the successful completion of each little step until the entire behavior is accomplished. For instance, Azrin and Foxx, in their book *Toilet Training in Less than a Day* (1974), demonstrated very clearly how to shape toilet training behavior. By reinforcing successive approximations of the final behavior, the end goal can be achieved. The crucial elements in using positive reinforcers are to use powerful reinforcers to reinforce quickly and frequently, and to reinforce small steps toward the final target behavior.

Contingency Contracting

Although the developmental level of the child may preclude the use of written contracts, with many children contingency contracting is a viable option. Simply put, contingency contracting is a written contract which spells out the reinforcement contingencies between the child and the therapist (Homme, Csanyi, Gonzales, & Rechs, 1970). The advantage of the written contract in behavior therapy is similar to the value of a contract in business. A written contract provides a tangible record which helps to reduce disagreements and misunderstandings between the parties to the contract.

The major elements of contingency contracting have been described elsewhere (Homme *et al.*, 1970; Ollendick & Cerny, 1981). Among other elements, the contract should (1) specify clearly the target behavior in behavioral terms (i.e., capable of being observed and measured); (2) describe the criteria to be reached for reinforcement; and (3) indicate the type, amount, and timing of the reinforcement. Both the child and the therapist must sign the contract, and others (e.g., teacher and parents) may wish to sign, too. Most of the considerations discussed in the earlier section on positive reinforcement also apply to contingency contracting. Gelfand and Hartmann (1984) made the point that the most important aspect of a contingency contract is that both the child and the therapist feel that the contract is fair. If the contract is seen as fair, it is assumed that the child will be more likely to comply.

DECREASING BEHAVIOR

In this section, we discuss methods for reducing the rate of behavior. Three main categories of approach are reviewed: reinforcement, punishment, and extinction.

Reinforcement

Reinforcement includes the differential reinforcement of other behavior (DRO), the differential reinforcement of incompatible behavior (DRI), time-out, and response cost.

DRO and DRI

DRO and DRI are best discussed together because DRI is simply a special case of DRO. Essentially, DRO is reinforcing any of the child's behavior other than the target behavior that needs to be decreased (Homer & Peterson, 1980). A special case of DRO is DRI. In DRI, selected behaviors, incompatible with the target behavior to be decreased, are reinforced. For example, if the hitting of peers is the behavior to be decreased, then incompatible behaviors may be playing cards or doing push-ups. The particular advantage of DRI is that it works quickly with violent, aggressive, disruptive behaviors. A significant advantage of DRI and DRO is that, in contrast to punishment procedures, where aversive stimuli are introduced, there are no negative emotional effects. Put another way, when a child is punished by mild electric shock, by spanking, or by other aversive physical actions, the child may develop anger and hate for the persons and/or situations where the aversive stimuli are introduced. By contrast, DRO or DRI can be employed without causing negative emotions in children. This, of course, is reasonable since the child is receiving a valued reinforcer with some regularity. It is also expected that the absence of negative affect will facilitate learning.

At this point, it is appropriate to comment on some of the treatment research on the use of various behavioral treatment methods for aggressive and disruptive behavior. As there have been relatively few investigations with brain-injured children, it becomes necessary to consider the rather well-developed behavior treatment literature with the developmentally disabled population. In a review paper, Matson and Taras (1989) examined behavior treatment techniques for decreasing aggressive and disruptive behavior in mentally retarded clients. The review makes it possible to estimate the relative effectiveness of various treatment methods. The authors found that

> The treatments that seemed to be most effective in terms of magnitude of changes from baseline to the end of treatment were DRI, aversive stimuli punishment, facial screening, and overcorrection. (p. 100)

Thus, it appears there is some evidence to support the use of DRI to decrease aggressive behaviors in a population of developmentally disabled persons.

Time-Out

Time-out is perhaps the most misunderstood of all behavioral techniques. The correct term is *time-out from positive reinforcement* (Gelfand & Hartmann, 1984). Essentially, ongoing positive reinforcement contingencies are suspended for a specified period of time if the child emits a certain behavior. This precise definition contrasts with the popular notion of time-out as time spent in a time-out room. Although many public-school behavior-modification programs utilize time-out rooms, the actual technique of time-out need not involve a room. Moreover, in early time-out programs with elementary-school children, the child to whom time-out was applied was not removed from the room. Rather, the child, unlike the other children, was not eligible for positive reinforcement. For example, each child who attends to a classroom demonstration could be given an M & M every two minutes. Assume that one child hits a classmate. The time-out could be as simple as withholding M & Ms for five minutes from the child who hit a classmate.

Two important considerations in the use of time-out are its duration and the characteristics of the room, if a room is used. Lengthy time-out intervals need not be used. Some authors have recommended a time-out interval of about four minutes (Hobbs & Forehand, 1977).

A second consideration is the time-out room. Clearly, there are safety and comfort issues. The child's contingency is the loss of positive reinforcement and not the unattractiveness of the time-out room. Time-out areas (not necessarily a room) should be clean, with adequate light and ventilation, and should allow for constant or very frequent observation by the staff or caregivers. It would be abusive to lock a child in a dark room for excessive periods of time.

Response Cost

The basic concept of response cost is a fine. As noted by Gelfand and Hartman (1984):

> In a response cost (RC) contingency, engaging in a specified prohibited behavior produces a loss of reinforcing stimuli and events. Most often, point, tokens, or money are removed contingent upon a child's making an incorrect response. (p. 141)

Perhaps the adult contingencies for exceeding speed limits (i.e., traffic tickets), parking in the wrong place (i.e., parking tickets), or keeping a library book for longer than two weeks (i.e., library fines) are helpful examples of response cost. For children, often-used response-cost contingencies include denial of privileges such as access to television and video games or going out for an afternoon.

The most important aspect of response cost is its emotional effect on children subjected to such contingencies. Simply put, the emotional effects are minimal. This effect is in marked contrast to that of punishment procedures, which often produce strong emotional responses and even hatred of the persons delivering the contingency. Perhaps children fail to make the connection between their behavior and the punishment or feel that punishment is never justified, regardless of the type and severity of their behavior. Because of the absence of negative emotional aftereffects, response cost is one of the most preferred methods of decreasing behavior.

The downside of response cost, however, is that sometimes it is overused. The child's parent or caregiver, in order to get *quick* behavior change, may employ so many response-cost contingencies that the child does not have access to any positive reinforcers (Kazdin, 1980). It is important to monitor carefully the use of response cost to ensure that the child will have a fair chance to avoid the response-cost contingency. Gelfand and Hartmann (1984) made the cogent recommendation that persons implementing the response-cost contingencies imagine themselves as the child and decide if they would feel fairly treated. Also, as always, it would be important to pair the response-cost contingency with some contingencies whereby the child could earn positive reinforcements. As the old saying suggests, you catch more flies with honey than with vinegar.

Punishment

Unfortunately, punishment techniques have often been associated with behavior modification by the lay public. Helped by popular fiction and movies such as *A Clockwork Orange,* many laypersons have formed negative attitudes toward behavior modification based on misinformation. Simply put, although punishment techniques may have a place in behavior modification, it is quite limited and circumscribed.

Gelfand and Hartmann (1984) defined punishment as "decreasing the rate of a particular response by applying an aversive stimulus or event contingent upon the emission of that response" (p. 137).

In the context of this chapter, punishment is the application of mildly aversive procedures. Some authors would describe punishment as including time-out or response cost. Earlier, the taking away of a positive reinforcer or response cost, was described under "Reinforcement." Punishment, however, can include severely aversive procedures, such as electric shock. Procedures of that magnitude of intensity are not described here. Such procedures require elaborate safeguards to protect the child from possible abuse and/or from physical injury.

By contrast, mild punishment, such as reprimands or overcorrection, is less apt to lead to abuse or to present the possibility of physical injury.

Reprimands

A reprimand is simply a verbal admonishment to the child to change his or her behavior. It can be as simple as "Just say no!" The keys to making reprimands effective include body language consistent with the verbal context of the reprimand; clear, consistent, and oft-repeated instructions about what to do; and paced reprimands at short intervals (i.e., seconds) repeated until the child is compliant.

It is important to realize that peer groups may play a role in the effectiveness of reprimands. In some groups of children, reprimands serve as attention to the child, and the child, of course, may prefer *any* form of attention to being ignored. Therefore, how the child sees the reprimand will mediate its effectiveness. On the bright side, reprimands are cheap, are not physically dangerous, and are only a mild form of punishment. On the dull side, reprimands are sometimes of limited effectiveness, and circumstances that are not easily manipulated may influence their effectiveness.

Overcorrections

There are two main types of overcorrection: positive-practice and restitutional (Foxx & Azrin, 1972, 1973). The essential element in overcorrection is physical repetition of acts that "socially correct" for inappropriate or negative actions by the child. The *over* portion of the word *overcorrection* means that the "correct" act is repeatedly performed to the point where it becomes mildly aversive to the child. Another way of looking at overcorrection is to view it as a "physical" version of response cost. However, with overcorrection, one is not fined but has to perform "positive" or "restitutional" physical acts an excessive number of times.

Gelfand and Hartmann (1984) described positive-practice overcorrection as consisting "of repetitive practice of more appropriate behaviors that are physically incompatible with the undesired acts" (p. 151).

Similarly, Gelfand and Hartmann (1984) described restitutional overcorrection as requiring "the child to make amends for any damage he (she) has done and to overcorrect or to improve on the original state of affairs" (p. 150).

The distinction between positive-practice and restitutional overcorrection is straightforward. If an object or a person is injured, then "restitution" must be made. What the child does to make restitution constitutes the basic act of the overcorrection procedure, but what makes it *over*correction is that the child has to repeat the basic act many many times. For example, a child who makes a mess on a floor might be required to wash the entire floor 10 times. Obviously, the basic act would have to be within the child's capacity both physically and psychologically.

In cases where no object or person has been injured, positive-practice overcorrection procedures may be used. For example, a child who performs socially inappropriate self-stimulation behaviors might be required to perform physical exercises which involve the same muscle groups but are physically incompatible with the self-stimulatory behaviors. Foxx and Azrin (1973), in a classic case report, described how they utilized neck exercises for 20 minutes contingent upon instances of a retarded female's self-stimulatory head movements. Additional frequently used positive-practice overcorrection procedures include tooth brushing for swearing, patterned head movements for head banging, and gentle touching and repeated apologies for aggressive and threatening behaviors (Foxx & Azrin, 1972).

The crucial common elements of overcorrection appear to be the following (Foxx & Azrin, 1972). First, the overcorrection behavior must be topographically related to the behavior to be decreased. Second, the initiation of the overcorrection procedure must immediately follow the behavior to be decreased. Third, the overcorrection act must be repeated to the extent that the child finds the procedures to be more of a bother than the behavior to be decreased is enjoyable.

Overcorrection has been demonstrated to be effective in decreasing aggressive, disruptive, and self-stimulatory behaviors (Azrin & Besalel, 1980). Overcorrection decreases selected self-injurious behaviors, such as head banging and eye poking, and should be attempted prior to using electric shock or physical restraint (Gelfand & Hartmann, 1984).

On the other hand, there are some problems with overcorrection. For one thing, it is difficult to predict how long or how many times an overcorrection procedure must be done. Durations and frequencies reported in the literature often range in duration from 10 seconds to 2 hours and in frequency from 10 to 30 times. The rule of thumb is to start low and work up if the shorter duration or lower frequency fails to prove itself effective (Luiselli, 1980).

Another problem with overcorrection is that it is a time-intensive and labor-intensive activity. If the child is unwilling to comply with the overcorrection act, physical force may be used to make him or her comply. This requires, at a minimum, one staff member per limb of the child for an extended period of time. Sometimes, caregivers balk at the allocation of such a high number of personnel per child. Indeed, there is at least one report (Kelly & Drabman, 1977) of a successful overcorrection procedure's being discontinued because of the amount of work necessary to implement the procedure. Nonetheless, the effectiveness of overcorrection argues for its use (Matson, Horne, Ollendick, & Ollendick, 1979).

Extinction

The last procedure for decreasing behaviors to be discussed in this chapter is extinction. Gelfand and Hartmann (1984) described extinction as: "a procedure in which reinforcement that previously followed an operant behavior is discontinued" (p. 132).

Essentially, extinction is when reinforcement is discontinued so that the behavior to be decreased will decrease. It is important to realize that, before one can use extinction, two things are necessary. First, one must know exactly what reinforcer or reinforcers are maintaining the behavior to be decreased. Second, one must be able to control access to the reinforcer or reinforcers. If either of these conditions (i.e., knowing the reinforcers and controlling access to the reinforcers) cannot be met, then it is futile to use extinction to decrease a behavior. For example, a child in school who acts out to get attention from his or her age-peers will be little affected if the teacher ignores him or her. If the teacher is able to control the responses of the age-peers, then perhaps the use of extinction as a method of decreasing the behavior could be contemplated.

There are two potential problems in using extinction. The first problem deals with time. Simply put, extinction takes a lot of time, especially if the behavior to be decreased has been on an intermittent, rather than a continuous, schedule of reinforcement.

As is well known in behavior modification research, a behavior that has been reinforced each time it occurs will decrease quickly if the reinforcement is stopped. Essentially, there is quick feedback that the reinforcement contingency no longer applies. By contrast, when the reinforcement schedule is a variable-interval or ratio, for example, the feedback is not so clear-cut.

The amount of time necessary for extinction to decrease a particular behavior can be a problem. In a common example, one child may exhibit aggressive behavior toward other children to gain a parent's or a teacher's attention. Although extinction could eventually work as a behavior reduction technique, the fact that it would take time, during which the other children are being hit, makes extinction a poor choice. Clearly, extinction should not be used if there is any possibility of injury to the child, to his or her peers, or to any other person.

A second problem with extinction deals with the child's pattern of responding after the reinforcer has been removed or discontinued. Essentially, there is often an exacerbation of responding by the child. Put another way, things get worse before they get better. The technical term for this pattern of responding is *extinction burst* (Gelfand & Hartmann, 1984). An example of this behavior can be seen in everyday life. Recall what happens when a child puts money in a soft-drink machine and nothing comes out after a selection has been made. Usually, the child will hit the selection button several times and will often kick the machine. This is a classic example of an extinction burst.

SUMMARY

This chapter presented a brief overview of selected treatment procedures for brain-injured children. The chapter reviewed both cognitive-behavioral and behavioral treatment procedures. The cognitive-behavioral techniques include problem solving and self-instructional techniques. The problem-solving techniques include a general orientation to problem solving, steps involving problem definition formulation, the generation of reasonable alternatives, methods of making decisions, and also methods for verifying the value and appropriateness of various decisions. Regarding self-instructional training, self-statement types and sequences of self-instructional training were both discussed. The more strictly behavioral treatment procedures include behavioral contingencies, instructional strategies, and motivational strategies. The discussion of behavioral contingencies included defining the target behavior, methods of behavioral assessment, and procedures for increasing a behavior. The instructional strategies include both direct verbal instruction and modeling procedures. The motivational strategies, positive reinforcement and contingency contracting, are fairly straightforward. Particular emphasis was placed on decreasing behaviors. A number of very specific techniques for decreasing behaviors were reviewed: the reinforcement-based methods of decreasing behavior, (the differential reinforcement of other behavior, the differential reinforcement of incompatible behaviors, time-out, and response cost), punishment (reprimands and overcorrection), and extinction.

REFERENCES

Azrin, N. H., & Besalel, V. A. (1980). *How to use overcorrection.* Lawrence, KS: H & H Enterprises.

Azrin, N. H., & Foxx, R. M. (1974). *Toilet training in less than a day.* New York: Simon & Schuster.

Bandura, A. (1969). *Principles of behavior modification.* New York: Holt, Rinehart & Winston.

Bandura, A. (1982). Self-efficiency mechanism in human agency. *American Psychologist, 37,* 122–147.

Blanchard, E. B. (1970). Relative contributions of modeling, informational influences and physical contact in the extinction of phobic behavior. *Journal of Abnormal Psychology, 76,* 55–61.

Dollard, J., & Miller, N. E. (1950). *Personality and psychotherapy.* New York: McGraw-Hill.

D'Zuvilla, T. J., & Goldfried, M. R. (1971). Problem solving and behavior modification. *Journal of Abnormal Psychology, 78,* 107–126.

Foxx, R. M., & Azrin, N. H. (1972). Restitution: A method of eliminating aggressive disruptive behavior of retarded and brain damaged patients. *Behavior Research and Therapy, 10,* 15–27.

Foxx, R. M., & Azrin, N. H. (1973). The elimination of autistic self-stimulating behavior by overcorrection. *Journal of Applied Behavior Analysis, 6,* 1–14.

Foxx, R. M., & Shapiro, S. T. (1978). The timeout ribbon: A nonexclusionary timeout procedure. *Journal of Applied Behavior Analysis, 11,* 125–136.

Gelfand, D. M., & Hartmann, D. P. (1984). *Child behavior analysis and therapy* (2nd ed.). New York: Pergamon Press.

Glass, D. C., & Singer, J. E. (1972). *Urban stress.* New York: Academic Press.

Goldfried, M. R., & Davison, G. C. (1976). *Clinical behavior therapy.* New York: Holt, Rinehart & Winston.

Hall, R. V. (1971). *Managing behavior: Basic principles.* Lawrence, KS: H & H Enterprises.

Hartmann, D. P., & Hall, R. V. (1976). The changing criterion design. *Journal of Applied Behavior Analysis, 9,* 527–532.

Hayes, S. C. (1981). Single case experimental design and empirical clinical practice. *Journal of Consulting and Clinical Psychology, 49,* 193–211.

Hersen, M., & Barlow, D. H. (1976). *Single case experimental designs: Strategies for studying behavior change.* New York: Pergamon Press.

Hobbs, S., & Forehand, A. (1977). Important parameters in the use of timeout with children: A reexamination. *Journal of Behavior Therapy and Experimental Psychiatry, 8,* 365–370.

Homer, A. L., & Peterson, L. (1980). Differential reinforcement of other behavior: A preferred response elimination procedure. *Behavior Therapy, 11,* 449–471.

Homme, L., Csanyi, A. P., Gonzales, M. A., & Rechs, J. R. (1970). *How to use contingency contracting in the classroom.* Champaign, IL: Research Press.

Horton, A. M., Jr. (1987). Luria's contributions to clinical and behavioral neuropsychology. *Neuropsychology, 1*(2), 39–44.

Horton, A. M., Jr., & Barrett, D. (1988). Neuropsychological assessment and behavior therapy: New directions in head trauma rehabilitation. *Journal of Head Trauma Rehabilitation, 3*(1), 57–64.

Horton, A. M., Jr., & Wedding, D. (1984). *Introduction to clinical and behavioral neuropsychology.* New York: Praeger.

Kazdin, A. E. (1975). Characteristics and trends in applied behavior analysis. *Journal of Applied Behavior Analysis, 8,* 332.

Kazdin, A. E. (1978). *History of behavior modification.* Baltimore, MD: University Park Press.

Kazdin, A. E. (1980). *Behavior modification in applied settings* (rev. ed.). Homewood, IL: Dorsey.

Kazdin, A. E. (1986). *Behavior modification in applied settings* (rev. ed.). Homewood, IL: Dorsey.

Kelly, J. A., & Drabman, R. S. (1977). Generalizing response suppression of self-injurious behavior through an overcorrection punishment procedure: A case study. *Behavior Therapy, 8,* 468–472.

Kendall, P. C. (1977). On the efficacious use of verbal self-instructional procedures with children. *Cognitive Therapy and Research, 1,* 331–341.

Kendall, P. C., & Braswell, L. (1985). *Cognitive-behavioral therapy for impulsive children.* New York: Guilford Press.

Kendall, P. C., & Finch, A. J. (1979). Developing nonimpulsive behavior in children's cognitive-behavioral strategies on self-control. In P. C. Kendall & S. D. Hollon (Eds.), *Cognitive-behavioral interventions: Theory, research, and procedure.* New York: Academic Press.

Luiselli, J. (1980). Programming overcorrection with children: What do the data indicate? *Journal of Clinical Child Psychology, 9,* 224–228.

Matson, J., Horne, A., Ollendick, D., & Ollendick, T. (1979). Overcorrection: A further evaluation of restitution and positive practice. *Journal of Behavior Therapy and Experimental Psychiatry, 10,* 295–298.

Matson, J. L. & Taras, M. (1989). A 20 year review of punishment procedures and alternative methods to treat problem behaviors in developmentally delayed persons. *Developmental Disabilities, 10,* 85–104.

Meichenbaum, D., & Goodman, J. (1971). Training impulsive children to talk to themselves: A means of developing self-control. *Journal of Abnormal Psychology, 77,* 115–126.

Ollendick, T. H., & Cavey, J. A. (1981). *Clinical behavior therapy with children.* New York: Plenum Press.

Premack, D. (1965). Reinforcement theory. In D. Levine (Ed.). *Nebraska Symposium on Motivation* (Vol. 13). Lincoln, NE: University of Nebraska Press.

Simon, H. (1966). *Administrative behavior.* New York: International University Press.

Skinner, B. F. (1953). *Science and human behavior.* New York: Macmillan.

6

Treatment Outcome

INTRODUCTION

There is an old hospital saying that therapy is a blanket that covers many sins. Perhaps in no place is this statement more true than in a discussion of the psychotherapy and behavior-change literature. It is perhaps no exaggeration to say that psychotherapy is an area in which little is known and even less can be proven. And indeed, the fact that one might work with children is no advantage in this area.

Nonetheless, the need and value of research on effective psychotherapy and behavior change methods for children would appear self-evident. Many children evidence specific developmental difficulties that are desperately in need of treatment. Among others, developmental learning delays, trauma brain injuries, and attentional problems are particularly salient. Well-done, well-documented research interventions would have the value of highlighting particularly effective techniques. These identified techniques could then be utilized to facilitate the treatment of brain-impaired children.

The purposes of this chapter are to briefly and selectively review some of the research literature with respect to behavioral approaches to the problems of brain-injured children. By way of illustration, some additional comments with respect to the problems of children with attentional problems are also considered. More specific treatment of children with developmental learning disorders is not attempted because of limitations of space. Readers wishing a more specific treatment with respect to developmental learning disorders might consult Hartlage and Telzrow's excellent book *Neuropsychological Assessment in Intervention with Children and*

Adolescents (1986). In order to provide the most appropriate context for a review of what research has already been undertaken, some brief words are first offered with respect to general reviews of psychotherapy and behavior change techniques with children.

It is perhaps somewhat difficult for members of the various mental health professions to accept, but nonetheless, the fact of the matter is that the value of psychotherapy in general, regardless of the age, sex, race, or clinical condition of the person treated, or the sort of treatment utilized, is currently not an entirely settled question. There is a fairly substantive debate regarding the effectiveness of any sort of behavioral change techniques. Also, increasing scrutiny of expenditures of public monies for psychological treatment is but one symptom of the ongoing health care controversy. To provide a perspective on this issue, some general comments are first made regarding the adult psychotherapy and behavior change literature, and then specific attention is devoted to the child psychotherapy and behavior change literature.

It would perhaps be very difficult to begin any discussion of the evaluation of behavior change techniques or psychotherapy without first remarking on the important review by Eysenck (1952; 1966) of adult psychotherapy, in which he severely questioned the efficacy of traditional psychotherapeutic practice. This work, of course, was done with adult patients, but it has implications also for those who work with children. Eysenck, quite simply, found that, essentially, the patients could be seen to fall in three roughly equal categories: those who got better, those who got worse, and those who stayed the same. He suggested that the traditional forms of therapy were no better than essentially no treatment at all.

Suffice it to say that Eysenck's comments elicited multiple responses from a variety of sources. One of the reactions to that review was a felt need to develop behavior therapy methods in the hope that they would be more effective. Interestingly, perhaps the companion review of the Eysenck review of the treatment of adults was one by Levitt (1957), who evaluated a number of studies of psychotherapy with children. He found no significant differences in improvement between those children who received psychotherapy (i.e. 67–78%) versus those children who didn't receive psychotherapy (73%) (Levitt, 1957). This was a fairly harsh critique of traditional behavior-change methods as applied to the problems of children. As would be expected, there were again multiple responses from various sources with respect to Levitt's results.

Perhaps in response to his critics, Levitt again reviewed the literature in 1963, over five years later, and found similar results. Again, the treated and untreated groups of children were virtually indistinguishable. Indeed, Levitt's (1963) second review appeared to suggest that perhaps treatment had a slightly less positive effect (65%), than non-treatment condition (73%).

Be that as it may, however, one thing that appeared to be fairly clear was that there was a definite need for specificity (Kazdin, 1988), that is to say, that the focus of psychotherapeutic reviews should be the question of what type of clients do best, with what type of therapist, employing what sort of treatment, over what period of time, and as assessed by which particular outcome measures.

At this point, some attention might be given to the interesting results of a new research methodology which holds significant promise for answering these questions: meta-analysis. Meta-analysis is perhaps one of the few new methods that have emerged in the last decade regarding the evaluation of psychotherapy and behavior change research.

Meta-analysis has emerged as a viable option to the traditional method of evaluating research literature. Essentially, the previous practice was to collect all studies that touched on a particular issue and then total up how many studies suggested there was a difference or positive result and the number of studies that failed to find any positive result. This method produced a basic "box score," in which, in the most common case, some studies showed positive results and some studies showed negative results. Quite simply, such a traditional box-score evaluation was distinctly lacking in precision (Smith & Glass, 1977).

As noted by Kazdin (1988), part of the problem was the fact that there were essentially no established rules for evaluating alternate studies based on the strength of effect or to make an overall judgment regarding a particular treatment in cases where there was any degree of disagreement among studies. Simply put, for a treatment or technique to be considered effective, there had to be a predominance of evidence in favor of the technique. One of many clear advantages of meta-analysis is that it provides a standard set of rules for combining the results of multiple research studies on a particular question (Smith & Glass, 1977). In addition, meta-analysis enables one to synthesize and summarize the research literature in a heuristic fashion (Kazdin, 1988).

Of course, an alternative view might be that, in some cases, one might be adding apples and oranges and thereby providing an intellectual fruit salad. An even less attractive thought would be that as the computer-literate point out, garbage in equals garbage out. Even with these misgivings, it might be clearly pointed out that meta-analysis is certainly in vogue, and it would be difficult to attempt to evaluate the child psychotherapy literature without at least mentioning the results of any relevant meta-analyses.

At this point, some consideration might be given to the way that an appropriate meta-analysis would be conducted. Essentially, meta-analysis rests on the concept of effect size (Smith & Glass, 1977). As noted by Kazdin (1988), effect size is calculated as the difference between the means of an experimental (treatment) and a control (no-treatment) group, divided by the standard deviation of the control group. Effect size constitutes the dependent measure for the meta-analysis. It is used by investigators as a summary statistic to examine the impact of other variables. The characteristics of the investigation (e.g., age of subjects, different types of treatment, and duration of treatment) become the independent variables (Kazdin, 1988).

Put another way, essentially one uses the control group as a metric for evaluating the effect size. The control group serves as a general normal curve, and the treatment group is superimposed on it. The magnitude of difference by which the treatment group differs from the control group is seen to represent the effect size, and the purpose of the meta-analysis is to put all these effect sizes together and calculate a mean effect size. One underlying assumption, of course, is that all control groups are virtually the same, which may be perhaps as rational as assuming that all distributions are normal. As can be seen clearly, there is ample warrant to do research on the meta-analysis method *itself!*

While there have been multiple meta-analyses of the psychotherapy literature, the conclusions of the first reasonably comprehensive meta-analysis of Smith and Glass (1977) still appears, generally, to hold firm. The large number of meta-analyses since Smith and Glass's first study appear, to a large extent, to have served to replicate their findings. Essentially, they had two conclusions. One is that psychotherapy or behavior-change sorts of treatments generally have a greater therapeutic effect than no-treatment control conditions. Thus, they showed that psychotherapy does have a clear benefit. While that conclusion was appreciated and well received, their second conclusion was less easy to accept. Essentially, they found that different treatments, such as psychodynamic theory or behavioral treatment, tended to be equally effective. Given the widely differing and very complex theoretical rationales for treatment as widely diverse as rational emotive therapy and gestalt therapy, it is easy to see why many had difficulty accepting the second conclusion. While some researchers had felt that the results indicated that cognitive-behaviorally oriented sorts of therapy (i.e., systematic desensitization, rational emotive therapy, and behavior modification) had demonstrated some slightly better results than others (Horton, 1982), this was not the conclusion of Smith and Glass (1977).

With respect to the treatment of children by psychotherapeutic or behavior-change methods, the Smith and Glass review (1977) did include studies of children, but they did not differentiate between children and adults in their conclusions. A later child-psychotherapy meta-analysis review by Casey and Berman (1985) was published in the *Psychological Bulletin*. This meta-analysis included some 75 studies published over a 30-year span. As would be expected, each study included the comparison of some form of therapeutic treatment with either a control group or some other treatment. Studies included in the meta-analysis included children from early childhood to the teenage years and included the usual sorts of individual therapy, such as psychodynamic, client-centered, and behavioral.

Essentially, as would be hoped, Casey and Berman (1985) found that the use of psychotherapeutic and behavior-change methods with children demonstrated a reasonable effect size. The effect size they found was .71, which indicates that the difference between the average experimental group and the average control group was almost three quarters of a standard deviation. While not outstanding, this is nonetheless roughly comparable to the results found by Smith and Glass (1977), and others, in terms of meta-analyses that included children and adults or only adults. With respect to alternate therapies, again the results were somewhat similar to those obtained with adults. Behavioral therapies had a mean effect size of .91, or essentially nine tenths of a standard deviation. By contrast, nonbehavioral therapies had a mean effect size of .40, or a little less than half a standard deviation.

Interestingly, the behavior therapies actually consist of both classical behavior therapies and those that are also considered primarily cognitive-behavioral. Moreover, in the review by Casey and Berman (1985), the cognitive-behavioral therapies appeared to have a lower effect size than the classical behavior therapies; that is, the cognitive-behavioral therapies had a .81 effect size, or roughly eight tenths of a standard deviation, whereas the classically behavioral therapies had an effect size of .96, which is almost a whole standard deviation, and the largest single effect size of any component (Casey & Berman, 1985). Interestingly, the non-behavioral therapies were divided into client-centered and dynamic, with the client-centered therapies having the effect size of .49, and the dynamic an effect size of .21 (Casey & Berman, 1985). While it is tempting to see certain types of therapies as "winners," perhaps the most reasonable comments are those presented by Kazdin (1988):

> First, psychotherapy appears to be better than no treatment. Second, the magnitude of these effects closely parallels those obtained with adults. Third, treatment differences, when evident, tend to favor behavioral rather than non-behavioral techniques. However, there are difficulties in reaching this latter conclusion because of the paucity of studies of non-behavioral techniques, and because of the finding that specific kinds of problems and specific measures often are associated with these different techniques. (p. 33)

The most important point to take away from Kazdin's comments is that the interactions of specific techniques with specific sorts of problems may be the most important consideration with respect to the effectiveness of various behavior-change techniques.

Along those lines, in the following section of this chapter some selected behavior-modification studies are briefly reviewed. Perhaps the most comprehensive work can be found in a chapter by Horton and Miller (1985), is a review of behavior modification strategies with children that surveys the literature from 1967 to 1984 (see Table 6.1, which reprints selected aspects of those studies). At that time, it was noted that only 2 studies of 19 had utilized group designs, that an additional two studies were multiple-group case studies, and that 3 studies were of single-subject design, that is, multiple-baseline or reversal design. The remainder of the studies, and that, of course, would be the majority, were uncontrolled case reports. While the brain-injured children treated included a wide variety of etiologies, such as closed-head injuries, cerebral palsy, Huntington's chorea, and others, nonetheless the fact that the majority of the studies were uncontrolled case reports suggests that increased methodological rigor and additional research are sorely needed. In an unpublished review of the literature from 1984 to the present, relatively little progress was documented. Horton (unpublished data) reviewed the "Psych Abstracts" and "Med-Line" data bases and found only a few studies. The first, by Ann V. Deaton (1987) in the *Journal of Learning Disabilities,* focused on behavior change strategies for children and adolescents with severe brain injuries, and she demonstrated, in a number of case examples, the efficacy of behavioral interventions. Similarly, Zencius, Wesolowski, and Burke (1989), in a paper in the journal *Brain Injury,* compared motivational systems with head-injured adolescents. They utilized behavioral contracting and point systems and response costs to ensure the attendance of two head-injured adolescents at class and therapy sessions and demonstrated significant effectiveness. In another paper, Schoen (1986) modified the non-compliant behavior of a six year old with brain damage through manipulation of instructional reinforcers. Unfortunately, these reports were relatively uncontrolled case studies and thus lack even elementary methodological controls for any possible alternate causation of the effects.

In conclusion, while it appears that there is some significant evidence over some 21 published reports that behavioral methods are effective with brain-injured children, nonetheless too little is known regarding the parameters of effectiveness and the most effective techniques in particular cases. While it is perhaps trite to say it, there is a clear need in this area for well-controlled and methodologically sophisticated treatment-group-design research. It is also very evident that increasing attention should be devoted to the ability of behavioral techniques to deal with the mental, emotional, and behavioral problems of brain-injured children.

RESEARCH ISSUES

As can be clearly seen from the following review of the treatment of children by behavioral means, there is a grave paucity of adequate research studies. While now one can only hope that in

TABLE 6.1 Behavior Modification/Therapy Studies with Brain-Injured Children

Author	Population	Method	Remarks
Blyth (1969)	Brain-damaged children; number unspecified	Social reinforcement and stimulus control and token economy	Improved behavior
Brannigan & Young (1978)	13-year-old male with minimal brain damage	Social skills training	Better social function and emotional control improved
Campbell & Stremel-Campbell (1982)	10-year-old cerebral palsy boy; multiple baseline design	Social praise, repetition of child's responses, answers to child's questions and a token	Language generalization was facilitated
Carlin & Armstrong (1968)	4 boys—2 with brain damage	Token rewards and fines	Improved social responsibility
Cinciripini, Epstein, & Kotanchik (1980)	7-year-old boy with cerebral palsy	Overcorrection for self-stimulation and differential reinforcement of attentional responses and behavior incompatible with self-stimulation	Behavioral treatment reduced self-stimulation and seizures and increased attention
Denton & Citron (1983)	20 adolescent males; 1/3 (N = 7) had closed head injury	Cognitive behavioral treatment for impulsivity	Improved self-control
Gerber, Major, Adams, & Spevack (1981)	16-year-old male with traumatic closed head injury—case study	Operant reward contingencies with motorcycle pictures as rewards for performing cognitive stimulation exercises	Increases on Raven's progressive matrices and subscales of Pictorial Test of Intelligence
Hall & Broden (1967)	3 children with central nervous system dysfunction	Social reinforcement	Children improved in target behaviors

Krumchy & Kores (1981)	Neurologically impaired pediatric inpatients	Reinforcement (praise, standing, and using binoculars)	Decrease of inappropriate behavior and improved appropriate behavior
Murray (1976)	Brain damaged child—case study	Time-out procedure	Tantrum behavior controlled
Muir & Milan (1982)	3 children, 2 with diagnoses of cerebral palsy and 1 with developmental delay and seizure disorder	Parents reinforced for child's progress with lottery tickets	Children improved in language skills
Reidz (1979)	7-year-old boy with brain damage	Verbal commands, praise, and manual guidance	Appropriate acting behavior was learned and generalized to home and school
Ribes-inesta & Guzman (1974)	14-year-old girl with deep brain lesion—case study	Time-out, electric shock, and slaps	Reduced behavior of placing non-edibles in the mouth
Salzinger, Feldman, & Portnoy (1970)	23 families with brain-damaged children (56% girls, 44% boys)—group case study	Parents instructed in behavior modification techniques	Parents who carried out the program reported success in changing their child's behavior
Sellick & Peck (1981)	2-year/4-month-old cerebral palsied boy—case study	In vivo behavioral flooding/extinction	Decreased fear of physical insecurity and positive generalization
Waye (1980)	16-year-old female with Huntington's chorea	Time-out contingencies and positive reinforcement	Decreased temper outbursts and public disrobing

the future this very important area will be adequately addressed, one thing that can be done at present is to discuss some of the important methodological issues that will be crucial for future effective treatment-outcome research. The ultimate research questions, of course, are what treatment conditions work, for what problems, under what circumstances, and so on.

In order to answer these ultimate research questions, a number of issues need to be addressed. The areas discussed here are those concerned with the characteristics of the children treated, the behavioral treatment conditions provided, the type and characteristics of the therapists who provide the treatment conditions, clinical assessment measures, and methodological and statistical research-design issues. With respect to the characteristics of the children treated, diagnostic questions were considered in Chapter 1. Issues with these children, however, go beyond diagnosis.

While a group of children might have a similar DSM-III-R diagnosis, they may, at the same time, vary considerably with respect to the severity, duration, and scope of their problems. For example, with attention-deficit–hyperactivity disorder (ADHD), some children may be "totally off the wall," whereas others may have a greater degree of self-control. Similarly, some children with developmental reading disorder may be totally illiterate, whereas others are able to glean some information from the printed page. However, there is often a failure to appreciate the fact that children may have multiple problems, and that matching children for multiple problems can be an exercise in total and complete frustration for a clinical child neuropsychology researcher. Simply put, what is needed is a greater degree of specification of the diagnostic or assessment criteria, which cover a wide variety of important domains.

Another important child-related issue involves variables that may moderate the ability of behavioral treatment conditions to effect change. Previous research on the behavioral treatment of brain-injured children has almost totally neglected this vital area of research. There are a variety of domains of personality structure, demographic characteristics, and socioeconomic variables that could be profitably explored. To mention just one of these, the developmental level of the child may be a very important consideration with respect to planning effective behavioral treatment. This is not to conceptualize a child's developmental level as simply age-related, but to operationalize it in a more meaningful and conceptually rich paradigm. Obviously, for an attention-deficit-disordered (ADD) child or a child with a traumatic brain injury, appreciating the intricacies of moral development could be a particularly difficult cognitive problem.

And of course, while a child's developmental level is an important variable, one should not neglect chronological age either. The possibility of Age X treatment interactions is certainly a notion worthy of intense scrutiny. For example, the age of onset of brain damage and the resulting neuropsychological sequelae are areas that have had a rich research history, as was mentioned in Chapter two. There are likely to be important treatment implications from this literature.

In addition, the child's gender is an important variable. Anyone who has dealt with children has to be struck by the larger number of referred males than females. While there may be a societal trend to discount or ignore gender differences, nonetheless they do occur, and there is considerable warrant from empirical research to determine if there is differential responding to selected behavioral treatment techniques by brain-injured girls and brain-injured boys. In some of the research literature that has been amassed (Kolvin, Garside, Nicol, MacMillan, Wolstenholem, & Leitch, 1981), there has been a suggestion that girls, if anything, generally responded better to various psychological treatments than boys. Also, there appear to be interaction effects of interest. While acting-out behaviors were more easily modified in girls, emotional-overactivity behaviors appeared to be easier to change in boys. The acute observer would wonder if it is easier to move a child in the direction of traditional sex typing than not. Other potential moderator variables of great significance, of course, are the child's demographic, socioeconomic, and personality characteristics, as well as those of the parents and other family members with whom the child resides. Simply put, issues such as child and family psychopathology, socioeconomic status, current and past parental marital satisfaction, and a host of other variables are likely to be quite important with respect to the eventual outcome of the behavioral treatment of a brain-injured child. Given the importance of this particular set of variables, it is somewhat surprising that relatively little has been done to study them. Recent work by researchers appears to be moving in this area, and one can only hope that their efforts will proceed apace.

TREATMENT ISSUES

One important issue or problem with respect to conducting a behavioral-treatment research-outcome study with brain-damaged children is whether the treatment has actually been applied. In some settings, this might be seen as an issue of treatment fidelity, that is to say, whether the treatment has actually happened. While it is well known that behavioral principles can be specified with a remarkable degree of precision, whether or not the parents or therapists or other staff at an institution or outpatient facility have applied these principles with an appropriate degree of judgment, insight, and alacrity is quite another question. Indeed, perhaps an important reason for many instances of the failure to find treatment effects in neuropsychological and behavior-therapy research literature may be less that the procedures, when adequately applied, are not effective than that the effective treatments may never have been appropriately applied. The typical treatment-research-outcome study infrequently includes clinical research measures that assess whether the behavioral treatment was adequately applied (Sechrest, West, Phillips, Redner, & Yeaton, 1979a). In the best of worlds, there would be a well-specified and clearly written treatment manual which would provide the appropriate treatments, and there would be careful documentation that the treatment was actually applied, as well as an independent review of the documentation that treatment was applied (Yeaton & Sechrest, 1981). As is clear to all, most people do not hold the illusion that they live in the best of worlds.

THERAPIST ISSUES

Important concerns with respect to the therapist are the therapist's training and her or his personal and social characteristics. With respect to training, in the typical behavioral-research-outcome study, the person or persons actually providing or implementing the treatment conditions may range from a high-school dropout employed part time to an individual trained at the Ph.D., Ed.D. or M.D. level. It is interesting to recall that, in clinical practice, the clear intent is to maximize the variable of therapist competence in order to improve the treatment outcome. By contrast, in research investigations, the intent is to control for the effect of the variable of therapist competence in order to look at the effects of a specific treatment. Clearly, multiple therapists are advantageous in research investigations so that the effects of very effective and less effective therapists may be balanced.

As might be expected, specific characteristics of therapists augment or ameliorate the specific direction and degree of behavioral change produced by the behavioral treatment conditions delivered. While the characteristics of therapists of children with brain injury have been relatively little studied, there is an extant data base of research on the general context of therapy with adults (Beutler, Crago, & Ariznendi, 1986) which may yield some hypotheses for further exploration. At this point, probably the most reasonable stance would be to suggest that it is very likely that therapist characteristics have influences on therapeutic work with children similar to those they have on work with adults. At the same time, the reservation that there are just as likely to be some significant differences that are as yet unspecified should also be kept in mind.

There are some methodological considerations that warrant discussion regarding therapist characteristics in terms of work with children: treatment administration and the types of characteristics which may be of importance. With respect to treatment administrators, in child treatment the actual person who delivers the treatment intervention is often not a professional therapist. For example, the individual delivering the intervention may be a parent, a teacher, a paraprofessional, or a peer. While it is clear that the characteristics that these individuals bring to the therapeutic situation may have an effect on the treatment outcome, conceptualizing their influences requires a dramatic expansion of the usual therapist-characteristics concept. To take but one example, it would appear straightforward that the mental health, intelligence, and personality characteristics of the parents who apply contingency management procedures to their behaviorally disturbed brain-injured child in the home could have a direct effect on the efficacy of these procedures. Another related concern is how a professional therapist might shape the behavior of other professionals and paraprofessionals in order to bring their behavior into line with a specified treatment program.

Another methodological consideration to be raised concerns the type of characteristics to be studied. Obviously, demographic characteristics such as age, ethnic status, education, and socioeconomic status are of immediate concern. In addition, personality and emotional variables, such as hysterical or obsessional tendencies, as well as warmth and empathy, merit very thoughtful consideration. In order not to reinvent the therapeutic wheel, one would wish to utilize what has already been learned over the last 30 or 40 years with respect to research on client-centered therapy approaches.

ASSESSMENT ISSUES

There are a number of issues with respect to assessment that could be reasonably considered. These should include the selection of the measures and techniques used to assess treatment outcome, process issues, satisfaction with the treatment provided, and the ease of administration of the treatment conditions. In addition, the issue of increasing prosocial functioning versus immediate symptom reduction should be considered, as well as the timing of follow-up assessment.

With respect to the assessment outcome measures, over the years there has been an evolving clinical consensus in this area. Essentially, the selection of outcome measures should follow the well known MultiTrait-MultiMethod Matrix (MTMMM) (Campbell & Fiske, 1959). That is to say, the outcome evaluation should be multifaceted, involving different methods, different points of view, and different domains of functioning (Kazdin & Wilson, 1978). Obviously, parents, teachers, and peers may have different perspectives on a child's functioning. In addition, the available list of methods of assessment might include behavioral observations, checklists, neuropsychological test performances, and self-reports by the child or a number of other individuals (Achenbach, 1985).

To a degree, the implicit assumption of using these multiple domains and multiple traits in assessment is that agreement among them provides a source of validity, or at least corroboration of the assessment results. The available evidence suggests that children are reasonably accurate in reporting their internal affective states but are less consistent in reporting their overt behavior (Edelbrock, Costello, Culcan, Conover, & Kalas, 1986). When multiple outcome measures fail to coincide, the onus is upon the clinician to make sense of the data. Clearly, in clinical child psychology, there has been a great reliance on child, parent, and teacher self-reports. In clinical child neuropsychology, there has been a greater reliance on specific neuropsychological test performances. In child behavior therapy, there has been a predominant reliance upon specific observations of overt behaviors. The challenge in all three areas of clinical and research inquiry will be to examine the interrelationships among the extant data and to provide empirical evidence and an adequate rationale for any continuing relationships.

Other types of measures that are of great importance include process measures, patient satisfaction indices, and techniques for gauging the ease of treatment administration. Each of these is very briefly discussed here.

Process measures involve tracking the process of change. For example, the old question from social psychology—"Do attitudes change before behaviors or behaviors change before attitudes?"—can, to a degree, be evaluated by process measures of treatment delivery. These measures can provide an understanding which will potentially be quite valuable in terms of the initial validation of a theory of therapeutic change. If one postulates that certain cognitive behavioral interventions are of prime importance for children, it will be important to show that changes in cognition underlie or closely coincide with overt behavioral improvement. If changes fail to demonstrate a temporal relationship, it will be difficult to argue that the theory has escaped falsification.

Another type of measure that has only recently been appreciated in terms of its importance is patient satisfaction. While perhaps most of the work on this measure has been done with adult populations, nonetheless it would appear self-evident that children should have some rights with respect to the selection of the treatment conditions that they would find most congenial. Obviously, dropping out of treatments or lack of adherence to the prescribed interventions may be mediated by the child's degree of satisfaction with the treatment regimen. It would appear reasonable, but possibly at this time not empirically proven, that a greater degree of child, parent, and teacher satisfaction with a treatment program would predict greater compliance by all with the actual prescribed treatment procedures. It may be that a treatment of slightly less effectiveness (e.g., systematic desensitization) might be preferable over one of greater established effectiveness (e.g., implosive therapy), because child, parent, and teacher satisfaction would predict greater compliance with the least difficult to preform and least emotionally demanding treatment procedures and therefore would mediate a higher degree of actual therapeutic change by the less demanding technique at the end of treatment. It might be noted that this is an area in which relatively little empirical research has been done, and that there are ample opportunities for future research in this very important area.

The last of the assessment measures to be covered here is the ease of administration of treatment conditions. Perhaps one of the most telling criticisms of the behavioral treatment of children is that the treatment works, but it requires a staffing ratio of approximately 8 to 1 or higher. Other treatment programs, which are of considerably less effectiveness but administratively can be staffed at a ratio of 1 to 1 (or much less), may be preferable to harried treatment-services administrators who fail to receive immediate, direct, and explicit feedback with respect to treatment effectiveness. In addition to issues such as cost, however, concerns such as the length of time necessary for the training of therapists, the complexity and dangerousness of the behavioral procedures to be implemented, and the robustness of the treatment interventions in the face of very lax and inconsistent application by possibly unenthusiastic treatment providers—all should be considered. In some cases, it may be that a treatment of less effectiveness, but with considerably greater ease of application, would be generally preferred over one of greater effectiveness that requires extraordinary efforts on the part of the treatment providers.

To cite but one example, one of the difficulties with respect to the treatment of institutionalized brain-injured children is overmedication. Providing these children with a drug that will sedate them is quick, easy, and relatively economical of institutional personnel resources. At the same time, a high-quality behavioral program that will teach the child positive prosocial behaviors and that can quickly reduce dangerous and/or obnoxious behaviors will require an initial and continuing investment of considerable time and quite a bit of fairly scarce professional expertise. While the long-term costs of overmedication, in terms of social and medical complications, may be considerable, short-term considerations too often determine immediate behavior.

At this point, the discussion shifts to the issue of immediate symptom reduction versus increasing positive prosocial behaviors. Quite clearly, behavioral problems, as well as others, can be conceptualized as either a dearth of appropriate functioning or an excess of inappropriate functioning. The reason for seeking treatment is more likely to be an excess of inappropriate functioning or very grossly maladaptive behaviors (e.g., physical attacks on others). The usual method of assessing the effects of treatment for these problems would be a prompt reduction of the physically dangerous and/or obnoxious behaviors to either a baseline of zero or an acceptably rare degree of occurrence. For example, for a child in school, the maladaptive behavior could be fighting, hitting, and verbal abuse of peers and authority figures. In many ways, a successful treatment outcome could be defined as the reduction of these potentially physically and psychologically harmful behaviors to a baseline of zero. While that is well and good and quite popular with anyone who was hit or verbally abused by that child, at the same time it should be realized that the reduction of dangerous and/or obnoxious behaviors does not necessarily result in an entirely successful treatment outcome. As noted by Kazdin (1988), the reduction of negative symptoms is not the same as effective positive prosocial functioning. Whether or not the child is able to initiate and sustain positive adaptive behaviors over time in a variety of social situations is an entirely different set of questions from whether he or she currently emits dangers and/or obnoxious behaviors that are harmful to others.

From a tactics point of view, the purpose of considering prosocial functioning as an issue is linked to the prognosis for the continued social, behavioral, and emotional functioning of the child. Very often, children who have behavioral problems also have very inadequate behavioral repertoires with respect to eliciting positive social reactions from others. If the child can be taught methods of interacting in a socially acceptable fashion and therefore may receive the respect, admiration, and positive regard of others in society, then it would seem quite likely that the child would not have to resort to negative behaviors to satisfy his or her needs for attention or social status. Again, as in the patient satisfaction area, the methodology for the effective assessment and quantification of positive prosocial behaviors is an evolving area. It is hoped that future work will focus upon this extremely important area.

Another area of importance with respect to assessment regards its timing. More particularly, consideration should be devoted to the timing of follow-up assessment. While it would seem rather straightforward that children, depending on the particular situation they are in, should be assessed early in the initiation of the treatment process, and also at multiple times throughout and at the end of formal treatment, it is less clear when they should be assessed at follow-up. In terms of validating that the treatment conditions worked, there is nothing quite so convincing as a series of comprehensive follow-up assessments conducted over a number of years. Clearly, a treatment that works quite well, but that allows a very dramatic degree of recidivism over one or two months, is considerably less desirable than a treatment that may work less efficiently to begin with, but that will sustain positive behavior changes in brain-injured children over a course of some years. For example, in the Kolvin *et al.* (1981) study, the children demonstrated different degrees of improvement based on the point in time at which the assessment was completed. Essentially, there was a "sleeper effect," in that improvements that were not effective immediately after treatment later emerged over a period of time after treatment. Apparently, untangling possible developmental or age effects with respect to the sleeper effect is quite an important task. It may very well be that some children will simply "grow out" of certain problems. With others, however, there may actually be a pattern of effects so that the treatment conditions can be manifested only over a considerable period of time.

One way of looking at this problem might be through the lens of patient self-involvement in treatment. A treatment program might appear to be highly effective initially when all of the important decisions are made by the child's therapist. If the child believes that the treatment worked only because the therapist was there, however, and the therapist leaves, then the child may be less involved in performing the sort of actions or in continuing to follow the procedures that would be required for the treatment to continue to be effective. Another sort of treatment, in which the child perceived the therapeutic effects as coming directly from the child's own personal efforts, might be, in the long run, more helpful, as the child would realize that he or she must continue to do certain things in order to be successful, and he or she would not perceive a great change in the transition from treatment to posttreatment. In short, to whose efforts the child attributes the therapeutic change may be crucial in maintaining the efforts. Clearly, this is a very tricky area, which will require much additional work to establish the principles and parameters necessary to guide child behavioral treatment.

RESEARCH DESIGN ISSUES

The purpose of this section is not to review selected true or quasi-experimental research designs as detailed in Campbell and Stanley (1963), but to discuss some elementary considerations with respect to designs and clinical research with children who have suffered brain injury. Two very important issues are very briefly considered. First, some considerations with respect to statistical power are quickly discussed, and second, issues with respect to the clinical significance of treatment results are briefly noted. The discussion of statistical power relates to Type II errors, or the possibility of rejecting the null hypothesis when it is false (Cohen, 1992). Put another way, it is failing to find a difference between two groups when there actually is a difference. As this mental concept can become quite complex, the intent in this discussion is only to sketch a few broad outlines. There is a danger in this approach, in that the concept may be oversimplified.

Essentially, how powerful a statistical test is depends on a number of factors: the number of subjects in the sample, the significance level selected, and the actual differences between the conditions that are to be compared. Cohen, in his 1977 book on statistical power analysis for the behavioral sciences, outlined the various parameters for estimating statistical power. As just mentioned, one of these is how many subjects are available for study, which is a rather straightforward concept in theory. Obtaining enough subjects, however, is often quite tricky in the actual practice of research. In addition, another parameter relates to the alpha level, which is the level of statistical significance chosen. Although the .05 level is quite commonly used, this choice is simply a matter of convention and tradition, and other levels, such as the .10, the .01, and the .001 levels, could be adequately justified in certain situations (Cohen, 1988).

The actual differences between the conditions that are to be compared is often difficult to determine. This determination requires assessing, given the sort of research that one is doing, whether or not a large effect should be seen or whether the effect might be medium-sized or small.

It is assumed, rightly or wrongly, that various areas of research have different levels of effects. For example, in IQ research, one would expect, for the sake of argument, that it might be specified that a standard deviation difference in IQ would be a large effect, that a half-standard-deviation difference would be a medium effect, and a quarter-standard-deviation difference would be a small effect. How does one calculate what would be the average effect size seen in a body of research? Essentially, one has to review the literature of previous research investigations in the area to be studied (Cohen, 1977). It is, of course, recognized that, in some cases, previous investigations may not be reasonable models and that, in other cases, the estimation of effect size is, to a large degree, a guess. If one errs on the side of conservatism, one would always assume that a reasonably small effect would be seen, and therefore this would cover the majority of cases. It should be recognized that even small effects, depending on the area of research, can be impressive (Prentice & Miller, 1992). Based on previous work by Cohen (1962), there is ample evidence to suggest that most studies published in important scientific journals are relatively weak in detecting small or medium-range effects. Actually, Cohen found that the medium probability of the studies in the *Journal of Abnormal and Social Psychology* was .48, or roughly 50/50, in terms of detecting group differences with a medium-sized effect. In other words, even if there was an effect, one would get almost the same results by just flipping a coin. This is clearly not the degree of scientific rigor that one should use to establish the scientific respectability of an area of research. While the actual calculation of effect size and statistical power goes beyond the scope intended for this chapter, nonetheless it might be mentioned that Cohen, in his 1977 book, and other publications

(Cohen, 1988, 1992) has provided tables for estimating the statistical power of various designs.

Sad but true, often the only variables within the control of the clinical child neuropsychology researcher are the levels of significance to be accepted and the number of subjects collected. Both of these parameters have their own sets of pitfalls. With respect to alpha level, while .05 is the standard level of accepted, if a researcher wishes to accept a less stringent level, such as the .10, he or she stands the risk of finding an effect when none exists. On the other hand, in terms of sample size, collecting an adequate sample can be very time-consuming and extremely expensive, depending on the specific research protocol in place. It is well to keep in mind that adequate statistical power often requires sample sizes in the range of 50, 100, or 200 per treatment cell, depending on the other variables and conditions involved in the power calculations. Quite clearly, collecting a sample size as large as 100 patients in a clinical research study can be quite difficult, not to mention very, very expensive and time-consuming. In the case of very-difficult-to-treat disorders or poorly motivated subjects, one might have sufficient subjects at the beginning of the study and then, because of subject attrition, find at the end of the study that one has too few subjects for an adequately powerful statistical test.

One issue that remains to be considered is that the actual effect size seen depends on the within-group variability of the observations obtained, so obtaining a more homogeneous sample could have significant advantages in terms of augmenting statistical power (Kazdin, 1988). One strategy might be to utilize a repeated-measures design to control for assessment error.

At this point, attention is directed to the concept of clinical significance. While statistical significance is often related to the alpha level to be accepted (as earlier noted, in many situations, this is set at the .05 level), nonetheless the concept of *clinical significance* implies whether or not the changes seen are of such a magnitude as to make a change in the real world. Put another way, is the brain-injured child after treatment indistinguishable in the relevant characteristics from a matched control of his or her age, gender, ethnic status, social class, and education (Kazdin, 1988)?

This is actually quite a stringent test, in that most current treatments can produce changes in terms of statistical analysis, but often, when one matches them with their norm group, the treated patients continue to have serious deficits in adaptive functioning. While on one hand the concept of *statistical significance* points out rather clearly and very forcefully how much additional work needs to be done, on the other hand the ultimate goal of any treatment is to ameliorate the deficits seen in a brain-injured child to the point where he or she is indistinguishable from other children from a carefully matched control group. It is to be hoped that future research investigators will include a careful consideration of the issues of clinical significance when designing clinical research studies.

Only by appreciating the clinical significance concept will it be possible to truly evaluate the actual worth of contemporary behavioral research. For example, 10 years ago, the behavioral treatment of obesity was noted to be quite successful in terms of obtaining statistical significance. A variety of behavioral treatment programs for overweight subjects were able to obtain statistically significant results. There were claims that weight control problems were essentially "cured." When one looks at the actual absolute results of the research, however, one finds that the average patient weight loss was approximately 8 pounds. While this loss was certainly better than nothing and better than what the other psychotherapeutic treatments available could provide, the fact remains that many individuals who were obese wished to lose, perhaps, 80 or more pounds, and a simple loss of 8 pounds was about as effective as emptying ashtrays on an airplane to lighten it. Clearly, the aim of behavioral treatment research with brain-injured children should be to achieve socially important clinical change. Anything less would truly fail to adequately meet the needs of the children and their parents.

SUMMARY

This chapter dealt with a number of important clinical research issues, including a review of a selective list of crucial considerations with respect to the psychotherapeutic treatment of children and the previous research conducted on it. Also, the available literature on meta-analysis was briefly discussed, along with its application to the behavioral treatment of children. The focus then shifted to a number of important methodological issues in the research on and treatment of children. Attention was focused on, among other vital concerns, patient variables, treatment variables, therapist variables, and assessment issues. In addition, at the end of the chapter, careful attention was devoted to two very important, but often overlooked, issues: the statistical power of clinical-research experimental designs and the question of whether the therapeutic change that may have taken place is of practical significance to the child and his or her family or significant others. These considerations are too often overlooked but are crucial to the development of meaningful treatment strategies.

The hope and clear expectation is that this chapter has provided a worthwhile overview of a few very important issues in outcome research on child behavioral treatment and has also provided some cogent suggestions about what might be done next and how it might best be done. Clearly, much remains to do!

REFERENCES

Achenbach, T. M. (1985). *Assessment and taxonomy of child and adolescent psychopathology.* Beverly Hills, CA: Sage.

Blyth, Z. (1969, July–August). Group treatment for handicapped children. *Journal of Psychiatric Nursing and Mental Health Services,* 172–173.

Beutler, L. E., Crago, M., & Ariznendi, T. G. (1986). Therapist variables and psychotherapy process and outcome. In S. L. Garfield & A. E. Bergin (Eds.), *Handbook of psychotherapy and behavior change* (3rd ed., pp. 257–310). New York: Wiley.

Brannigan, G., & Young, R. (1978). Social skills training with the MBD adolescent: A case study. *Academic Therapy, 13*(4), 401–404.

Campbell, D. T., & Fiske, D. W. (1959). Convergent and discriminant validation by the multitrait-multimethod matrix. *Psychological Bulletin, 52,* 81–105.

Campbell, D. T., & Stanley, J. L. (1963). *Experimental, and quasi-experimental designs for research.* Chicago: Rand McNally.

Campbell, C., & Stremel-Campbell, K. (1982). Programming "loose training" as a strategy to facilitate language generalization. *Journal of Applied Behavior Analysis, 15,* 295–301.

Carlin, A. S., & Armstrong, H. E. (1968). Rewarding social responsibility in disturbed children: A group play technique. *Psychotherapy: Theory, research, and practice, 5,* 169–174.

Casey, R. J., & Berman, J. S. (1985). The outcome of psychotherapy with children. *Psychological Bulletin, 98,* 388–400.

Cinciripini, P., Epstein, L., & Kotanchik, N. (1980). Behavioral intervention for self-stimulatory, attending, and seizure behavior in a cerebral palsied child. *Journal of Behavior Therapy and Experimental Psychiatry, 11,* 313–316.

Cohen, J. (1962). The statistical power of abnormal-social psychological research: A review. *Journal of Abnormal and Social Psychology, 65,* 145–153.

Cohen, J. (1977). *Statistical power analysis for the behavioral sciences.* New York: Academic Press.

Cohen, J. (1988). *Statistical power analysis for the behavioral sciences* (2nd ed.). New York: Academic Press.

Cohen, J. (1992). A power primer. *Psychological Bulletin, 112,* 155–159.

Deaton, A. (1987). Behavioral change strategies for children and adolescents with severe brain injury. *Journal of Learning Disabilities, 20*(10), 581–589.

Denton, A., & Citron, C. (1983, August). *The development of group intervention strategies for impulsive adolescents with cognitive and language deficits.* Paper presented at the annual convention of the American Psychological Association, Anaheim, CA.

Edelbrock, C. S., & Costello, A. J., Culcan, M. K., Conover, N. C., & Kalas, R. (1986). Parent-child agreement on child psychiatric symptoms assessed by structured interview. *Journal of Child Psychology and Psychiatry, 27,* 181–190.

Eysenck, H. J. (1952). Effects of psychotherapy: An evaluation. *Journal of Consulting Psychology, 16,* 119–124.

Eysenck, H. J. (1966). *The effects of psychotherapy.* New York: International Universities Press.

Gerber, G., Major, M., Adams, J., & Spevack, M. (1981). *Stimulation of cognitive functioning in a young severely-impaired closed head injury patient: The role of behavior modification strategies.* Paper presented at the meeting of the Association for Advancement of Behavior Therapy, Toronto.

Hall, R. V., & Broden, M. (1967). Behavior changes in brain-injured children through social reinforcement. *Journal of Experimental Child Psychology, 5,* 463–479.

Hartlage, L. C., & Telzrow, C. F. (1986). *Neuropsychological assessment in intervention with children and adolescents.* Sarasota, FL: Professional Resources Exchange.

Horton, A. M., Jr. (1982). Introduction to the psychotherapy of the aging. In A. M. Horton, Jr. (Ed.), *Mental health interventions for the aging* (pp. 1–17). New York: Praeger.

Horton, A. M., Jr., & Miller, W. G. (1986). Neuropsychology and behavior therapy. In M. Hensen, R. M. Gisler, & P. M. Miller (Eds.), *Progress in behavior modification* (Vol. 19, pp. 1–55). Orlando, FL: Academic Press.

Kazdin, A. E. (1988). *Child psychotherapy.* New York: Pergamon Press.

Kazdin, A. E., & Wilson, G. T. (1978). *Evaluation of behavior therapy: Evidence in research strategies.* Cambridge, MA: Ballinger.

Kolvin, I., Garside, R. F., Nicol, A. R., MacMillan, A., Wolstenholme, F., &

Leitch, I. M. (1981). *Help starts here: The maladjusted child in the ordinary school*. London: Tavistock.

Kumchy, C., & Koris, P. (1981). Behavioral management of a neurologically impaired pediatric inpatient. *Archives of Physical Medicine and Rehabilitation, 62*, 289–291.

Levitt, E. E. (1957). The results of psychotherapy with children: An evaluation. *Journal of Consulting Psychology, 21*, 1989–1996.

Levitt, E. E. (1963). Psychotherapy with children: A further evaluation. *Behavior Research and Therapy, 60*, 326–329.

Muir, K., & Milan, M. (1982). Parent reinforcement for child achievement: The use of a lottery to maximize parent training effects. *Journal of Applied Behavioral Analysis, 15*(3), 455–460.

Murray, M. E. (1976). Modified time-out procedures for controlling tantrum behavior in public places. *Behavior Therapy, 7*, 412–413.

Prentice, D. A. & Miller, D. T. (1992). When small effects are impressive. *Psychological Bulletin, 112*, 160–164.

Reidz, T. (1979). Training appropriate eating behavior in a pediatric rehabilitation setting: Case study. *Archives of Physical Medicine and Rehabilitation, 60*(5), 226–230.

Ribes-inesta, E., & Guzman, E. (1974). Effectiveness of several suppression procedures in eliminating a high-probability response in a severely brain-damaged child. *Interamerican Journal of Psychology, 8*, 29–39.

Salzinger, K., Feldman, R. S., & Portnoy, S. (1970). Training parents of brain-injured children in the use of operant conditioning procedures. *Behavior Therapy, 1*, 4–32.

Schoen, S. F. (1986). Decreasing noncompliance in a severely multihandicapped child. *Psychology in the Schools, 23*(1), 88–94.

Sechrest, L., West, S. G., Phillips, M. A., Redner, R., & Yeaton, W. (1979). Some neglected problems in evaluation research: Strength and integrative treatments. In L. Sechrest, S. G. West, M. A. Phillips, R. Redner, & W. Weaton (Eds.), *Evaluation studies: Review annual*, Vol. 4 (pp 15–35). Beverly Hills, CA: Sage.

Sellick, K., & Peck, C. (1981). Behavioral treatment of fear in a child with cerebral palsy using a flooding procedure. *Archives of Physical Medicine and Rehabilitation, 62*(8), 398–400.

Smith, M. L., & Glass, G. V. (1977). Metanalysis of psychotherapy outcome studies. *American Psychologist, 31*, 750–760.

Waye, M. (1980). Treatment of an adolescent behavior disorder with a diagnosis of Huntington's chorea. *Journal of Behavior Therapy and Experimental Psychiatry, 11*, 239–242.

Yeaton, W. H., & Sechrest, L. (1981). Critical dimension in the choice and maintenance of successful treatment: Strength, integrity and effectiveness. *Journal of Consulting and Clinical Psychology, 49*, 156–167.

7

Single-Subject Research Design

with WILLIAM G. MILLER

In this chapter attention is devoted to the single-subject research design. As noted by Horton and Wedding (1984):

> Leaving issues of accountability aside for the moment, the major consideration of the patient's clinical needs demands a hard-headed empirical approach to evaluation. Within-subject designs have major advantages over group research in this area. (p. 198)

Given their unique flexibility, single-subject research designs can provide relevant answers to several questions, including whether a treatment works, whether one form of treatment works better than another form of treatment, whether the child prefers one form of treatment, and what level of treatment is optimal (Hayes, 1981). This stress on single-subject research is in no way intended to deny the value of traditional group research. As noted by Agras and Berkowitz (1980), the single-subject research design, as one facet of clinical research, is as defensible as laboratory analogue studies, the evaluation of treatment parameters, and long-term outcome studies.

Each facet has a special value in a progressive model of clinical research. The special value of single-subject research designs is, of course, that the effect of an intervention can be seen fairly rapidly (Barlow, Hayes, & Nelson, 1984).

Here, a cursory introduction is given to the most commonly used single-subject research designs. The four research designs described are the reversal design, the multiple-baseline design, the changing-criterion design, and the alternating-treatment design. Readers desiring a more detailed description of the logic and application of these and other single-subject research designs should consult either the classic Hersen and Barlow (1976) text *Single Case Experimental Designs: Strategies for Studying Behavior Change,* or the revised edition (Barlow & Hersen, 1985). A variety of other excellent references are available (Barlow, *et al.*, 1984; Gelfand & Hartmann, 1984; Kazdin, 1982; Webster, McCaffrey, & Scott, 1986). As suggested by Barlow, *et al.* (1984) the variety of possible single-subject research designs is limited only by the clinical-research–practitioners' imagination and ingenuity.

REVERSAL DESIGN

The reversal design, or the ABAB design, is perhaps the most commonly used single-subject research design (Kazdin, 1975). The logic of the design is that experimental control is demonstrated by the effect of alternate presentation and removal of the clinical intervention over time (Kazdin, 1986). The steps of the reversal design are as follows: First, there is a baseline phase, when the target behavior is recorded at its free operant level. Second, there is an intervention phase, when the experimental procedure is introduced. Third, there is a withdrawal of the experimental condition and return to the baseline condition. Fourth, the experimental procedure is once again introduced (Hall, 1971). The alternating baseline and intervention phases are indicated in design shorthand as ABAB (i.e., A = baseline phase; B = intervention phase). The ABAB design is the most commonly used format. It is possible, however, to have different lengths and different varieties (e.g., ABA and ABABAB).

An example will illustrate the application of the reversal design. Suppose a brain-injured child is physically violent toward his or her peers. A typical intervention would be to utilize the behavior modification technique of time-out (i.e., the child has to go to a quiet room for a time period contingent upon the violent behavior). In the first phase (A), the target behavior (physical violence toward age-peers) is reliably recorded for a number of days. In the second phase (B), the child is placed in the time-out room for a short period of time whenever there is an incident of physical violence toward age-peers. In the third phase (A2), the time-out is no longer in effect, and the conditions of the first phase resume. The fourth phase (B2) involves a reinstitution of the time-out contingency. The acid test of the intervention is whether or not the target behavior changes in response to the phase changes.

With increased demonstrations of responsiveness of the target behavior to phase change, the more convincing is the assumption of functional control of the target behavior (Gelfand & Hartmann, 1984).

The reversal design has some very positive features which promote its use. First, it allows dramatic proof of the power of the clinical intervention. Second, the reversal design controls for a number of alternate explanations of the behavior change. Third, the reversal design can have a positive effect on the child by demonstrating the role of the stimuli involved in the problem (Baer, Wolf, & Risley, 1968). Finally, the reversal design makes it clear when the child needs additional treatment for appropriate responding (Hayes, 1981).

The reversal design also has some negative features that preclude its use in certain situations. The major difficulty is that, for practical and ethical reasons, it may not be possible to reinstitute the baseline condition. In the example used above, one could understand the reluctance of the brain-injured child's age-peers to once again be subjected to physical violence (Horton & Wedding, 1984).

Other potential problems include the possibility that the treatment might have introduced lasting and irreversible changes or that there might be lingering effects of treatment that would obscure the demonstration of experimental control of behavior in the reversal design (Gelfand & Hartmann, 1984). (See Figure 7.1 for an example of a typical reversal design.)

MULTIPLE-BASELINE DESIGN

The multiple-baseline design is used less often than the reversal design (Kazdin, 1978). Although both the reversal design and the multiple-baseline design have a long history in applied behavioral analysis (Baer, *et al.*, 1968), the multiple-baseline design re-

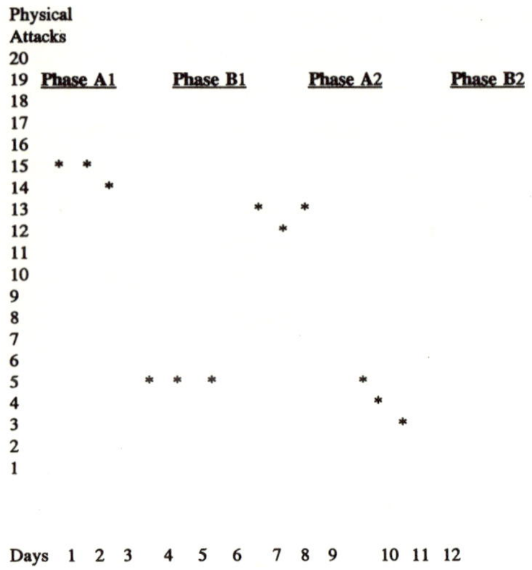

Figure 7.1. A typical reversal design (ABAB).

quires more elaborate efforts on the part of the clinician. As observed by Gelfand and Hartmann (1984), "Multiple baseline designs typically involve keeping data on two or more behaviors that will be modified sequentially with the same treatment procedure" (p. 69).

Simply stated, the effect of the experimental treatment is demonstrated when the target behavior is either increased or decreased when the experimental treatment is applied to different baselines at different times (Kazdin, 1975).

The multiple-baseline design can be of several types: across subjects, behaviors, and/or settings. The logic of the design is fairly simple and straightforward. First, baselines must be obtained and must be both reliable and stable. Second, the experimental treatment is introduced for one randomly selected behavior (or subject or setting) while the other behavior (or subject or setting) is also observed. Third, after a stable baseline is obtained, another untreated baseline is randomly selected, and the experimental treatment is introduced. Fourth, this process is continued until the experimental treatment has been introduced for every baseline.

In the best of situations, the initial baselines are stable, the treated baseline changes, and the untreated baseline remains unchanged. Therefore, experimental control can be demonstrated sequentially across the multiple baselines. If the baselines are unchanged prior to treatment and change only after treatment, then there is considerable evidence to suggest that the treatment was responsible for the behavior change (Gelfand & Hartmann, 1984).

The secret to making this design work is to have independent baselines. Put another way, the behaviors, settings, and subjects must not be related to each other in such a way that the treatment of one will influence another. Perhaps an example would clarify this point. Assume that there are three children who have problems with physical attacks on age-peers. Because of the nature of the attacks, the use of a reversal design would be contraindicated. By contrast, the use of a multiple-baseline design would enable the clinician to demonstrate experimental control without having to allow the child to resume his or her physical attacks on age-peers. One foreseeable problem, however, would be if the children are in a group and the child selected to be treated first is observed by the other children. The other children might decide to decrease physical attacks simply to avoid the possibility of time-out. For purposes of demonstrating experimental control, the experimental treatment should be introduced when the other children are not in a position to be aware of the potential consequences of their behavior.

Although not reintroducing the problem behavior is a very important advantage of the multiple-baseline design, there are some limitations in this design: the need for stable baselines prior to intervention, the amount of time and effort required to collect data on the multiple baselines, and the difficulties encountered in finding independent behaviors (Gelfand & Hartmann, 1984).

Perhaps the most crucial of these problems is the need for independent multiple baselines. This need is particularly acute in clinical neuropsychology, as the recovery of function after brain injury often presents unique problems (Horton & Wedding, 1984). As discussed in Chapter 2, certain neuropsychological abilities may recover spontaneously after cerebral insult, and as might be expected, different neuropsychological abilities recover at different rates (Bach-y-Rita, 1981). Horton and Wedding, (1984) quoted Thomas J. Boll, a prominent clinical child neuropsychologist, as describing a gross general pattern of motor abilities recovering first, followed by language ability, and later by cognitive processes. Boll, a Wisconsin farm boy in his youth, memorably de-

```
        Phase A

Physical Attacks
                         Subject 1

20        * * * I                           Phase B1
15              I
10              I
5               I * * *   * * *   * * *
________________________________________________________________

Subject 2

20        * * *   * * *  I                  Phase B2
15                       I
10                       I
5                        I   * * *   *  *  *
________________________________________________________________

Subject 3

20        * * *   * * *   * * * I           Phase B3
15                              I
10                              I
5                               I   *  *  *
________________________________________________________________

Days      1 2 3   4 5 6   7 8 9    10 11 12
```

Figure 7.2. A typical multiple baseline design.

scribed cognition as "the last cow to come in the barn." Horton and Wedding (1984) observed:

> One can see that if a novice neuropsychologist designed a multiple baseline study with a single brain-injured subject and used a motor measure (finger tapping) for a baseline, a language measure (Reitan-Indiana Aphasia Screening Test) for the second baseline, and a cognitive measure (Trail-Making Test) for a third, then one could see how if the intervention was applied in that sequence (i.e., motor first, then language, and last cognition), then it would be possible to demonstrate that a completely ineffective treatment showed changes over time as the intervention was applied. (p. 201)

Clearly, recovery of function is an important issue in devising multiple-baseline studies with brain-injured children (Horton & Wedding, 1984). Figure 7.2 demonstrates a typical multiple-baseline design.

CHANGING-CRITERION DESIGN

The logic of the changing-criterion design is quite ingenious. Essentially, a series of graduated arbitrary criteria for a given behavior is specified, and if the behavior matches the criteria repeatedly, the intervention is assumed to be responsible. The logic that warrants postulating experimental control rests upon the degree to which the behavior changes match the arbitrary set levels (Hayes, 1981). This design is most appropriate when the target behavior can change in only one direction. Hartman and Hall (1976) noted similarities between the changing-criterion design and the multiple-baseline design. First, each phase of the treatment can be used as a baseline to evaluate later phases. Second, the successive changes in the changing-criterion design are similar to the replicated changes in the multiple-baseline design. On the other hand, the two designs are dissimilar in that the changing-criterion design does not require extended baseline phases.

If we use the same example as in the previous two designs, the changing-criterion design is straightforward. Assume the number of physical attacks is averaging 14 per day. Next, assume the criterion level could be decreased to fewer than 10 and after that to fewer than 4. If the target behavior decreases in response to the criterion changes, one can assume that the target behavior is under experimental control. Another way of conceptualizing this relationship is to think of the changes as similar to an effective behavior-shaping program. See Figure 7.3 for an example of a changing-criterion design.

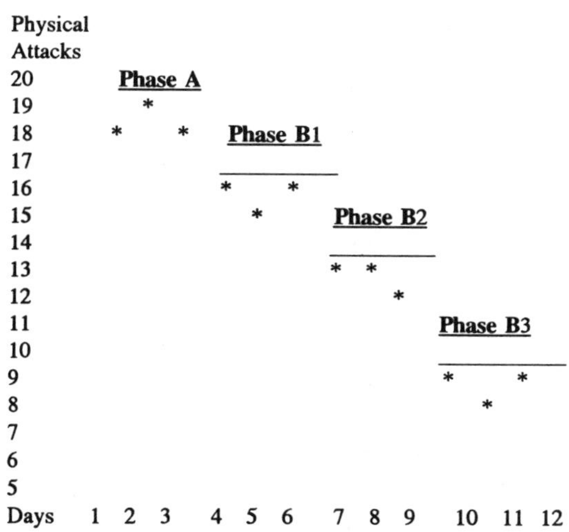

Figure 7.3. A typical changing criterion design.

At this point, comments on the positive and negative features of the changing-criterion design are appropriate. On the positive side, the changing-criterion design does not require a baseline phase of great length. In addition, the gradual nature of goal attainment of the changing-criterion design matches the usual progression of behavior change found in clinical work with children. On the other hand, however, there are times when the demonstration of experimental control may be quite difficult. Level changes may be too dramatic, the behavior changes may be more than expected, or the target behavior may be too variable (Gelfand & Hartmann, 1984). There are a number of alternatives to deal with these problems, and the strategies are well described elsewhere (Gelfand & Hartmann, 1984; Kazdin, 1982).

ALTERNATING-TREATMENT DESIGN

The logic of the alternate-treatment design is that two different treatments are alternated quickly, and counterbalancing is used to control all other features so that the effects of the different treatments are evident (Barlow & Hayes, 1979). Phrased another way, Treatments A and B are assigned to different treatment sessions in a random fashion. The target behavior is examined for whether one series of treatments has been more effective than the other series. Alternate-treatment designs are unique in that they allow for the comparison of two or more treatments within a single child.

Experimental control is demonstrated by comparing the baseline with the treatment phases and, later, the treatment phases with each other. The fact that specific treatment assignment is random aids in ruling out maturational effects and other sources of experimental error.

An example using the child who attacks age-peers may make the above material clearer. At this point, assume that the issue in question is which of the two effective treatments is most effective. Figure 7.4 presents hypothetical data for this research design. Baseline data are collected for a period of time, and then the two treatments are alternately applied to the target problem in separate treatment sessions. If one of the treatments is superior to the other, then it should demonstrate more dramatic changes in the

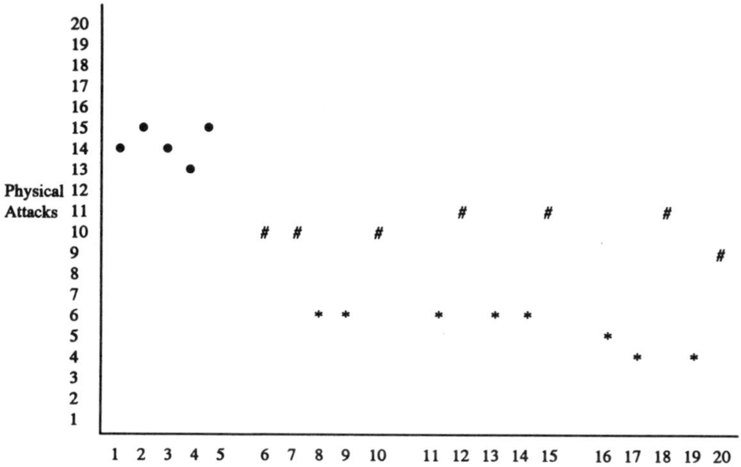

Figure 7.4. Hypothetical data for an alternating treatments design.

level of the target behavior. If treatment effects are weak, then the two treatment baselines will not show any appreciable separation.

The alternating-treatment design has a number of positive points. Chief among these is the fact that it allows the comparison of multiple different treatments. It is the only single-subject research design which allows this comparison (Barlow & Hayes, 1979). An additional advantage of the alternating-treatment design is that it does not require a reversal phase. Given the possible ethical and/or legal problems that a return to baseline of physical attacks on children could produce, one can see how valuable not requiring a reversal phase can be (Gelfand & Hartmann, 1984).

On the other hand, there are some negative aspects of the alternating-treatment design. First, it requires that the treatments work quickly and that the effect is brief. An additional problem with the alternating-treatment design is interference from multiple treatments or, put another way, interactions in the alternation of the treatments (Barlow & Hayes, 1979). The crux of the matter is that the treatment effects may be present only after the multiple treatments are alternated and *not* when the apparently most effective treatment is applied by itself. The problem of interaction in a counterbalance design is similar to the problem with the group Latin-square design (Campbell & Stanley, 1963). Ways of dealing with some of these problems are discussed in detail in other sources (Barlow & Hayes, 1979; Gelfand & Hartmann, 1984; Shapiro, Kazdin, & McGonigle, 1982).

In closing this section on the alternating-treatment design, it might be mentioned that this design has been used rarely in comparison with other single-subject research designs, such as the multiple-baseline or reversal designs. Given the unique strengths of the alternating-treatment design for addressing questions of the comparative effects of different treatments, however, it is likely that the alternating-treatment design will see greater usage in the coming years.

STATISTICAL ANALYSIS OF SINGLE-SUBJECT DESIGNS

There is considerable controversy regarding the use of statistical analysis in single-subject design (Kazdin, 1976). The traditional method was to "eyeball" the graphed data and decide subjectively if a treatment effect was present. Given that this subjective judgment may vary, the use of statistical procedures should be encouraged. The reader is referred to Kazdin's chapter (1976) in the classic Hersen and Barlow text *Single-Case Experimental Designs: Strategies for Studying Behavior Change* (1976). Additional valuable references are Edgington (1982), Gelfand and Hartmann (1984), and Kazdin (1982).

SUMMARY

This chapter dealt with single-subject research designs. Essentially, a single-subject research design provides an opportunity to verify the worth of procedures without having to assemble a large group of subjects. Four single-subject research designs were discussed: the reversal, or ABAB, design; the multiple-baseline design; the changing-criterion design; and the alternating-treatment design. Essentially, in the reversal design, treatment is alternated and the trick is to see if the child improves when the treatment is not there. In the multiple-baseline design, treatment is targeted at different behaviors at different times. In the changing-criterion design, quite simply, the criterion for reinforcement or punishment changes over time. In the alternating-treatment design, different treatments are applied in a random, alternating manner, and the effects of the various treatments on the child's behavior are determined. In this chapter, the basic logic of each design, an example of how each design would be applied, and the strengths and weaknesses of each design were covered. In addition, there was a brief mention of possible statistical analysis of single-subject design.

REFERENCES

Agras, W. S., & Berkowitz, R. (1980). Clinical research in behavior therapy: Halfway there? *Behavior Therapy, 11*, 472–488.

Bach-y-Rita, P. (1980). *Recovery of function: Theoretical considerations for brain injury rehabilitation.* Baltimore: University Park Press.

Baer, D. M., Wolf, M., & Risley, T. R. (1968). Some current dimensions of applied behavior analysis. *Journal of Applied Behavior Analysis, 1*, 91–97.

Barlow, D. H., & Hayes, S. C. (1979). Alternating treatments design: One strategy for comparing the effects of two treatments in a single subject. *Journal of Applied Behavior Analysis, 12*, 199–210.

Barlow, D. H., Hayes, S. C., & Nelson, R. O. (1984). *The scientist-practitioner.* New York: Pergamon Press.

Barlow, D. H., & Hersen, M. (1985). *Single case experimental designs: Strategies for studying behavior change* (2nd ed.). New York: Pergamon Press.

Campbell, D. T., & Stanley, J. C. (1963). *Experimental and quasi-experimental designs for research.* Chicago: Rand McNally.

Edgington, E. J. (1982). Nonparametric tests for single-subject multiple schedule experiments. *Behavioral Assessment, 4*, 83–91.

Gelfand, D. M., & Hartmann, D. P. (1984). *Child behavior analysis and therapy.* New York: Pergamon Press.

Hall, R. V. (1971). *Managing behavior: Basic principles.* Lawrence, KS: H & H Enterprises.

Hartmann, D. P., & Hall, R. V. (1976). The changing criterion design. *Journal of Applied Behavior Analysis, 9*, 527–532.

Hayes, S. C. (1981). Single case experimental design and empirical clinical practice. *Journal of Consulting and Clinical Psychology, 49*, 193–211.

Hersen, M., & Barlow, D. H. (1976). *Single case experimental designs: Strategies for studying behavior change.* New York: Pergamon Press.

Horton, A. M., Jr., & Wedding, D. (1984). *Introduction to clinical and behavioral neuropsychology.* New York: Praeger.

Kazdin, A. E. (1975). Characteristics and trends in applied behavior analysis. *Journal of Applied Behavior Analysis, 8*, 332.

Kazdin, A. E. (1976). Statistical analyses for single-case experimental designs.

In M. Hersen & D. H. Barlow (Eds.), *Single-case experimental designs*. New York: Pergamon Press.

Kazdin, A. E. (1978). *History of behavior modification*. Baltimore, MD: University Park Press.

Kazdin, A. E. (1986). *Behavior modification in applied settings* (Rev. ed.). Homewood, IL: Dorsey.

Kazdin, A. E. (1982). *Single-case research designs, methods for clinical and applied settings*. New York: Oxford University Press.

Shapiro, E. S., Kazdin, A. E., & McGonigle, J. J. (1982). Multiple-treatment interference in the simultaneous- or alternating-treatments design. *Behavioral Assessment, 4,* 105–115.

Webster, J. S., McCaffrey, R., & Scott, R. R. (1986). Single case design for neuropsychology. In D. Wedding, A. M. Horton, Jr., & J. S. Webster (Eds.), *The neuropsychology handbook*. New York: Springer.

8

Case Studies

INTRODUCTION

The purpose of this chapter of case studies is to illustrate the process of assembling a child neuropsychological report and also a detailed behavior management plan. Cases were intentionally chosen to provide extreme examples of the difficuties of providing neuropsychological and behavior modification services. It is expected that the cases will prove instructive to the beginning clinician.

An important consideration in child clinical neuropsychology is the choice of assessment strategies. Put another way, does the child neuropsychologist use a "fixed-battery" approach, a "flexible-battery" approach, or an "individualized-assessment" approach. Generally speaking, a fixed battery is an already-assembled group of neuropsychological tests such as the age-appropriate downward modification of the Halstead-Reitan Neuropsychological Battery (HRNB) or the children's version of the Lubria-Nebraska Neuropsychological Battery (LNNB-CR). A flexible battery is usually a consistent core set of neuropsychological tests, which is often augmented with additional tests depending upon the referral question, the case history, and how the child does in his or her initial responses to the core battery of neuropsychological tests. By contrast, the individual-assessment approach involves the tailoring of the neuropsychological test battery to the specific problems of the child. As in the flexible-battery approach, this may include the initial referral question, the case history, and how the child does in his or her responses to the neuropsychological tests that are administered. In Chapter 3, some of the many considerations regarding the selection of one of the approaches over another were enumerated.

To a large extent, the controversial aspects of selecting a *single* approach over the others are exaggerated. Most clinical child neuropsychologists have a core set of neuropsychological tests they use, and in some cases, these include the entire age-appropriate Halstead-Reitan or children's Luria-Nebraska. When supplementation with additional measures is required, then they freely add other neuropsychological, educational, and emotional/personality tests. A more pressing and important issue is the range and depth of coverage of neuropsychological testing. Some inadequate clinicians would add the Trail Making Test (TMT) to a standard psychoeducational battery (e.g., the age-appropriate Wechsler, Wide Range Achievement Test—Revised, Bender Visual-Motor Gestalt Test, and Draw-A-Person) and call it an individual-assessment neuropsychological battery despite the fact that there are very grave omissions in terms of the coverage of important neuropsychological functions.

One clear advantage of using a fixed battery is that some effort has gone into working out the coverage of important neuropsychological functions. The clear advantage of using a flexible battery, that of flexibility, can be gained by adding more tests. The problem, however, becomes at what point the child is overtested so that the tests are more expensive than they should be and the child is excessively burdened by long hours of testing. These are vexing questions that are not to be resolved here.

The following case studies illustrate one strategy for dealing with only a few of these concerns. As can be seen, certain tests, primarily from the Halstead-Reitan tradition, are used with almost every case, and some measures are also drawn from the children's version of the Luria-Nebraska and other sources. These were picked to illustrate the fixed-battery or a limited flexible-battery approach. Given the initial nature of this book, it was decided not to include cases illustrating an individualized-assessment approach. Tailoring neuropsychological tests to children's problems is a very difficult task and should be a strategy reserved for the most senior of clinical child neuropsychologists. Thus, with those cautions set out, the following case studies are presented for inspection. All were clinical referrals and reflect real-life experience in child neuropsychology.

INTRODUCTION TO E.D.

This young man presented with a common problem of children, attention-deficit–hyperactivity disorder (ADHD). In this case, the child's situation was complicated by the stress attendant on a blended family. Also, the psychiatric history in blood relatives served to reinforce questions of personality contributions. An important point in the recommendations section is the use of "response cost" to control acting-out behavior. Given the possibility of a codiagnosis of conduct disorder, effective management recommendations were even more important than usual.

NEUROPSYCHOLOGICAL DATA FORM

Identifying data

Name: E.D.	Education: 6 years
Age: 12 years	Handedness: Right
Sex: Male	Marital status: Never married
Race: White	Occupation: Student

Intellectual/cognitive functions

Wechsler Intelligence Scale for Children—Revised (WISC-R)

Verbal subtests	*Scale scores*
Information	14
Similarities	14
Arithmetic	10
Vocabulary	13
Comprehension	15
Digit Span	8
VIQ = 119	

Performance subtests	*Scale scores*
Picture Completion	15
Picture Arrangement	12
Block Design	18
Object Assembly	13
Coding	11
PIQ = 128	

FSIQ = 126

Academic achievement

Wide Range Achievement Test—Revised (WRAT-R)

Subject areas	*Scale scores*	*Percentiles*	*Grade-equivalent score*
Reading	110	75	9B
Spelling	93	22	6B
Arithmetic	98	45	7E

Tactile functions

Single or Double Simultaneous Suppression

Right side	*Left side*
No errors	No errors

Finger Agnosia

Right hand	*Left hand*
1 error/10 trials	1 error/10 trials

Fingertip Number Writing

Right hand	*Left hand*
3 errors/10 trials	3 errors/10 trials

Auditory functions

Single or Double Simultaneous Stimulation

Right side	*Left side*
No errors	No errors

Rhythm Test: NA

Visual functions

Single or Double Simultaneous Stimulation

Right side	*Left side*
No errors	No errors

Trail Making Test, Part A: 16 sec

Spatial Relations Section of Reitan-Indiana Aphasia Screening Test: No deficits

MOTOR SKILLS

Finger Tapping Test

Right hand	*Left hand*
40.2	32.8

Dominance: Right-handed
Mixed eye and foot dominance

LANGUAGE

Aphasia Section of Reitan-Indiana Aphasia Screening Test: Errors on spelling and mental math items

Good verbal fluency

EXECUTIVE FUNCTIONS

Trail Making Test, Part B: 42 sec

ATTENTION/MEMORY FUNCTIONS:

Digit Span: 8 (scale score)
Hyperactivity Questionnaire: Impaired
Attention Deficit Questionnaire: Impaired
Child Luria-Nebraska, Memory Subtest: 43T (above average)

NEUROPSYCHOLOGICAL EVALUATION

CONFIDENTIAL

NAME: E.D.

AGE: 12 years

RACE: White

SEX: Male

EDUCATION: Sixth grade

HANDEDNESS: Right

OCCUPATION: Student

MARITAL STATUS: Never married

DATE OF EVALUATION: XXXX

REASON FOR REFERRAL

The patient was referred for neuropsychological evaluation because of his difficulties in school.

TESTS ADMINISTERED

Wechsler Intelligence Scale for Children—Revised (WISC-R); Wide Range Achievement Test—Revised (WRAT-R); Finger Tapping Test; Reitan Klove Lateral Dominance Examination; Reitan Klove Sensory Perceptual Examination; Trail Making Test; Reitan-Indiana Aphasia Screening Test; Speech Sounds Perception Test; Hyperactivity/Minimal Brain Dysfunction Questionnaire; Screening Form for Attention Deficit Disorder; Memory Subtest of the Luria-Nebraska Neuropsychological Battery; Millon Adolescent Personality Inventory.

BEHAVIORAL OBSERVATIONS

Appearance and Behavior: The patient is a young boy who appears approximately his stated age. The patient's dress is neat and his posture is comfortable. His facial expression is unremarkable. His interview behavior was somewhat passive; however, his motor activity appeared to be somewhat increased. With respect to speech behavior, it was somewhat soft and reduced. His flow of thought was within normal limits, and mood and affect also appeared to be within normal limits. With respect to current thought content, he appeared to be slightly suspicious of his stepmother, but otherwise his thought content was appropriate to the situation. There is no evidence for hallucinations or delusions, and the child was oriented to time, place, and person. He was brought to the interview by his stepmother and picked up by his father.

Chief Complaints: The patient's problems, as reported by him, are difficulties in school and an inability to concentrate. He reported that the difficulties arose in the second half of the past school year, that he was put on medication at the end of the school year, and that the medication helped a little bit. His stepmother reported that he has difficulties with focusing in school. More specifically, he has difficulty staying on track. She stated that he previously earned a Group IQ score of 103 and noted that they are currently seeing Dr. X for family therapy and help in terms of organization and management for the child. So far, they have had three visits, the stepmother reported. The father reported the child's problems as school problems, poor grades, and not paying attention.

BACKGROUND INFORMATION

Health History: The patient was reported to have been a sickly baby and to have a number of allergies and poor appetite. Apparently there was an illness in the first year of life that was significant. More specifically, this appeared to have been a virus when the child was only 2 weeks old, and in addition, there was a report that the umbilical cord had been wrapped around his neck but later became unwrapped. The child went to day care at age 3 and had to spend two years in kindergarten, as he was reported at that time to be somewhat immature and unfocused. He entered school at age 6 and has required special help for attention-deficit disorder (ADD) in the regular classroom. With respect to his pediatric medical history, he has had ear infections and broken bones, but no hospitalizations or other serious illnesses. He did, however, take Ritalin for the last four days of school in the past school year. The dosage was apparently 10 mg, and the child lost his appetite. Reports regarding the effectiveness of Ritalin in this brief period of time are mixed. The stepmother states there was no effect, while the child states it was somewhat helpful. Regarding family health history, there is no history of seizures in the family; however, the patient's biological mother and her brother have possible ADD symptoms. In addition, there are allergies in the family: The patient's sister, as well as the patient, has had allergy treatment for a considerable period of time, and the father has had treatment for allergies. With respect to the family psychiatric history, the patient's biological mother was reported to have problems with both alcoholism and manic-depressive illness. Apparently, she has a bipolar disorder and is currently on lithium and recovering from alcoholism.

Social History: The patient's biological mother and father divorced, and the father remarried. The patient's birth order at this point is somewhat complicated. In his biological family of origin, he is in a sibship of two, with one sister two years older. Nonetheless, it is noteworthy that, in effect, he is in a sibship of four, with, of course, his older sister and two younger sisters. The immediately younger sister is his stepsister, the daughter of his stepmother from an earlier marriage. His youngest sister, age 4, is his half-sister, as she is the biological daughter of his father and his stepmother. The older sister is described as somewhat withdrawn, but with an IQ of 130+. Remarkably, the patient's older sister is described as a "C" student. It should be noted that an older stepsister, who was adopted, is no longer in the home. With respect to the patient's parents, his biological father works as a civil servant, his stepmother works as a teacher in a private school, and his biological mother works as a legal secretary. The biological mother was reported to have been a college dropout and fired from a number of jobs. Apparently, the patient sees his biological mother on weekends.

Avocational Activities: When asked what he does for fun, the patient indicated that he draws, rides his bike, and plays with his friends.

ANALYSIS OF NEUROPSYCHOLOGICAL TEST RESULTS

A comprehensive battery of neuropsychological tests was administered: measures of intellectual ability, academic achievement, sensorimotor abilities, visual-spatial skills, language functioning, mental set shifting executive functions, attention, memory, and emotional/personality functioning.

Intellectual/Cognitive Functions: On the WISC-R, the patient earned a Verbal IQ (119) that fell in the upper portion of the high-average range, a Performance IQ (128) that fell in the superior range, and a Full Scale IQ (126) that also fell in the superior range. With respect to Verbal IQ subtests, the patient did best on a subtest that assessed his understanding of everyday rules and regulations and did most poorly on a subtest that assessed his attention and concentration skills. On the Performance IQ subtests, the patient did best on a subtest that assessed his spatial relationships ability and did most poorly on a subtest that required him to demonstrate clerical speed and accuracy skills. With respect to the general overall profile, it was noteworthy in that the profile low points were on the subtests Arithmetic, Digit Span, and Coding. Such a constellation suggests that the patient is quite low on the "freedom-from-distractibility" factor. Such a pattern is very often associated with ADD symptoms.

Academic Achievement: On the WRAT-R, the patient's reading score fell at the 75th percentile, and that would translate into a grade equivalent of beginning ninth grade. On the spelling subtest, the patient obtained a percentile ranking of the 22nd percentile and a grade equivaent rating of beginning sixth grade. On the arithmetic subtest the patient obtained a percentile ranking of the 45th percentile and a grade equivalent score of ending seventh grade. While his reading ability appears to be roughly along the lines of expectation (given his Verbal IQ), his performance with respect to spelling and arithmetic is somewhat discrepant from expectations.

Sensorimotor Abilities: On the Reitan Klove Lateral Dominance Examination, the patient was strongly right-handed but demonstrated mixed dominance for eye preference and foot preference. On the Finger Tapping Test, the patient scored within normal limits for both the right and the left hand. With respect to basic primary visual, auditory, and tactile perception functions, the patient did not exhibit suppression to single or double simultaneous stimulation in any of these three primary modalities, a result suggesting that all are intact. With respect to higher level tactual perceptual processes, however, there was mild impairment in both the identification of a touched finger and also the perception of single digits written on the fingertips. The level of impairment was mild but bilaterally present on both tasks.

Visual-Spatial Skills: The patient's visual-spatial abilities appeared quite adequate regardless of whether the task involved spatial relations, visual tracking, or assembling puzzles.

Language Abilities: The patient's general language skills appear intact. He did show some errors on a spelling task and also on a mental math item, but he was fairly adequate with respect to naming, writing, reading, repeating, recalling, and left–right orientation. On the Speech Sounds Perception Test, he scored above average, and his verbal fluency in the interview was quite good.

Mental Set Shifting/Executive Functions: The patient demonstrated some difficulties when a task required him to keep more than one aspect of a situation in mind at the same time, and to make decisions rapidly, based on that data matrix.

Attention/Memory: The patient demonstrated some difficulties with respect to attention and concentration skills. Moreover, on the Screening Questionnaires for Hyperactivity/Minimal Brain Dysfunction and Attention Deficit Disorder, the patient scored in the impaired range on both, a result suggesting he might qualify for a diagnosis of ADHD. On the Memory subtest of the Luria-Nebraska Neuropsychological Battery—Children's Revision, the patient's score was well above average.

Emotional/Personality Functions: On the Millon Adolescent Personality Inventory (MAPI), the patient obtained a valid and reliable report. With respect to behavioral correlates, he scored quite highly on impulse control and social conformity. This result would suggest that the patient may be somewhat impulsive and at times thoughtless with respect to attention to events in his life. Youngsters who have completed this personality test in a similar manner have sometimes been found to be difficult to manage in scholastic and other settings. At times, they respond angrily to the typical restraints and regulations of structured settings. Under the stress of such difficulties, this youngster's academic performance may slip below expectations based on his intellectual level. With respect to concerns expressed by the patient, he has a remarkable number of strengths and one rather glaring concern. For example, the patient's self-concept, personal esteem, comfort with his body, maturity, sexual acceptance, security with peers, social tolerance, and academic confidence are all quite positive. On the other hand, however, there is evidence of considerable difficulty with respect to family relationships. His family is seen by this youth as a source and focus of attention and conflict. Apparently, conflicts within the home take up a great deal of his emotional energy. With respect to personality style, the youngster may be seen as sociable, confident, forceful, and sensitive. To a degree, the patient has a strong sense of himself and may at times expect special recognition and consideration without assuming reciprocal obligations. In addition, the patient may attempt to present an image of strength and bold competitiveness and a willingness to assume risks, and threats of punishment could serve to reinforce his feelings of rebellion. While quite charming, clever, and stimulating under nonstressful social conditions, the patient under a degree of stress is likely to demonstrate feelings of being treated unfairly and is easily provoked to anger and irritability. A degree of suspicion of those in authority may incline him toward acting-out behaviors.

SUMMARY/FORMULATION

This 12-year-old white, right-handed male, who has obtained six years of education, is functioning in the superior range of measured intellectual abilities. There appears to be considerable evidence for a diagnosis of ADHD. In addition, personality test data and interview data suggest the patient might also qualify for a diagnosis of conduct disorder, group type. Evidence for neuropsychological impairment appears to be secondary to that for the ADD symptoms. Major areas of deficit appeared to be in attention, mental set shifting, and complex tactual perceptual-discrimination processes. In terms of academic abilities, his spelling and arithmetic skills, although not markedly below grade level, are somewhat below what one might expect given the patient's level of intellectual ability. Areas of strength include the patient's visual-spatial skills, basic sensory perceptual modalities, reading skills, and short-term memory skills. Personality test data and interview data both suggest current family-related difficulties that exacerbate personality predispositions to be self-absorbed and nonconformist.

RECOMMENDATIONS

Future Assessment: Regarding additional assessment, a repeat referral for neuropsychological evaluation in one to two years would probably be appropriate to assess the degree of progress that the patient will hopefully make.

Treatment: With respect to therapeutic interventions, the patient and his family are already being seen for family therapy, and at the time, the patient was evaluated, three therapy sessions had been held. It might be suggested that this patient is likely to be an unwilling participant in therapy and entered therapy only under family pressure. It may be that the youngster will attribute his problems to others and will attempt to manipulate the therapist and provoke disapproval and criticism. Rapport building would benefit from empathetic understanding of the patient's difficulties. The patient's suspiciousness will make building the necessary sense of trust and developing a constructive treatment alliance difficult. A highly structured and very directive approach toward school- and family-related problems may be profitable. An important issue to consider in terms of conducting treatment is the fact that the patient appears to have difficulties with mental set shifting. Therefore, it will be important to ascertain the degree to which he appreciates therapeutic insights.

Management: It is important to realize that this patient's abilities to think through problems and exercise good judgment, and to critically analyze the effects of his personal behaviors on others, are at least mildly impaired. Significant others in his environment should realize this and anticipate problems and difficulties and make adjustments for the patient. One cognitive behavioral strategy that may prove helpful would be to teach the patient to self-instruct himself when presented with complex social situations. Self-instructional techniques might be utilized whenever the patient begins to become angry or feels that his rights and privileges have been transgressed by those in positions of authority. Behavior modification would certainly seem to be appropriate; one thing to keep in mind, however, is that patients with personality structures similar to that of this patient usually do poorly under conditions of punishment. A more profitable strategy is to utilize a combination of positive reinforcement and response cost to modify their behavior. Response cost usually consists of allowing the patient to have access to certain privileges or reinforcers, and then making that access contingent upon continued good behavior. Generally speaking, this demonstrates far superior results to the imposition of aversive stimuli in a typical punishment paradigm. In terms of structure, it would appear that this young man will need greater structure than others, as he has particular difficulties with respect to impulsivity. The difficulty will be that often the patient will feel that the imposition of structure is a diminution of his freedom of action and therefore will react negatively. Perhaps, a contractual approach, whereby the patient is given a degree of input with respect to family decisions, would prove useful.

Comment: The deficits of this young man, who is without marked physical impairment and who presents with a very charming and clever social appearance, may represent something of a puzzle to others. It will be important for persons in his living situation to realize that there is a degree of neuropsychological deficit present, and that, therefore, expectations of the patient's future performance will have to be adequately tailored to fit his pattern of mental abilities. While medical implications go beyond the expertise of this examiner, it would seem apparent that pharmacological strategies might be considered by the physician responsible for this young man's medical care.

DISCUSSION OF E.D.

This case is an interesting example of the neuropsychological test profile often seen in ADHD children. The "freedom-from-distractibility" profile on the WISC-R is well known in the literature. Another important consideration is the use of IQ data to set expectations for academic achievement levels. Failure to consider intellectual levels could result in a misdiagnosis of a child with significant difficulties.

INTRODUCTION TO A.R.

This case presents an interesting mix of cognitive, personality, achievement, and neuropsychological factors. Again, attention-deficit disorder was a major consideration in the assessment of neuropsychological deficits. This young man was an adolescent, and the Wechsler Adult Intelligence Scale—Revised was used because of his age.

NEUROPSYCHOLOGICAL DATA FORM

Identifying Data

Name: A.R.	Education: 11 years
Age: 17 years	Handedness: Right
Sex: Male	Marital Status: Never married
Race: Black	Occupation: Student

Intellectual/Cognitive Functions

Wechsler Adult Intelligence Scale—Revised (WAIS-R)

Verbal subtests	*Scale scores*
Information	10
Similarities	8
Arithmetic	7
Vocabulary	7

Comprehension	9
Digit Span	10
VIQ = 100	

Performance subtests	*Scale scores*
Picture Completion	11
Picture Arrangement	9
Block Design	12
Object Assembly	12
Digit Symbol	10
PIQ = 110	

FSIQ = 105

Academic achievement

Wide Range Achievement Test—Revised (WRAT-R)

Subject areas	*Percentiles*	*Grade-equivalent score*
Reading	58	12E
Arithmetic	8	7B

Tactile functions

Single or Double Simultaneous Suppression

Right side	*Left side*
No errors	No errors

Finger Agnosia

Right hand	*Left hand*
No errors	No errors

Auditory functions

Single or Double Simultaneous Stimulation

Right side	*Left side*
No errors	No errors

Speech Sounds Perception Test: 5 errors (WNL)
Rhythm Test: 2 errors (WNL)

Visual functions

Spatial Relations Section of Reitan-Indiana Aphasia Screening Test: Adequate

Motor skills

Right hand	*Left hand*
46.4	44.4

Trail Making Test, Part A: 24 sec

Language

Aphasia Section of Reitan-Indiana Aphasia Screening Test: Errors on reading, naming, writing, spelling (adequate for age)

Executive Functions

Trail Making Test, Part B: 42 sec (WNL)
Category Test: 38 errors (WNL)

Attention/Memory Functions

Digit Span: 10 (scale score)
Wechsler Memory Scale subtest: Mental Control = 8/9
Hyperactivity/MBD Questionnaire: 24 (impaired)
Wechsler Memory Scale subtest: Logical Memory = 23 (WNL)
Wechsler Memory Scale subtest: Visual Reproduction 14 (WNL)

Stroop Color Word Test (*t*-score reversal):
Word: 59
Color: 62
Color-Word: 57

NEUROPSYCHOLOGICAL EVALUATION

CONFIDENTIAL

NAME: A.R.

SEX: Male

RACE: Black

AGE: 17 years

EDUCATION: 11 years

DATE OF EVALUATION: XXXX

REASON FOR REFERRAL

The patient was referred for neuropsychological evaluation to determine the nature and extent of cognitive deficits.

TESTS ADMINISTERED

Wechsler Adult Intelligence Scale—Revised (WAIS-R); Reading and Arithmetic Subtests of the Wide Range Achievement Test—Revised (WRAT-R); Reitan-Klove Sensory Perceptual Examination; Speech Sounds Perception Test; Rhythm Test; Reitan-Indiana Aphasia Screening Test; Finger Tapping Test; Trail Making Test; Category Test; Stroop Color-Word Test; Selected Subtests from the Wechsler Memory Scale and Hyperactivity Minimal Brain Dysfunction Questionnaire.

INTERVIEW OBSERVATIONS

The patient was normal in appearance and appropriately dressed. There was no evidence of unusual motor activity or abnormal interview behavior. The patient's speech was somewhat soft, but the flow of thought was normal, and mood and affect were also within normal limits. Regarding thought content, there were some thoughts of suicide, but no evidence of hallucinations or delusions, and the patient was well oriented.

Chief Complaints: The patient describes himself as feeling well physically and fine emotionally. He denies hallucinations but feels sometimes that people are against him. He said that he would be nervous if he were in a dark place, and that he does feel, at times, depressed. He denied any thoughts of killing someone else but did admit to past thoughts of killing himself. He denied any current intent to commit suicide. He indicated he has trouble sleeping when it is cold and remembering things when they are boring. With respect to current behavioral issues, these include aggressiveness. In the past, he noted, there has been a history of truancy and destructiveness. The patient also noted that he is already being seen for counseling.

BACKGROUND INFORMATION

There was no note of prenatal pregnancy problems. In addition, there is no report of maternal prenatal substance abuse, and the patient appears to have exceeded most developmental milestones. The patient did indicate a problem with colic in infancy, and that he was bottle-fed for more than 10 months. With respect to childhood history, there was a report of a family member's death. The patient reported that he entered kindergarten at age 5 and elementary school at age 6. With respect to special-education placements in grades 3–5, he was in a special reading program. The patient denied any sort of hospitalization or entry into substance abuse programs. In addition, serious illness was denied. With respect to individual and family counseling, he described going to X Service to see a therapist for therapy for depression. With respect to his family that are living in the home currently, these include his mother and sister. Interestingly, the patient had reported three younger brothers but did not note that they are currently living with him. In addition, the patient denied being married or having any children. Moreover, the patient denied any history of seizures, attention-deficit disorder or communication disorder, or allergies in his family.

ANALYSIS OF NEUROPSYCHOLOGICAL TEST RESULTS

A battery of neuropsychological tests was administered, including tests of psychometric intelligence, adaptive ability, language skills, and measure of memory, sensory and tactual perceptual functioning, and motor skill. Utilization of this battery provides the opportunity to assess the overall level of adequacy of performance of an individual across a broad range of higher level mental abilities, as well as lower level functions such as motor and sensory skills. In addition, specific signs of impairment or disorder of function may be elicited. Moreover, specific signs of impairment can be seen on examination for constructional dyspraxia and sensory suppression. The relationship between areas of adequacy of performance and areas of deficit are also examined with respect to their implications for adequacy or impairment of related brain functions. Finally, the comparative efficacy of the two sides of the body can be compared across perceptual, sensory, and motor functions. Utilization of these four complementary inferential methods provides a series of checks and balances against which to examine the individual tests, and it provides a series of screens through which the data must pass before conclusions can be reached.

Intellectual/Cognitive Functions: On the WAIS-R, the patient earned a Verbal IQ (100) that falls in the average range, a Performance IQ (110) that falls in the lower portion of the high-average range, and a Full Scale IQ (105) that falls in the average range. There is not a significant difference between the Verbal and Performance IQs, which would suggest relative equivalence of the patient's overall ability to utilize and reproduce previously learned verbal material and his ability in the area of visual-spatial problem solving. With respect to the subtests, on the verbal scale the patient did best on subtests that assessed his attention and concentration skills and also his general fund of information. The patient did most poorly, however, on subtests that required him to define words orally, and to solve orally presented arithmetic problems. On the performance subtests, the patient did best on subtests that required him to solve puzzles and to make a design out of blocks. The patient did most poorly in a subtest that required him to put cartoon pictures in a meaningful sequence. There was not a dramatic amount of variation between or among the subtests.

Academic Achievement: On the Reading portion of the WRAT-R, the patient earned a percentile ranking of 58 and a grade equivalent of exiting 12th grade. On the Arithmetic subtest, the patient earned a percentile ranking of 8 and a grade equivalent of beginning 7th grade. It would appear that his reading achievement is within normal limits, but there are some difficulties with respect to mathematics achievement.

Tactile Functions: The patient did not exhibit tactile suppressions to single or double simultaneous stimulation, a result suggesting that his primary tactile functions are intact. With respect to higher level tactile perceptual processes, there were no difficulties on either hand when the task was the identification of a touched finger.

Auditory Functions: The patient did not demonstrate auditory suppressions to single or double simultaneous stimulation, a result suggesting that his primary auditory areas are intact. In addition, his phonemic discrimination of speech sounds and his rhythmic pattern discrimination abilities were also both intact.

Visual Functions: The patient's visual perceptual skills appeared to be adequate, and his visual organizational/spatial skills fall within normal limits.

Motor Functions: On a test of motor speed, the patient's right hand was slightly slowed, though the left hand fell within normal limits. Similarly, on a complex task that involved visual tracking, as well as a perceptual motor response from the dominant hand, the patient's performance fell within normal limits.

Language: The patient did demonstrate some difficulty in comprehending a verbal communication, but for the most part, his language abilities are unimpaired. The patient was able to read, name, write, and spell with relative adequacy.

Abstraction/Concept Formation Abilities: The patient demonstrated no impairment in concept formation skills or in understanding cause-and-effect relationships. In addition, the patient had no difficulty in performing a set-shifting task that required him to devote attention to more than one aspect of a situation simultaneously.

Attention/Memory: On a test that required a certain amount of cognitive flexibility, the patient scored in a low-average/questionably impaired range. While his automatic-level attentional skills appear to be relatively adequate, nonetheless on a questionnaire designed to assess the possibility of Attention-Deficit–Hyperactivity Disorder, the patient scored well within the impaired range. It may be that the patient has difficulty when required to direct his attention to a specific situation over a period of time. With respect to memory abilities, the patient's short-term verbal and short-term nonverbal memory appears to fall within normal limits.

SUMMARY/FORMULATION

This 17-year-old black male, who has obtained 11 years of education, is currently functioning in the average range of measured intellectual abilities. There is questionable evidence of neuropsychological impairment. The evidence of neuropsychological impairment that does exist probably would be best explained by the hypothesis of an attention-deficit disorder, residual type. Areas of deficit include motor functioning with the right hand and some possible difficulties of a mild nature with cognitive flexibility. The data for even those areas of deficit are relatively weak. Of course, the patient's difficulties with respect to arithmetic skills are an area of concern. Relative areas of strength include the patient's overall intellectual functioning and reading abilities, as well as his sensory perceptual skills and generally adequate language and concept-formation abilities. The information regarding personality functioning gathered in the interview failed to reveal syndromes of immediate clinical interest.

RECOMMENDATIONS

Future Assessment: Regarding additional assessment, the possibility of trying this young man on a small dose of stimulant medication might be considered by a psychiatrist. Of particular concern in this case also are the patient's thoughts of suicide. While there was no evidence of severe current psychiatric syndromes evident in the clinical interview, it would appear wise to have this individual carefully monitored. As it appeared that he was currently being seen for counseling, this might be done in the context of that relationship.

Treatment: With respect to therapeutic intervention, the patient clearly would appear to be in need of counseling to help him sort out his problems in terms of viewing the world.

Management: The best situations for this patient to achieve would be those that involve a minimum of interpersonal interactions and relatively straightforward tasks with explicit guidelines for decisions.

DISCUSSION OF A.R.

The mild neuropsychological deficits that this young man presented were a cause for caution. It is easy to overdiagnose a condition as difficult to quantify as attention-deficit disorder. In addition, emotional problems are also factors that can interfere with adequate cooperation in neuropsychological assessment. The neuropsychologist must be careful to fully utilize the services of child psychiatrists, pediatricians, and pediatric neurologists in difficult cases. As impressive as neuropsychological testing procedures are, nonetheless, they fail to span the entire range of assessment and treatment options. To not involve other specialists when their unique expertise is needed would be a grave error.

INTRODUCTION TO H.C.

Neurological problems can cause poor school achievement. In this case, a child with a pediatric medical history that was positive for seizures was also to be assessed for attention-deficit-hyperactivity disorder. It was particularly vexing to attempt to determine to what extent the academic problems were related to which of these conditions.

NEUROPSYCHOLOGICAL DATA FORM

Identifying Data

Name: H.C.	Education: Entering grade 6
Age: 10 years	Handedness: Right
Sex: Male	Marital status: Never married
Race: White	Occupation: Student

Intellectual/Cognitive Functions

Wechsler Intelligence Scale for Children—Revised (WISC-R)

Verbal subtests	*Scale scores*
Information	13
Similarities	15
Arithmetic	9
Vocabulary	10
Comprehension	11
(Digit Span)	(11)
VIQ = 109	

Performance subtests	*Scale scores*
Picture Completion	14
Picture Arrangement	13
Block Design	9
Object Assembly	12
Coding	5
(Mazes)	(8)
PIQ = 104	

FSIQ = 107

Academic achievement

Wide Range Achievement Test—Revised (WRAT-R)

Subject areas	*Percentiles*	*Grade = equivalent score*
Reading	23	3E
Arithmetic	21	4B

Tactile functions

Single or Double Simultaneous Suppression

Right side	*Left side*
One error	One error

Finger Agnosia

Right hand	*Left hand*
No errors	No errors

Fingertip Number Writing

Right hand	*Left hand*
13 errors	7 errors

Auditory functions

Single or Double Simultaneous Stimulation

Right side	*Left side*
No errors	No errors

Visual functions

Single or Double Simultaneous Stimulation

Right side	*Left side*
No errors	No errors

Spatial Relations Section of Reitan-Indiana Aphasia Screening Test: Within normal limits

Motor skills

Finger Tapping Test

Right hand	*Left hand*
33.2 (mild impairment)	30.2 (mild impairment)

Language

Aphasia Section of Reitan-Indiana Aphasia Screening Test: Within normal limits with a spelling error

Executive Functions

Mazes = scale score 8

Attention Functions

Digit Span: 11 (scale score)
Counting backward: 1 error
Hyperactivity/Minimal Brain Dysfunction Questionnaire: Impaired

NEUROPSYCHOLOGICAL EVALUATION

CONFIDENTIAL

NAME: H.C.

SEX: Male

RACE: White

AGE: 10 years

EDUCATION: Entering sixth grade

REASON FOR REFERRAL

The patient was referred for neuropsychological evaluation to determine the nature and extent of cognitive deficits.

TESTS ADMINISTERED

Wechsler Intelligence Scale for Children—Revised (WISC-R); Reading and Arithmetic Subtests of the Wide Range Achievement Test—Revised (WRAT-R); Reitan-Klove Sensory Perceptual Examination; Reitan-Indiana Aphasia Screening Test; Finger Tapping Test; Hyperactivity/Minimal Brain Dysfunction Questionnaire; counting backwards tasks.

INTERVIEW OBSERVATIONS

The patient's behavior in the interview situation was generally within normal limits. His appearance and dress were unremarkable, and his motor activity and speech behavior fell within normal limits. His flow of thought processes appeared normal as well, as were also his mood and affect and current thought content.

BACKGROUND INFORMATION

With respect to the child's health history, the following problems were noted prenatally: toxemia, preeclampsia, and edema, as well as excessive vomiting and pressure problems. With respect to the route of delivery, it was vaginal, and labor was induced. Regarding maternal prenatal substance abuse, this included smoking one pack of cigarettes per day. Regarding developmental milestones, most were achieved within expected limits. It is noteworthy that the patient was able to walk alone at 12 months rather than 13 months. The child entered kindergarten at 4½ years, and his age at elementary school entrance was 5½. There were no retentions; the child's pediatric medical history was noteworthy for seizures and a fever of greater than 102°F for longer than 24 hours. Apparently, the patient was hospitalized at 16 months overnight and had severe seizures due to high fever. Regarding medications taken during childhood, these include phenobarbital, which is an anticonvulsant. Regarding family history, the people that live with the patient include his mother, his father, four brothers, and one sister. Other siblings do not live at home. These include two sisters and one brother. There was no history in the family, other than in the patient's twin brother, of attention-deficit disorder or mental retardation or communication disorders. There is, however, a history of allergies, such as hay fever and an allergy to penicillin. In addition, diabetes has been noted both in the paternal father and great-grandfather and the maternal grandmother. Educationally, the patient is to enter sixth grade, and his grades are either average or failing.

Chief Complaints: With respect to physical problems, the patient indicated there have been seizures or "blanking spells"; these apparently started in the 16th month, and there was one seizure with fever. In addition, the patient has motor problems with respect to writing. His behavioral problems include hypersensitivity to criticism and some personality changes. Moreover, the patient is noted to have low motivation, poor attention, and academic problems. Apparently, the anticonvulsant medication was used for approximately one year after the onset of seizures at 16 months.

ANALYSIS OF NEUROPSYCHOLOGICAL TEST RESULTS

A battery of neuropsychological tests was administered, including measures of psychometric intelligence, adaptive ability, language skills, and measures of sensory perceptual ability and motor skills. Utilization of this battery provides the opportunity to assess the overall level of adequacy of performance of an individual across a broad range of higher level mental abilities, as well as lower level functions such as motor and sensory skills.

Intellectual/Cognitive Functions: On the WISC-R, the patient earned a Verbal IQ (109), which falls in the upper portion of the normal range; a Performance IQ (104) that fell in the average range; and a Full Scale IQ (107) that also fell within the normal range. There was not a significant discrepancy between the Verbal and Performance IQs, a result suggesting a relative equivalence of the patient's general fund of information and overall ability to utilize and reproduce previously learned verbal material, as well as ability in the area of visual-spatial problem solving. With respect to the verbal subtests, the patient did best on a subtest that required him to verbally express the relationship between two words, and he did most poorly on a subtest that required him to solve orally presented arithmetic problems. On the performance subtests, the patient did best on a subtest that required him to pick out the missing detail in a picture, and he did most poorly on a subtest that required him to demonstrate clerical speed and accuracy skills.

Academic Achievement: On the WRAT-R, the patient's score on the Reading portion was at the 23rd percentile, which would translate into a grade equivalent of exiting third grade. On the Arithmetic subtest, the patient earned a percentile ranking of the 21st percentile and a grade-equivalent score of beginning fourth grade.

Sensory Perceptual Functions: The patient did not exhibit tactile suppressions to single stimulation and had only one error on each side with respect to tactile double simultaneous stimulation. These errors probably were the results of wandering attention, and his primary tactile functions may be intact. This suggestion is supported by the patient's ability to identify a touched finger; the patient was errorless on both hands on that task. Nonetheless, on a more sensitive measure, in his ability to identify single-digit numbers written on the fingertips, the patient demonstrated some bilateral difficulties. Indeed, the patient made 13 errors out of 20 trials with the right hand and 7 errors out of 20 trials with the left hand. Both levels of impairment would be seen as suggesting at least moderate difficulty, and if anything, it appears that the right hand performs less ably than the left. With respect to auditory functions, the patient did not demonstrate auditory suppressions to single or double simultaneous stimulation, a result suggesting that his primary auditory areas are intact. Similarly, the patient did not exhibit visual suppressions to single or double simultaneous stimulation, a result suggesting that his primary visual areas are intact. In addition, his visual organizational/spatial skills appear to be within relatively normal limits.

Motor Abilities: On a measure of motor speed, the patient scored in the mildly impaired range with both hands. There was not an unusual relationship between the two sides of the body, a result suggesting that this was a general, as opposed to a lateralized, effect.

Language: On a language-screening measure, the patient generally performed within normal limits, although he did have an error on a relatively simple spelling task. The patient did relatively adequately, however, on very simple reading, repeating, writing, and naming tasks.

Executive Functions/Planning: On a measure designed to assess the patient's ability to foresee consequences, he scored in the low-average range.

Attentional Functions: The patient's automatic level of attention skills appeared relatively adequate; however, when more complex tasks were employed which would require him to maintain a level of mental effort over time, the patient demonstrated some difficulties. Moreover, on a questionnaire designed to assess hyperactivity symptoms, the patient's behavior was reported as falling in a range suggestive of attention-deficit–hyperactivity disorder.

SUMMARY/FORMULATION

This 10-year-old white male, who is entering the sixth grade, is currently functioning in the average range of measured intellectual abilities. There appears to be some mild evidence of neuropsychological impairment. The patient's major areas of deficit include complex tactile perceptual/discrimination skills, motor speed, and his ability to maintain focused attention over a considerable period of time. The patient's strengths include his general language abilities and intellectual skills. Academic achievement appears to be somewhat low in this case.

RECOMMENDATIONS

Future Assessment: Regarding additional assessment, a neuropsychological reevaluation in one year would appear indicated. With respect to the evidence of a possible attention-deficit–hyperactivity disorder, it would be wise to have this child's medication regime reviewed by a physician, either a pediatrician or a child psychiatrist. A stimulant medication probably should be considered by a medical professional. An issue that should be carefully evaluated is that the patient has had a history of seizures, and this may have bearing on the advisability of prescribing a stimulant medication.

Treatment: It appears clear that the patient's ability to attend to tasks for a considerable length of time, as well as his ability to focus mentally efficient efforts on a specific task, is somewhat compromised. As much as possible, it would be advisable to reduce the level of distracting stimuli in the child's classroom and home situations. An important factor to add to this person's situation would be structure and supervision with respect to organizing his activities. Individual tutoring in academic subjects could be helpful and should be provided.

DISCUSSION OF H.C.

This case was quite complex. It was quite difficult to decide how many of the child's problems were due either to the history of seizures or to the possible ADHD. In such cases, the best strategy is often to focus on the problems identified by the child's pattern of strengths and weaknesses, and to use these as a basis for recommendations. In many cases, the needed treatment can be determined by this strategy even if an exact diagnosis cannot.

INTRODUCTION TO I.T.

Poor school achievement is an important reason for neuropsychological assessment. The mix of diagnoses includes possible learning disabilities, attention-deficit-disorder symptoms, emotional problems, and poor motivation. Children can, of course, have one, two, or many interlocking problems. The task for the neuropsychologist is to sort the problems out, assign weights to each, and recommend appropriate remedial strategies.

NEUROPSYCHOLOGICAL DATA FORM

Identifying Data

Name: I.T.	Education: Grade 10
Age: 15 years	Handedness: Mixed (left)
Sex: Male	Marital status: Never married
Race: Black	Occupation: Student

Intellectual/Cognitive Functions

Wechsler Intelligence Scale for Children—Revised (WISC-R)

Verbal subtests	*Scale scores*
Information	14
Similarities	11
Arithmetic	13
Vocabulary	12
Comprehension	8
(Digit Span)	(10)
VIQ = 109	

Performance subtests	*Scale scores*
Picture Completion	14
Picture Arrangement	9
Block Design	17

Object Assembly	8
Coding	9

PIQ = 109

FSIQ = 110

Academic achievement

Wide Range Achievement Test—Revised (WRAT-R)

Subject areas	*Scale scores*	*Percentiles*	*Grade-equivalent score*
Reading	115	84	12+
Spelling	124	95	12+
Arithmetic	104	61	11B

Tactile functions

Single or Double Simultaneous Suppression

Right side	*Left side*
No errors	2 inconsistencies

Finger Agnosia

Right hand	*Left hand*
No errors	No errors

Fingertip Number Writing

Right hand	*Left hand*
3 errors	2 errors

Auditory functions

Single or Double Simultaneous Stimulation

Right side	*Left side*
No errors	No errors

Visual functions

Single or Double Simultaneous Stimulation

Right side	*Left side*
No errors	No errors

VISUAL PERCEPTION

Trail Making Test, Part A: 24 sec
Spatial Relations Section of Reitan-Indiana Aphasia Screening Test: Within normal limits

MOTOR SKILLS

Finger Tapping Test

Left hand (dominant)	*Right hand (nondominant)*
46	58

LANGUAGE

Animal Naming Test: Within normal limits

EXECUTIVE FUNCTIONS

Trail Making Test, Part B: 61 sec

ATTENTION FUNCTIONS

Digit Span: 8
Stroop Color-Word Test: Word = 64T; Color = 66T; Color-Word = 60T (T = scores reversed)

NEUROPSYCHOLOGICAL EVALUATION

CONFIDENTIAL

NAME: I.T.

SEX: Male

RACE: Black

AGE: 15 years

EDUCATION: Grade 10

HANDEDNESS: Mixed

OCCUPATION: Student

MARITAL STATUS: Never married

REASON FOR REFERRAL

The patient was referred for neuropsychological evaluation because he is encountering school and social difficulties.

TESTS ADMINISTERED

Wechsler Intelligence Scale for Children—Revised (WISC-R); Stroop Color-Word Test; Trail Making Test; Spatial Relations Portion of the Reitan-Indiana Aphasia Screening Test; Reitan-Klove Sensory Perceptual Examination; Animal Naming Test; Portions of the Reitan-Klove Lateral Dominance Examination; Wide Range Achievement Test—Revised (WRAT-R); Millon Adolescent Personality Inventory (MAPI); Finger Tapping Test.

INTERVIEW OBSERVATIONS

Appearance and Behavior: The patient was dressed neatly. His posture was initially somewhat anxious, but later he settled into a more comfortable sitting pattern. The client's behavior toward the examiner was generally cooperative. No abnormal actions were noted. With respect to motor behavior, he demonstrated some self-stimulatory behaviors. These included tapping his fingers and playing with objects on the desk. These self-stimulatory behaviors were particularly noted after lunch.

Mental Status: With respect to emotional state, the patient's affect was generally appropriate. With respect to mood, he appeared slightly anxious and, for a brief period, was angry. Predominantly, however, the patient's mood appeared within normal limits. Thought processes were inferred from speech, and generally, the patient's thought processes were logical in form and normal in flow. The patient reported that he had had some suicidal thoughts in the past, but he has no plan to commit suicide.

Chief Complaint: The patient's mother reported that her son's grades are failing, and that he procrastinates when performing his homework. She stated that her son would rather draw than do his schoolwork. The mother describes a motivation problem and notes that her son has incompletes, with six weeks to make them up, and that it is difficult to get him focused on his work. The mother notes that the problem has had an onset since middle school, and that the difficulty with schoolwork has really become a problem this year. With respect to consequences, the mother stated that she had tried contracts and structuring homework time. The mother also noted that her son is somewhat isolated and withdrawn in peer relationships, and that he uses his art ability to gain social reinforcement from others.

The patient also reported that he is not doing his schoolwork, and that this is a source of conflict. The patient stated that doing his schoolwork has been a problem since the sixth grade, that he is ambivalent regarding the value of putting in a great deal of effort, and that he has feelings of failure and is afraid of possibly flunking his academic subjects. The patient agreed also that he has few friends, and that he feels lonely at times. He also acknowledged that he avoids peers and is somewhat withdrawn.

BACKGROUND

With respect to the patient's childhood and adolescent history, the following comments are offered. With respect to delivery history, the route of delivery was vaginal, and the induced labor was not traumatic. The patient had a low birth weight. With respect to developmental milestones, the patient could sit alone at 6 months and could crawl on all four extremities at 7–8 months. The patient could walk alone at 13 months and was toilet-trained after almost 3 years. Infancy problems included feeding difficulties and colic. It is noteworthy that the patient was born with a foot deformity. The patient's feet apparently turned inward, and he had to wear special shoes for the first year of his life. The patient has a childhood history of sibling conflict with his single sibling, a sister three years younger than he. The patient entered kindergarten at age 5 and first grade at age 6. He apparently was specially placed in gifted-and-talented/honors classes. There is a history of counseling in that the patient was enrolled in play therapy at age 5. There apparently were problems at home and in the neighborhood. The patient was in therapy for six to nine months. The patient also had problems with balance and difficulties with his eyes, as well as difficulties fighting with his peers. The patient did not have many friends, and this difficulty has continued. The patient's family consists of his mother, age 38, who is an M.S.W. and works in social services. His father, age 40, has a bachelor's degree in sociology and works as a manager for a fast-food restaurant. His sister, age 12, is in seventh grade and has no problems that are known. The patient's family health history is noteworthy in that his father's mother had epilepsy, and it was reported that she died from seizures. As earlier alluded to, the patient is in grade 10 at a public school, and he has been given a number of incompletes. Apparently, in the first quarter, the patient was getting A's and is now in the third quarter getting C− grades, except in computers and art. He did relatively well the year before. It is noted that he is currently in an open classroom. With respect to physical problems, he does seem to have some motor difficulties, as he appears clumsy at times, and it was reported that he had had coordination problems as a child and he has difficulties with hand–eye coordination and sports. He does relatively well in martial arts, swimming, and other individualized sports. With respect to behavioral problems, he has difficulty with noncompliance. In school, he puts forth effort only in activities in which he is motivated. Also, it is noteworthy that he has lied on occasion regarding homework. In addition, the patient was described as somewhat hypersensitive to criticism and also has a bad temper, sometimes throwing objects at walls and breaking his possessions. As was earlier alluded to, he has a very low motivation in school and participates in no activities with other children. He works primarily in solitary pursuits such as drawing, which he loves, and also in computer activites.

ANALYSIS OF TEST RESULTS

Intellectual/Cognitive Functions: On the WISC-R, the patient earned a Verbal IQ (109) that falls in the upper portion of the average range, and a Performance IQ (109) that also falls in the upper portion of the average range. His Full Scale IQ (110) falls in the lower portion of the high-average range. With respect to the Verbal IQ subtests, the patient did best on a subtest that assessed his general fund of information, and he did most poorly on a subtest which assessed his ability to follow everyday rules and regulations and to exercise social judgment. On the Performance scale subtests, the patient did best on a subtest that assessed his spatial relations abilities, and he did most poorly on a subtest that required him to solve puzzles.

Academic Achievement: On the WRAT-R, the patient obtained a Reading score that fell in the 84th percentile, and that translated into a grade equivalent score of 12 years or more. On the Spelling subtest, he obtained a percentile rank in the 95th percentile and again had a grade equivalent of 12 years or better. On the Arithmetic subtest, he obtained a percentile ranking in the 61st percentile and a grade-equivalent score that falls in the beginning portion of grade 11. Relative to his intellectual values on the WISC-R, these achievement test scores suggest the patient is doing better in terms of academic achievement than one would predict from his obtained IQ scores.

Tactile Functions: The patient did not exhibit tactile suppressions to single or double simultaneous stimulation, a result suggesting that his primary tactile functions are intact. With respect to higher level tactile perceptual processes, his identification of a touched finger was relatively adequate. The patient demonstrated some mild difficulties with perception of numbers written on the fingertips. This evidence of imperception was present bilaterally.

Visual Functions: The patient did not exhibit visual suppressions to single or double simultaneous stimulation, a result suggesting that his primary areas are intact. His visual perceptual abilities appeared to be excellent, and his visual-spatial/organizational skills were good.

Auditory Functions: The patient did not demonstrate auditory suppression to single or double simultaneous stimulation, a result suggesting that his primary areas are intact. Similarly, there was no suggestion in the interview that the patient had a clinically significant hearing deficit.

Motor Skills: The patient's gross motor skills appear adequate. On the sections of the Reitan-Kove Lateral Dominance Examination that were performed, the patient showed a pattern of mixed dominance. It is noteworthy that the patient does write with the left hand. On a name-writing test, the patient's speed with the preferred hand was within normal limits, and similarly, the relationship between the preferred and nonpreferred hand was unremarkable. On a measure of motor speed, however, the preferred hand (left upper extremity) was slower than the nonpreferred hand (right upper extremity). This relationship is essentially opposite what is usually found. Usually, one expects the dominant or preferred hand to be somewhat faster than the nondominant or nonpreferred hand. The motor speed of the patient with the dominant hand was also slow on visual tracking tasks.

Language Skills: The patient's general language abilities appeared to be grossly intact. There was no clear-cut evidence in the interview of difficulties with expressive or receptive language. His verbal fluency, which was assessed by the Animal Naming task, appeared to be quite good.

Executive Functions/Cognitive Flexibility: The patient demonstrated mild to moderate difficulty with respect to flexibility in thinking and the ability to consider more than one aspect of a situation at the same time. The patient is also likely to have significant difficulty in resisting distractions and in dealing with multiple competing stimuli.

Attention: The patient's performance on attentional and concentration tasks was quite inconsistent. In some cases, he was able to obtain relatively adequate scores, and in other cases, he was significantly less adequate. It may be that motivational and/or mental stamina considerations played a role in the set of results.

Emotional/Personality Functions: On the MAPI, the patient's profile was quite alarming. Specifically, the patient expressed or self-reported difficulties with respect to self-concept, personal esteem, body comfort, sexual acceptance, peer security, social tolerance, family rapport, and academic confidence. A central difficulty for this young man appears to be his pervasive sense of dissatisfaction with himself as a person, as well as his low confidence in his ability to formulate a successful personal identity. He appears to find himself of low worth and has an unwillingness to believe that others could regard him positively. He appears to have concerns regarding his physical maturation, his sexual impulses and fears, and his relationships with peers. This young man appears to be dismayed about his academic performance and finds little personal relevance in the course work or extracurricular scholastic activities. With respect to personality pattern, the patient scored high on dimensions suggesting inhibition and sensitivity. This would suggest that his behavior is likely to be characterized by a pervasive apprehensiveness, restlessness, and variable moods. There may be extended and alternating periods of dejection and self-deprecation, as well as episodes of irritability, anger, and isolation. He apparenty feels quite alienated from others, yet at the same time has a feeling of alienation from himself, creating a constant undercurrent within him of tension and anger. With respect to behavioral correlates, similar patients are often described as somewhat rebellious and socially noncompliant. School, social, and future vocational difficulties are possible.

SUMMARY/FORMULATION

This 15-year-old black, left-handed male, who is currently in the 10th grade, is functioning in the lower portion of the high-average range of measured intellectual ability. There appears to be evidence of at least mild neuropsychological impairment. Major areas of deficit include mental flexibility, attention and concentration skills, and motor speed with the dominant hand. Major areas of strength are his general fund of information; reading skills; math ability; spelling skills; basic sensory areas with respect to tactile, auditory, and visual functions; visual perceptual skills; and spatial relations. Psychometric data are also consistent with a hypothesis of some significant emotional disturbance. Relevant diagnostic statements would suggest that the patient is similar to other adolescents who have been diagnosed as having "avoidant disorder of adolescence with overanxious disorder features." Other possibly related diagnostic statements would include borderline personality disorder and identity disorder. With respect to learning disabilities, the patient is, if anything, an overachiever in terms of his academic skill levels relative to his measured intellectual level. Nonetheless, there appears to be a degree of neuropsychological impairment which is impairing his social and academic functioning to a very significant degree.

RECOMMENDATIONS

Future Assessment: Regarding additional assessment, referral for a repeat neuropsychological evauation in one year is certainly indicated. In addition, the patient could profit from a psychiatric evaluation to determine the advisability of additional medication-based therapy.

Treatment: With respect to therapeutic intervention, the patient clearly appears to be in need of psychotherapy. After a period of individual psychotherapy, the patient might be tried in group therapy, where the other group members are age-equivalent adolescents. It should be noted, however, that, because of dependency conflicts and a general mistrust of others, it will be very difficult for this young man to fully enter into a therapeutic relationship. The initial stage of therapy will consist of the patient's engaging in maneuvers to test the sincerity and motives of the therapist. It will be important that the therapeutic goals be set relatively modestly, as this patient is likely to change very slowly. The important additional issues to consider in conducting treatment are the patient's difficulties with resisting distractions, and his lowered cognitive-flexibility skills. All of these factors could make individual and/or group therapy extremely difficult. When one adds the patient's extremely low self-esteem, the problem is only multiplied.

Management: The patient will need to be given careful, and at times repeated verbal instructions in very simple words and in short, distinctly spoken sentences. It is important to realize that the patient's current ability to adjust to new situations and to critically analyze the effect of his personal behaviors on others is at least moderately impaired. Significant others in his environment should realize this and anticipate problems and difficulties. It will be important to give him repeated feedback through his particularly strong visual modality. An important factor to add to this young man's situation will be structure and close supervision. It would probably be best for him not to be in an open classroom, but to be in a situation where the degree of stimulus bombardment is relatively controlled. In a more controlled setting, he would have a better opportunity to handle his scholastic requirements. This patient appears to have significant strengths and a clear preference for art- and computer-related activities; these might be utilized as incentives for him to complete less preferred activities and activities of a scholastic nature. It would also seem wise to arrange for the child to be individually tutored in his academic subjects. This might possibly be done on a one-to-one basis and in addition to his normal school hours.

COMMENTS

Despite a general appearance of adequacy, it is important to realize that this young man's actual level of cognitive functioning has been compromised. Although his achievement levels are relatively adequate, it is most likely that he is able to achieve above-average scholastic performance only with extreme difficulty, and at considerable cost with respect to mental energy and emotional stamina. The fact that this patient is without physical deficit may mask the fact that he does have a degree of cognitive difficulty. It will be important for persons in his living situation to realize that there is a degree of neuropsychological deficit present. Expectations of his future performance will need to be adequately tailored to fit his current level and pattern of mental skills. Similarly, parental expectations with respect to academic achievement levels may need to be carefully considered and discussed in light of the findings in this report.

DISCUSSION OF I.T.

Perhaps the most striking feature of this young man's test results is the evidence of emotional problems. Clearly, a psychiatric referral was necessary. Also, the fact that the child's achievement levels were in excess of usual expectations suggested possible emotional burnout. It is often difficult with teenagers to decide how many of their social difficulties can be attributed to normal developmental changes and how many to serious emotional problems.

It was difficult to be confident regarding specific organic factors in this case. It is worth noting that brain injury in children has three specific patterns. It may arise early and maintain a rather constant presence throughout the child's life, or it may appear early and seem to disappear as the child matures; various brain areas may take over what might have been the impaired function. The third pattern is the most problematical: Sometimes, children sustain a brain injury early in life, yet there is no apparent difficulty present in the child's repertoire of skills until the child, in the process of maturation, finds that the impaired area or structure is suddenly essential for some higher level cognitive task.

INTRODUCTION TO "JOHN"

This case study details a behavior modification plan for a young man with organic personality disorder as well as a number of serious medical problems. This behavior modification plan was selected to demonstrate how behavioral techniques are utilized in a truly challenging case. The multiple-problems situation is too often a clinical reality but is too infrequently seen in the published literature.

BEHAVIOR MODIFICATION PLAN

NAME: "John"

BEHAVIOR MODIFYING DRUGS: No current medications

RATIONALE

John is a 14-year-old nonverbal ambulatory white male who is mildly mentally retarded and also carries a diagnosis of bilateral deafness, grand mal seizure (inactive), and organic personality disorder. He has a personal hearing aid which is worn in his right ear. John was recently admitted to a residential care program; previously, he had attended other institutions. Because of a long history of aggressive, noncompliant, disruptive behaviors, he has been dismissed from various institutions. Also, at times, his sexual behavior has been judged inappropriate. Recently, he was dismissed from another program. After his dismissal, his mother attempted to manage him at home, but this proved unsuccessful. In the past, he has been on antipsychotic drugs. He was admitted to the intensive behavior program at the state medical center and was discharged from there recently.

Currently, he receives communication therapy twice a week and appears to be making reasonable progress. He is usually able to communicate with others in a generally adequate manner by using signs and facial gestures. A good worker with reasonably adequate skills relative to other clients, he does have some interpersonal problems. For example, he is sometimes quite bossy and has difficulty sharing materials with other clients. Though he does carry a diagnosis of seizure disorder, it has not apparently recurred since his first seizure attack four years ago.

Most of the time his maladaptive aggressive behaviors occur when he is trying to escape the demands of others or is not having his own demands met as soon as possible. His aggressive behaviors, such as assault, agitating peers, and property destruction, make him a danger to himself and others. Also, his aggressive behaviors have interfered with his progress in the social and vocational domains.

Functional Analysis

Antecedents for his aggressive behaviors are as follows:

1. Staff requests that he doesn't wish to comply with.
2. Failure to get his demands met.

Consequences include:

1. He is allowed to escape from completing a task or request.
2. He gets attention from staff and other clients.

At this point, it has been decided to consider the aggressive behaviors a major problem and to consider the inappropriate sexual behaviors with the other clients a subset of aggressive behaviors. It is expected that, as the aggressive behaviors are decreased, the inappropriate touching will also be decreased. This will be monitored empirically to demonstrate if there is interdependency between these behaviors. Future independent behavior programming to target the inappropriate touching behavior may be necessary.

Data needed for this analysis were collected by behavioral observations, chart reviews, and interviews with the client and other staff members.

Aggressive behaviors were monitored by an interval recording procedure. Reliability checks were conducted on seven occasions and revealed 100% accuracy of measurement. Over a four-month period, John demonstrated 22 incidents of aggressive behavior. His average number of incidents per month was 5.5. The actual monthly totals were 9 for January, 3 for February, 8 for March, and 2 for April.

The purpose of this program is to reduce the number of aggressive behaviors. The target behaviors to be decreased include assault, agitating peers, and property destruction.

BEHAVIOR MANAGEMENT PROGRAM PLAN

GENERAL PROCEDURES

Since the client's aggressive behavior could result in serious physical harm to himself, this plan should be implemented by staff trained in the physical management of behavior. Failure to follow the prescribed procedures by a person or persons trained in the physical management of aggression could result in physical injury to the client, to other clients, or to staff.

REINFORCERS

Reinforcers have been identified through interviews and observations of free-operant behavior. Reinforcers are to include sips of a soft drink or small pieces of candy, cake, or fruit, as well as access to favorite magazines, drawing, art supplies, games, and letter-writing materials. Reinforcers should be accompanied by a verbal restatement of the contingencies and by specific praise. Given this client's special disabilities, gestures and hand signals might also be used. Reinforcers should be rotated to avoid satiation with any single item. At variable intervals, a special reward might be given if John is demonstrating acceptable target-incompatible behaviors. This could be programmed by letting him cut a deck of cards, and if he gets a face card, then he gets a special reward. Staff members are responsible for shuffling the deck after each reinforcement opportunity.

METHODS

REINFORCEMENT OF INCOMPATIBLE BEHAVIORS

CONDITIONS

1. If John participates in any of the following target behaviors to be increased that are incompatible with aggressive behaviors during a 15-minute period. Adaptive target behaviors to be increased include:

a. Working with puzzles
b. Sports activities
c. Working quietly
d. Watching TV
e. Listening to the radio
f. Interacting positively with other clients
g. Sitting quietly
h. Looking at pictures in magazines

2. If John has behaviors incompatible with his target behaviors to be decreased for 1 hour.

CONSEQUENCES

1. Then staff members should, using a positive, friendly tone of voice, tell him, "If you are working [or some other behavior] then you'll get a sip of soda [or some other reinforcer]." The staff member should also use gestures and appropriate facial expressions in order to communicate the reinforcer contingency to John. At that time, he should be provided with a specific reinforcer. Reinforcers include:

a. Pieces of candy
b. Sips of a soft drink
c. Small pieces of cake
d. Small pieces of fruit

2. Then he will be given the opportunity to cut a deck of cards. If he gets a face card, then he'll get a special reward. Staff members are responsible for shuffling the deck after each reinforcement opportunity. Special rewards include the following:

a. Access to favorite magazines
b. Access to drawing and art supplies
c. Access to favorite games
d. Access to letter-writing materials

He should be specifically reinforced verbally and with gestures and facial expressions by staff members saying, "Very good, that's doing very well," and demonstrating by signs and gestures that he is also doing well. Regardless of whether or not he receives a reinforcer at the hourly interval, staff members should remind him by gesture, sign language, and verbal contingency that he will have another chance at a special reinforcer at the end of the next hour.

CORRECTIVE PROCEDURE FOR AGGRESSIVE BEHAVIOR

1. If John starts to exhibit aggressive behaviors which are defined as:

a. Assault
b. Agitating peers

c. Property destruction
d. Inappropriately touching other clients

2. Then staff members are to give no reinforcers for at least 30 minutes following any aggressive behavior. If John performs aggressive behaviors, then he should be subject to overcorrection procedures. For example, overcorrection can be either positive practice or restitution. In positive practice overcorrection, the client should be made to perform a positive physical behavior to make up for his negative physical behavior. The positive physical behavior should use the same muscle group as the aggressive behavior but perform a positive physical activity. Similarly, restitution overcorrection means that, if he breaks something, he has to fix it over and over again for a high number of times. For example, if he hits the wall, then he must wash the wall for 3 minutes or do physical exercise for a 3- to 10-minute period (physical exercise must be within his fitness level and medically approved). The idea is not to punish him in an aversive manner, but to teach him positive things he can do with the same muscle group. Staff members should not reinforce any aggressive behavior with attention in any form. Staff members should, while the patient is performing the overcorrection procedure, restate the reinforcement contingency, which is "If you do well, then you will receive reinforcements." Also, staff members should demonstrate the reinforcement contingency by facial expression and gesture.

3. If John refuses to undergo the overcorrection procedure willingly, staff members will physically ensure that he goes through this procedure. Staff members will not allow him to do any other activities until he completes his overcorrection activities, which are made up of physical activities that are physically incompatible with the aggressive behavior that initiated the overcorrection procedure.

SOCIALIZATION PROCEDURES

1. At least once per day on the evening shift (socialization module), John will respond correctly when asked the questions attached to this program entitled "Socialization Questions."

2. Staff will help John answer the questions correctly (if necessary). The socialization module may include other topics.

SOCIALIZATION QUESTIONS

Q: How do you get good things to eat and drink?

A: Do things like work with puzzles, work quietly, talk to other people pleasantly, and sit quietly and watch TV.

Q: What do you do if you're angry at something that happens on the unit?

A: Don't yell, find my group leader or shift supervisor, keep my voice low, and talk to them.

Q: What do you do if you're angry at another resident?

A: Ignore them, do not yell, and ask the evening group leader or shift supervisor to give me some help to work out the problem.

Q: What do you do if you feel like you're going to hit someone?

A: Sit down on the floor away from others, calm down, count slowly to 10, and then find the group leader or shift leader to talk with.

Q: What happens if I go around hitting others or breaking things?

A: Then I don't get reinforced, and I have to do some physical activity like cleaning a wall for a period of time.

Comment on "John"

As is clear from the behavior modification plan, aggressive behaviors were seen as "John's" major difficulty. It is well to note that these aggressive behaviors very likely blocked the emission of more prosocial behaviors. The plan included a behavioral functional analysis that made a decision as to which behaviors to target first for change. Other problem behaviors were observed to see if reduction in the targeted behaviors also produced reductions in the other problem behaviors. The behavior modification plan included prompts for positive adaptive behaviors incompatible with aggressive behaviors, and it paired both social and tangible reinforcers. In addition, there was a provision for variable-interval reinforcement, as he received a special reward only after selecting a face card from a deck of cards. The variable nature of the reinforcement was planned to maintain a higher level of responding than simple fixed-interval responding. The use of a deck of cards made the variable-interval procedure practical to administer by program-level staff.

SUMMARY

The above cases represent a number of important clinical referral issues. Many of the crucial issues, such as co-morbidity, appropriate remediation strategies, and the most effective behavior modification and behavior therapy techniques, are areas that are currently undergoing detailed research scrutiny. Thus, final answers are not available. As can be seen, in most assessment cases a core set of measures was utilized, and some additional supplementation with other neuropsychological, psychological, educational, and emotional/personality tests occurred, depending upon various clinical concerns and specific issues.

The intent of each case study was to integrate neuropsychological test findings from a number of diverse areas of functioning into a meaningful focus and to expand upon this focus by providing insights into how these diverse findings could be applied to significant clinical, behavioral, psychological, social, educational, and emotional problems of the children assessed.

While there is an assumption that these assessments and the treatment planning effectively described the child's neuropsychological status, conceptualized the findings in a reasonable formulation, and integrated and recast the formulation into a cogent, realistic, and practical set of treatment and management recommendations, nonetheless it would be well to be modest. In many ways, the practice of clinical child neuropsychology remains an enigma. There have been very few sound research studies in child neuropsychology, and only a limited number of the available assessment tools meet the most rudimentary standards of validity, reliability, and normative data. There is much to learn regarding the neuropsychology of children. In truth, our current knowledge is comparable more to that of a toddler than to that of a mature adult. Clearly, the coming years will be filled with excitement and wonder as our knowledge of these areas increases.

Index